The

# Flight of the
# Creative Class

The

New Global

Competition for Talent

The

# Flight of the
# Creative Class

RICHARD FLORIDA

HarperBusiness
*An Imprint of* HarperCollins*Publishers*

HarperCollins books may be purchased for educational, business, or sales promotional
use. For information, please write: Special Markets Department, HarperCollins Publishers
Inc., 10 East 53rd Street, New York, NY 10022.

FIRST EDITION

*Designed by Sarah Maya Gubkin*

Library of Congress Cataloging-in-Publication Data

Florida, Richard L.
    The flight of the creative class: the new global competition for talent /
Richard Florida.
        p.   cm.
    Includes index.
    ISBN 0-06-075690-X
    1. Intellectual capital—United States.   2. Creative ability—Economic aspects—
United States.   3. Technological innovations—Economic aspects—United States.
4. United States—Emigration and immigration—Economic aspects.   5. United
States—Economic conditions.   I. Title.

HD53.F65   2004
331.12'791—dc22                                                    2004060663

05   06   07   08   09   DIX/RRD   10   9   8   7   6   5   4   3   2   1

For Eleanor Florida

*As long as I have any choice in the matter, I will live only in a country where civil liberty, tolerance, and equality of all citizens before the law are the rule.*
—ALBERT EINSTEIN, upon coming to the USA, 1933

# Contents

# 1

# The Flight of the Creative Class

*Nothing is more revealing than movement.*
—MARTHA GRAHAM (1894–1991),
dancer and choreographer

In March of 2003, I had the opportunity to meet Peter Jackson, the
Academy Award–winning director of the *Lord of the Rings* trilogy, at
his film complex in lush, green, otherworldly Wellington, New
Zealand. Jackson has done something unlikely in Wellington, a small-
ish but exciting cosmopolitan city of roughly 400,000, and one certainly not previously considered a global cultural capital. He has built
a permanent facility there that is considered one of the world's most
sophisticated filmmaking complexes. And he did it in New Zealand
for a reason.

Jackson, a Wellington native, realized what many American cities
discovered during the 1990s: that paradigm-busting creative industries

could single-handedly change the way cities flourish while driving dynamic and widespread economic change. It took Jackson and his partners a while to raise the resources, but they eventually purchased an abandoned paint factory that, emblematic in its adaptive transformation and reuse, emerged as the studio responsible for the most breathtaking trilogy of films ever made. He realized, Jackson told me, that with the allure of the *Lord of the Rings* movies he would be able to attract a diverse array of creative talent from around the world, enticing the best cinematographers, costume designers, sound technicians, computer-graphic artists, model builders, editors, and animators to New Zealand.

Sure enough, during my visit to Wellington, I met dozens of Americans from universities such as the University of California at Berkeley and MIT working alongside talented filmmakers from Europe and Asia. Many had begun the process of establishing residency in New Zealand, ready to relinquish their American citizenship for what they saw as greener creative pastures. One of them, a digital wunderkind from the San Francisco Bay area, told me he was launching his new high-tech start-up in Wellington because of the technology infrastructure and environment there, which in his case created advantages that trumped even Silicon Valley. As we walked past a world map with pins stuck in employees' native countries, the head of digital animation joked that the organization looked more like the UN than a film production studio.

Think about this. In an industry synonymous with America's international economic and cultural might, film production, the single greatest project in recent cinematic history was internationally funded and crafted by the best filmmakers from around the world. But not in Hollywood.

When Hollywood produces movies, it creates jobs for directors, actors, and key grips in California. Because of the astounding level of technical innovation required by films of *Rings'* magnitude—in areas from computer graphics and animation to sound design—such a project also germinates whole new companies, and even new nationwide industries. George Lucas's *Star Wars* films, for instance, almost single-handedly sparked the advancement of everything from video games to product tie-in marketing. The lion's share of economic benefits from the *Rings* trilogy, though, is likely to accrue not to the United States but to New Zealand. In an equally mighty display of economic irony, Jackson's remake of *King Kong* is also being put together in Wellington, with a budget running upward of $150 million.

Peter Jackson's accomplishment in tiny Wellington hasn't factored into any of the ongoing debates over global economic competitiveness. But the United States of America is now facing its greatest challenge since the dawn of the Industrial Revolution. This challenge has little to do with business costs and even less with manufacturing prowess. And, no, the main competitive threats are not China or India. Our country—for generations known around the world as the land of opportunity and innovation—may well be on the verge of losing its creative competitive edge.

The core of this challenge is what I've come to see as the *new global competition for talent,* a phenomenon that promises to radically reshape the world in the coming decades. No longer will economic might amass in countries according to their natural resources, manufacturing excellence, military dominance, or even scientific and technological prowess. Today, the terms of competition revolve around a central axis: a nation's ability to mobilize, attract, and retain human creative talent. Every key dimension of international economic leadership, from manufacturing excellence to scientific and technological advancement, will depend on this ability.

This new global competition for talent creates a serious threat to the United States' long-standing economic hegemony on three overlapping fronts. First, a wide range of countries around the world are increasing their ability to compete for global talent. Second, the United States is undermining its own ability to compete for that talent. And third, the U.S. is failing to cultivate and harness the full creative capabilities of its own people in ways that position it to compete effectively.

The global talent pool and the high-end, high-margin creative industries that used to be the sole province of the U.S. and the crucial source of its prosperity have begun to disperse around the globe. A host of countries—Ireland, Finland, Canada, Sweden, Australia, and

New Zealand among them—are investing in higher education, producing creative people, and churning out cutting-edge products, from cellular phones to computer software to blockbuster movies. Many of them have learned from the United States' success and are shoring up their efforts to attract foreign talent—including Americans. If even a few of these rising nations draw away, say, 2 percent each of America's creative workforce, the effect on our economy will be enormous. The United States may well have been the Goliath of the twentieth-century global economy, but it will take just a half-dozen twenty-first-century Davids to begin to wear it down.

Unfortunately, the majority of U.S. political leaders, academics, and business analysts fail to grasp the true reason behind America's remarkable success in innovation, economic growth, and prosperity. It's not simply a generous endowment of natural resources, the size of our market, or some indigenous Yankee ingenuity that has powered our global competitiveness for more than a century. America's growth miracle turns on one key factor: its openness to new ideas, which has allowed it to dominate the global competition for talent, and in doing so harness the creative energies of its own people—and, indeed, the world's.

The United States may have ushered in the era of high-tech industry and perpetual innovation, but it is by no means our nation's manifest destiny to stay on top. To remain innovative, America must continue to attract the world's sharpest and most creative minds. And to do that, it needs to invest in the further development, from both internal and external sources, of its talent base. Because wherever talent goes, innovation, creativity, and economic growth are sure to follow.

## The Open Society and the Talent Advantage

In many ways, of course, the United States is still the world's center of ingenuity. Its GDP tops $10 trillion, and it is home to great universities, Silicon Valley, and many of the most dynamic companies in information technology, biotech, entertainment, and countless other fields. The U.S. led the world into the high-tech age by virtue of several important developments in its political, social, and economic landscapes. In the years following World War II, federal funding for basic research jumped considerably, as did the number of people earning a higher education, thanks in part to the GI Bill. In the private sector, the newly formed venture-capital industry provided an avenue for bringing research ideas to market. The social movements of the 1960s popularized the idea of openness; to be different was no longer to be an outcast but to be admired. Freedom of expression and experimentation allowed new technologies and cultural forms, from biotechnology to alternative rock, to flourish.

But the United States—and this point bears repeating—doesn't have some intrinsic advantage in the production of creative people, new ideas, or start-up companies. Its real advantage lies in its ability to attract these economic drivers from around the world. Of critical importance to American success in this last century has been a tremendous influx of global talent. These were powerhouse entrepreneurs and industry builders who molded every facet of American life, from steel titan Andrew Carnegie to financial wizard August Belmont to investor and mega-philanthropist George Soros. These were people who changed how we eat, drink, and entertain ourselves: Adolphus Busch in beer, Oscar Mayer in hot dogs, and film mogul Samuel Goldwyn. From Polish-born cosmetics magnate Helena Rubenstein to clothing queen Liz Claiborne, a Belgian, they affected the way we look, to ourselves and to the rest of the world. Turkish-born music magnate Ahmet Ertegun, founder of Atlantic Records, single-handedly shaped the face of American music, recording the defining sounds of an era: John Coltrane, Charles Mingus, Ray Charles, Bobby Darin, Aretha Franklin, Cream, and Led Zeppelin.

Immigrants have, of course, helped power America's economic growth engine since the dawn of the republic. But in the 1930s, the U.S. began to attract a steady stream of scientific, intellectual, cultural, and entrepreneurial talent in the form of Europeans fleeing fascism and communism. Italian-born Enrico Fermi and German Albert Einstein, who left Fascist Italy and Nazi Germany in the 1930s, were two of many who helped make the American university system and its innovative infrastructure second to none. America's rise to preeminence in the high-tech age would have been nearly unimaginable without imported talent. There was Russian-born David Sarnoff, the electronics and television visionary who guided RCA, one of the leading technology companies of its day, and went on to found NBC. By midcentury, General Georges Doriot, a Parisian, founded American Research and Development, America's first venture-capital firm, and was the initial investor in Digital Equipment, originator of the minicomputer revolution. In our own time, Hungarian Andy Grove helped to build Intel and America's semiconductor industry.

This stream of incoming talent surged to new levels in the 1980s and 1990s, thanks to more liberal immigration policies and a booming economy. In the 1990s alone, more than 11 million new people came to America, and today the immigrant population numbers more than 30 million, or 11 percent of the entire population. This 1990s wave of immigration was the largest in American history, and it drew creative talent from all corners of the globe, including high-tech luminaries such as Sergey Brin, the Moscow-born cofounder of Google, and Hotmail cofounder Sabeer Bhatia, who grew up in Bangalore. Yahoo's Jerry Yang of Taiwan, Pierre Omidyar, the French-born founder of eBay, and open-source software luminary Linus Torvalds from Finland helped to revolutionize in everything from the way we develop software to the way we buy things. A duo emblematic of the high-tech wave was German Andreas von Bechtolsheim and Indian Vinod Khosla, cofounders of Sun Microsystems and two of the earliest angel investors in Google. Khosla has become one of today's leading venture capitalists.

A growing number of America's leading Fortune 100 companies are headed by immigrants. Coca-Cola's top executive, E. Neville Isdell, was born in Ireland; Alcoa's Alain Belda was born in French Morocco and later became a Brazilian citizen; Pfizer's Hank McKinnell is Canadian; and Pharmacia's president and CEO, Fed Hassan, was born in Pakistan. Eli Lilly, NCR, Goodyear, and Philip Morris are also steered by foreign-born top executives. Until recently, McDonald's was headed by an Australian and Kellogg's by a Cuban. And who could forget Indian-born managing director of McKinsey and Company, Rajat

Gupta, a transplant to New York, Scandinavia, and then Chicago, who oversees the worldwide operations of the $1.3 billion transnational corporation. My own research indicates that CEOs of at least fifty of America's leading five hundred companies were born outside the U.S.

Immigrants are even more prevalent in the entrepreneurial start-up companies that power so much of American economic growth. Foreign-born CEOs ran seventy-two of *Inc.* 500 companies in the late 1990s, and immigrant entrepreneurs accounted for 30 percent of all Silicon Valley start-ups during the 1990s, accounting for nearly $20 billion in sales and more than seventy thousand jobs.[1] Foreign-born scientists and engineers make up huge percentages of our science and technology infrastructure, including roughly half of all our graduate-level computer scientists, and account for a disproportionate share of the most important discoveries in these and other key areas.[2]

Powered by an open-door policy to global talent coupled with huge investments in research and technology, the United States blew the doors of the creative age wide open. Today, some 40 million people, or more than 30 percent of our total workforce, are members of what I have termed the "creative class," employed in fields ranging from science and engineering to architecture and design, and from arts, music, and entertainment to the creative professions of law, business and finance, health care, and related fields. This creative sector of the economy currently accounts for nearly half of all wage and salary income (some $2 trillion)—almost as much as the manufacturing and service sectors combined.

## The New Global Competition for Talent

Now the competition for creative talent is heating up in all corners of the globe. Some 150 million people, or 2.5 percent of the world's population, live outside their country of birth.[3] The United States, with its 30 million foreign-born inhabitants, is home to one in five of these global migrants. But already, the percentage of the population represented by immigrants is higher in Canada (at 18 percent) and Australia (22 percent) than it is in the U.S. More and more countries are coming to understand that lasting economic advantage relies on attracting and retaining talented people, rather than simply competing for goods, services, and capital.

The competition is coming from two kinds of countries. On the one side, advanced economies with stable or shrinking populations are scouring the world for new talent pools, especially to fill looming gaps in key high-tech industries. As Pete Hodgson, New Zealand's minister for research, science, and technology, recently explained to me, "We no longer think of immigration as a gatekeeping function but as a talent-attraction function necessary for economic growth." On the other side, emerging economies—from Ireland and India to China, Korea, and Taiwan—are scrambling to attract back their own best and brightest and in some cases to poach from one another.

A close look at the international statistics shows the United States may already be losing its global edge. Along with Irene Tinagli, a doctoral student at Carnegie Mellon University, and using data from the International Labour Organisation (ILO), I compared some forty-five nations worldwide on several measures of creativity and competitiveness. The creative class, according to our estimates, numbers between 100 and 150 million for the countries where data are available. The United States lays claim to between 20 and 30 percent of that total global creative class pool. But while the U.S. may have the advantage in raw numbers, the creative class already represents a larger percentage of the workforce in several other countries than it does here. Far from being the world leader, we are not even in the top five.

When our U.S. data is adjusted for comparability to the ILO figures, the United States comes in at eleventh place worldwide. The creative class constitutes around a third of the workforce in Ireland, Belgium, Australia, and the Netherlands; and it accounts for roughly a quarter of the workforce in six other countries: New Zealand, Estonia, the United Kingdom, Canada, Finland, and Iceland. Even more impressively, when "technicians" are included in our broader analysis, the creative class rises to more than 40 percent in eight countries: the Netherlands (47 percent), Sweden (42 percent), Switzerland (42 percent), Denmark (42 percent), Norway (42 percent), Belgium (41 percent), Finland (41 percent), and Germany (40 percent). Nearly all the remaining countries employ more than 30 percent of their workforce in a creative economy job. What's more, the growth rate of the creative class in several nations has been phenomenal over the past decade or so. The percentage of people in creative occupations in New Zealand jumped from 19 percent in 1991 to 27 percent in 2002, while Ireland nearly doubled its creative class employment over the same period, from 19 to 34 percent of the workforce. Singapore's creative class grew from 17 percent in 1993 to 25 percent in 2002.

Our key indicator of worldwide economic competitiveness we call the Global Creativity Index, or GCI. It measures the creative competitiveness of nations according to my 3 Ts of economic growth: Technology, Talent, and Tolerance. The United States places fourth on this index behind Sweden, Japan, and Finland. Switzerland, Denmark, the Netherlands, and even tiny Iceland are not far behind—and closing fast.

In today's economy, where creativity and competitiveness go hand in hand, it's not surprising that our GCI rankings correlate closely with the results of other studies of international competitiveness. Finland ranks first, and the United States second—followed by Taiwan, Denmark, and Norway—on the 2004 Growth Competitiveness Index, a comprehensive measure of competitiveness developed for the Davos World Economic Forum. Harvard Business School's Michael Porter ranked the United States as the world's most competitive nation in his initial 1995 Innovation Index. According to Porter's projections, by 2005 the U.S. will have tumbled to sixth among the seventeen member countries of the Organization for Economic Co-operation and Development (OECD)—trailing Japan, Finland, Switzerland, Denmark, and Sweden. The 2004 Globalization Index developed by A. T. Kearney and published in *Foreign Policy* places the United States in seventh, behind Ireland, Singapore, Switzerland, the Netherlands, Finland, and Canada.[4] Perhaps most startlingly, the U.S. has for the first time ever slipped out of the top ten on the Index of Economic Freedom, a ranking put together by the Heritage Foundation and the *Wall Street Journal* that considers everything from fiscal burdens and government regulation to monetary and trade policy. The drop can be explained in part by the United States' slightly lower score, but an equally important factor is the improving performance of creative economy competitors—Sweden, Canada, Finland, Australia, Ireland, and others.

While in the aggregate statistical sense it often seems to be nations that compete for creative talent, when it comes down to it, creative people choose *regions*. They don't simply think of the United States versus England, Sweden versus Canada, or Australia versus Denmark. They think of Silicon Valley versus Cambridge, Stockholm versus Vancouver, or Sydney versus Copenhagen. The fact that many regions around the world are cultivating the attributes necessary to become successful creative centers makes this competition even fiercer.

For the better part of the past century, the United States held a clear edge in this regard; its cities were among the most open, the most exciting, and the most economically robust in the world. With some fifty city-regions that are each home to more than a million people, U.S. population centers offer varied bundles of economic opportunities and lifestyle options—from cosmopolitan global centers of finance, entertainment, and high technology to quality-of-life communities, major industrial centers, and buzzing university towns. But now the same forces of globalization that have reshaped our industrial system are acting on these cities and regions, and on the people who populate them. The elite of any society have, of course, always been highly mobile; what's distinct about our times is the extent to which more and more people are developing the cultural, political, and economic freedom to choose where to live and work globally.

U.S. cities are now challenged by the double threat of what I call the "global talent magnets" and "global Austins." The first category includes large, world-class cities such as London and Amsterdam, Toronto and Vancouver, and Sydney and Melbourne, which already boast percentages of immigrants on a par with or greater than New York or Los Angeles, and are aggressively competing for the world's best technological, entrepreneurial, and culturally creative talent. The global Austins, regions like Bangalore, Tel Aviv, Singapore, Taipei, and even Beijing and Shanghai, are recruiting foreign technology companies, bolstering their higher-education systems, investing aggressively in research and development, and expanding their cultural and lifestyle amenities. These places are attracting their own back from Silicon Valley and other leading U.S. centers, and dramatically increasing their ability to retain homegrown talent and to become magnets for regional talent.

## The Closing of America?

All of this might not pose such a dilemma for the United States if we weren't so critically dependent upon foreign talent in our economy in general and in our core creative fields especially. Our high-tech engine, for instance, couldn't function without this talent. Already in the U.S., nearly one-quarter of all scientists and engineers, 40 percent of all engineering professors, and more than half of all PhDs in engineering, computer science, and the life sciences hail from foreign countries. Former director of the U.S. Census and Columbia University professor Kenneth Prewitt says the U.S. will increasingly depend on these "replacement people"—foreign talent that rushes in to plug the gaping holes left in our workforce by an aging demographic—to provide key skills and grow new industries.[5] But that may not be as easy as it once was, as the United States increasingly confronts genuine competition for this talent. Some believe a reverse brain drain may be in the offing.[6]

Students are a leading indicator of global talent flows. The countries and regions that attract them not only have a leg up in keeping them around to fill critical positions, but also in attracting other pools of foreign talent—scientists, researchers, inventors, and entrepreneurs. For decades, international students have flocked to the United States to take advantage of its world-class higher education. According to the Institute of International Education, the body that grants Fulbright Scholarships, roughly 585,000 foreign students attended U.S. colleges and universities in the 2002–2003 academic year alone. This number is up from less than 50,000 in 1960. International education also contributed $12.9 billion to the U.S. economy in that year.

In 1999, the Council on Competitiveness warned that the United States could not count on funneling the international students who came to study at elite universities into our high-tech labor market. In 2003, the number of student visas issued by the U.S. dropped by 8 percent after falling 20 percent in 2002—the two largest drops since the government began tracking student statistics in 1952. And the rejection rate for student visas hit a record 35 percent in 2003, up from the previous record of 34 percent in 2002. International student applications for fall 2004 admission dropped sharply at 90 percent of the graduate schools responding to a June 2004 survey by the Council of Graduate Schools. The average decline was nearly a third. Signs don't point to a turnaround anytime soon, either. The Educational Testing Service found that one-third fewer international students applied to take the Graduate Record Exam (GRE) for the 2004 academic year than in 2003.

Foreign students face considerable obstacles to studying in the United States. The rejection rate for cultural exchange visas, used by many medical students, rose from 5.1 percent in 2001 to 7.8 percent in 2003, according to the *New York Times*. The number of students whose visas were rejected rose from 27.6 percent in 2001 to 35.2 percent in 2003. James Langer, vice president of the National Academy of Sciences, spoke plainly about what the drop in foreign students could mean at a May 2004 luncheon for the United States Senate Science and Technology Caucus: "Applications to many leading U.S. graduate schools from students in China, India, Russia, and elsewhere are already down by 30% or more, and there is evidence that these students are going elsewhere for advanced degrees. International scientific organizations, such as the International Union of Pure and Applied Physics, are refusing to hold conferences here." In short, as Langer concludes, "American science is being isolated from the rest of the world."

It would be comforting to think that restricting foreign immigration would open up more places for homegrown talent in the top American graduate programs and research facilities. The U.S. has many brilliant young people, but not nearly enough to satisfy the demand this nation's powerhouse economy has created—and certainly not when we take into account the impending baby-boomer retirements. In 2003, for instance, a vast artificial intelligence project at MIT had to be jettisoned because the university couldn't find enough graduate students who weren't foreigners and who could thus clear new security regulations.

Other countries are taking full advantage of America's apparent disregard for the value of foreign talent. Indeed, for many of them it's hard to imagine a better opportunity to skim off the cream of the international crop. Already, the United Kingdom, Germany, France, Australia, and Japan take in nearly 100,000 more students combined than the United States. Leading British, Australian, and Canadian universities boast that they are receiving their best applicant pools ever, made up increasingly of students who say they are applying there instead of the United States.

Students are only the tip of the iceberg, a glimpse of larger, deeper, and more dangerous subsurface flows. The total number of immigrants fell by 34 percent in 2003, the steepest decline since 1953. And while the U.S. added 4.25 million immigrants between 2000 and 2004, the rate of immigration slowed dramatically after peaking in 2000, according to a detailed analysis by the Center for Immigration Studies.[7] The economic costs are considerable. Visa delays have cost U.S. businesses roughly $30 billion in two years, according to a June 2004 study by a consortium of industry groups. Nearly three-quarters of the 141 companies that responded to the survey, reported having problems processing business visas since 2002, and the average financial impact per company was nearly a million dollars.

Almost every major American industry from high-tech to entertainment is feeling the repercussions of what seem unnecessarily isolationist U.S. economic and policy decisions. The last-minute diversion of Cat Stevens's (now Yusuf Islam) plane made international headlines and made the U.S. the butt of jokes worldwide. But our cultural problems go deeper than sloppy preventive security and the expenses incurred to the airline industry and the unfortunate copassengers of suspected singer-songwriters. A large and growing number of prominent international musicians, from celebrated opera singers to cutting-edge electronic musicians and world music acts, have been forced to cancel their American tours after being denied visas or encountering other hassles entering the United States. These cancellations in and of themselves won't have a big impact on the U.S. economy, but think of the influence on American artists, let alone on the multibillion-dollar music business.

America's music industry has for decades been the world's standard setter. The songs of American artists are heard on radio stations from Caracas to Istanbul. They're an integral part of the worldwide appeal of popular culture, and a major contributor to what Harvard's Joseph Nye calls our "soft power." The profits earned from American music exports help keep America's balance-of-payments deficits from getting too far into the red. Part of what makes American music so vital is its ability to absorb and incorporate the sounds of other countries—from American hip-hop picking up Caribbean reggae and Indian Bhangara beats, to hard rock musicians using industrial instrumentation from Germany. These may seem a litany of small inconveniences, but they're more than that. For American artists and fans, not being able to see touring foreign bands is the equivalent of the computer industry not getting access to the latest chips: It dulls the competitive edge.

Our increasingly restrictive climate may ironically be undermining aspects of our national security. Kofi Annan, United Nations secretary-general; Vicente Fox, president of Mexico; and Prince Saud Faisal, Saudi Arabia's foreign affairs minister, are just a few of the many foreign political and business leaders who studied at U.S. universities. As John Paden, a professor of international studies at George Mason University, and Peter Singer of the Brookings Institution write: "As students at American schools, [foreign leaders] developed strong ties to the country, laying the foundation for the productive relationships they have relied on later in their careers. American security has greatly profited as a result." But, they continue: "Unfortunately, Washington's present homeland security policy, shaped by panic-driven regulations and unfunded or ill-crafted mandates, is undermining and harming America's broader foreign policy," breeding resentment around the world over ever more restrictive visa and immigration policies. Our policy of openness, they conclude, is being supplanted by a new regime of restriction that seems "bent on turning the next generation . . . away." [8]

Open flows of people to and from the United States create powerful reciprocal benefits: increasing the economic opportunities open to foreign-born people, creating wealth in U.S. communities, and contributing to economic development and cultural change in countries badly in need of both. Instead of a brain drain, argues Annalee Saxenian, Dean of the School of Information Management and Systems, University of California at Berkeley, what is really occurring is a form of *brain circulation*, which can be beneficial to all. Trade experts like Columbia University's Jagdish Bhagwati also argue that an open international immigration framework provides huge benefits to the global economy. Or, as an *Economist* magazine survey of the field succinctly puts it: "The potential economic benefits to the world of liberalizing migration dwarf those from removing trade barriers." [9] The current restrictive bent of U.S. policy, if it is allowed to continue, threatens to undermine the manifold benefits that stem from this cycle of brain circulation.

While broad trends can be revealing, it is the individual cases that are the real eye-openers. What if, for example, Vinod Khosla, the cofounder of Sun Microsystems and venture-capital luminary who has backed so many blockbuster companies, had stayed in India? Or if Google's Sergey Brin had decided to apply his entrepreneurial talents in Europe? These are people whose creative genius has affected the trajectory of entire industries; their breakthroughs and business acumen have generated new companies and industries and completely remade existing ones. Already, though, rankings of individual companies' competitiveness yield results similar to those of the national indicators mentioned above. According to *BusinessWeek*'s 2004 Information Technology 100, for instance, only six of the world's top twenty-five most competitive high-tech companies are U.S.-based, while fourteen are in Asia. Given the escalating global competition for talent, do we really want to turn away even a few Vinod Khoslas or Brins?

Our recent circle-the-wagons mentality has also caused leading American scientists and engineers to leave the country. Roger Pedersen, a pioneer in the field of stem-cell research, left the University of

California, San Francisco, for Cambridge University in England. There, high-level stem-cell research is sponsored by the government—a sharp contrast to the United States, where the Bush administration has effectively banned federal funding of stem-cell research. Unfortunately, Pedersen's departure may be among the first of many. I have heard from and interviewed literally hundreds of scientists and engineers, not to mention artists and cultural creatives, who say they're already looking to leave the U.S. for better opportunities and "better lives" in Europe, Canada, Australia, and New Zealand. Not only does our increasing antagonism to openness—be it scientific, cultural, or economic—frustrate foreigners; now it's taking a toll on our own population's view of the United States.

Taken individually, none of those facts would be cause for concern about the future of the United States. It remains, when all is said and done, a culturally and economically rich country with diverse and impressive strengths. Cumulatively, though, the data create an unsettling picture of a nation that's allowing its long-standing advantage in talent and creativity to decay. Add to that greater security concerns and a highly politicized scientific climate, and it's easy to see why the nation is becoming less and less attractive to the world's brightest minds.

## The Challenge at Hand

The United States today faces its greatest competitive challenge of the past century, perhaps of its young life. The reason is basic: The key factor of the global economy is no longer goods, services, or flows of capital, but the competition for people. The ability to attract people is a dynamic and sensitive process. New centers of the global creative economy can emerge quickly; established players can lose position. It's a wide-open game, and the playing field is leveling every day.

Companies have always sought to attract the best talent: The difference today is that instead of bringing that talent to their existing locations, companies are setting up facilities where the talent already exists. Talent is the "biggest magnet" for globalized innovation, according to a 2004 *Economist* magazine survey of 104 leading multi-national companies.[10] Remember how quickly regions like Austin or Seattle rose to the top of the pack among U.S. regions. The same thing can happen—and is already happening—around the world. Now we're seeing the "jobs go to the people" phenomenon in global centers from Dublin to Wellington. As a result, the real foreign threat to the American economy is not terrorism; it's that we may make creative and talented people stop wanting to come here.

But, make no mistake, the United States cannot pin its economic future only on importing the huge amount of foreign talent its creative economy demands. It must also tap into the indigenous talent it already has. Many people have spoken and written about the need to better prepare our workforce for the global economy and to better educate our children. Though they suggest different approaches to satisfying these needs, the needs themselves are no-brainers. Beyond these very basics, though—calling for better classrooms or workforce retraining programs—the implications of the creative economy have yet to be fully understood by either major political party or by American leadership in general.

At the root of this problem is the fact that the rise of the creative economy is exacerbating economic inequality and stoking the flames of social and political tension. It's not just that our kids need more and better math and art classes, or that many factory workers and farmers require adjustment programs or entrepreneurial opportunities to transition more smoothly into the global economy—though all of this is indeed necessary. At the heart of these apparently unrelated symptoms is an underlying sickness: the aggravation and intensification of the fundamental class divide in America. Our society is growing more unequal both between regions and within them. While roughly 30 percent of our national workforce enjoys the ability to use their creativity at work and get paid for it, they leave the remaining 70 percent holding on dearly to far lower-paying service or manufacturing jobs—stalled in place on the ladder of socioeconomic mobility.

Worse still is the growing impression that while, on the one side, a latte-swilling clique of yuppies rocket up that ladder and pour money into gentrifying urban neighborhoods, on the other side, a coffer-draining gang of CEO and Wall Street robber barons rakes in the bonuses and erects immense McMansions in the suburbs. Stuck in the middle are growing numbers of Americans—liberal, conservative, and independent—united only in their growing distaste for this elite. True to reality or not, this impression is poisoning the political air we breathe, setting in motion a politics of anxiety and reaction that retards America's ability to exploit the full economic potential of the creative age.

The regionally uneven nature of the creative economy's development—the way that the beacons of the new creative class draw disproportionately from the nation's talent pools—further reinforces these divisions. And within those very creative centers—the San Franciscos, Bostons, Washington D.C.s, and Seattles—economic inequality is worse than anywhere else in the nation. Add to that the fact that housing has become almost completely unaffordable to middle-class and working-class people in these cities, and we see another overlapping class divide: There are those who own property, and those who can't buy into the system. Caught somewhere in between are the young but not yet established scientists, engineers, and other creative types these cities will need for long-term growth.

Interestingly, as more and more public attention turns toward the culture wars and political divide between red and blue America, it's almost as if the deep economic divisions that plague us are too intense and problematic even to be mentioned. But the class divide in this society is too deep and too fundamental to be swept under the rug or wished away: Sooner or later we will have to deal with it.

We've seen these divisions before; every society has. The rise of the industrial economy split our society into two classes, even as it increased overall technology, productivity, and wealth. What we need now is something as large-scale as the New Deal, a feat of political and economic mastery that simultaneously spurred the American industrial engine while allowing regular working people to earn a bigger paycheck. This enabled them to buy suburban homes, fuel the mass production of cars and appliances, and best of all educate their children, creating for a limited time a true ladder of upward mobility.

To begin to solve these problems, we must recognize the fact that every single human being is creative. We can no longer prosper and succeed by taking advantage of the creative energies of 30 or even 40 percent of our workforce, leaving the vast reservoir of the other 70 percent untapped. Rather, we must work to build a fully *creative society* by instituting mechanisms and policies that ameliorate the deep-seated tensions caused by the creative economy. Moving from merely creative economic production to this creative social structure is the only way forward.

The solutions go far beyond old conceptions of big government: An activist public sector alone cannot solve them, just as the markets alone cannot. Discovering and implementing the solutions to the growing disconnections and disparities of the creative age will take an effort immense enough to make the land-grant colleges, the public-school system, the GI Bill, the creation of a national R&D investment program, and indeed the New Deal itself look modest by comparison. This effort will require the energies of all—business, government, universities, the civic sector, and especially the average American citizen, who is ultimately the key source from which the collective energy of our entire nation must be drawn.

But where is this effort to build the equivalent of the canal systems, the port systems, the railroad and highway infrastructures of the creative age? How can our leadership be so collectively clueless in the face of what may be the most ferocious onslaught of global competition in more than a century? How to set about constructing the education and innovation systems that our times require if we are to flourish as a society and as a good global neighbor? How will we prepare our people—especially the 70 percent who, until now, have been offered few opportunities to match the insecurities of the modern-day global economy?

## The Argument for a Creative Society

This book examines the new global competition for talent and the challenges it brings with it—for the United States and the world. Part One traces the rise of the creative economy, identifying the factors that have propelled it forward as well as those that have limited its full emergence. Chapter 2 shows how important openness to people is to economic growth, and why long-run economic success turns on harnessing the full creative potential of each and every human being. It does this in part by addressing the ongoing debate over my theory of creativity and economic growth. Chapter 3 looks historically at the American economic experience, arguing that it was shaped fundamentally by openness to new people and ideas.

Part Two turns to the escalating global competition for talent. Chapter 4 examines how the United States is faring in this competition, examining our growing restrictiveness toward foreign talent. Chapter 5 turns to the rise of significant competitors to America's creative economy dominance. The globalization of talent, this chapter argues, is the driving force of the creative economy. In contrast to other factors of production, talent is mobile, and people can and do pick where they want to go. Chapter 5 also provides rankings on the creative class and on a new Global Creativity Index (based on measures of technology, talent, and tolerance) for some forty-five countries worldwide. Chapter 6 looks at how cities around the world are increasing their ability to compete for talent and harness the energy of their own creative people. In the end, it will be these cities, not just the countries that contain them or the companies that populate them, that will either draw or drive away global creative talent.

It is often said new competitors rarely provide the death knell for established powers; the fatal wounds are almost always self-inflicted. Part Three examines the internal problems facing the United States as it adapts to the creative age. The rise of the creative economy is reinforcing and exacerbating the fundamental class divide in the United States, creating a new economic geography of class along economic and social lines. Chapter 7 shows how the creative economy is reinforcing economic inequality producing a greater divide between regional haves and have-nots and also generating greater inequality within the leading creative centers themselves. In particular, it looks at the high levels of income inequality and other social and economic problems in the United States as by-products or "externalities" of the creative age. While such externalities are nearly always associated with the rise of new economic systems, the United States today seems unwilling to address them and moreover fails to recognize that the real issue with inequality is not social or moral: It's that inequality represents a waste of human creative potential. Chapter 8 examines the political and cultural divisions that affect the ability of the United States to respond to new challenges. While theories of political polarization are overdrawn, the United States is beset by a level of cultural and political division that may make it hard for us to address the core problems we confront. The key question is not whether the United States can get its act together but how fast it can do so relative to other competitors.

Chapter 9 concludes the book by outlining an agenda for the future, identifying in broad terms what the U.S. and other nations might do to cultivate the creative energies of people and to prosper in the creative age. Without a doubt, the U.S. has tremendous competitive and transformative capabilities. Now, for the first time in decades, they will truly be put to the test.

**Part I**

# The Creative Age

# 2

# Creativity Matters

*Imagination is the living power and prime agent of all human perception.*                                    —SAMUEL TAYLOR COLERIDGE

True to the old Chinese curse, we live in interesting times. The transformation we are experiencing is one of epochal proportions, as big as—perhaps bigger than—anything we have experienced in more than a century. Our economy is morphing in new ways every day, from an older industrial system founded on raw materials to a creative economy bound only by the limits of human talent and imagination. This fundamental shift in the way the economy is organized is also causing sweeping changes in the way we work, the way we use our time, our lifestyles and leisure, the kind of communities we choose to live in, and the personal and familial identities we construct.

Because this radical revamping of the ways we work, live, play, and think is still only in its adolescence, our times are fraught with contradiction. Take a look around. What do you see? Pure human genius and innovation accompanied by pure human greed and destruction. The breakdown of hierarchical order accompanied by the breakdown of social cohesion and economic certainty. Dizzying prosperity accompanied by extreme poverty. These are the social and economic conditions that define our world. How to understand them? Where did they come from? Where, most importantly, are they taking us?

## The Rise of the Creative Economy

In recent decades, a series of gradual changes in our economy and society have combined to give us a fundamentally new system of working and living. I call the age we are entering the creative age because the key factor propelling us forward is the rise of creativity as the prime mover of our economy. Not just technology or information, but human creativity.

Innovation doesn't come magically from an invisible hand. As Stanford University economist Paul Romer has long argued, great advances have always sprung from ideas.[1] Ideas don't fall from the sky; they come from people. People write the software. People design the products. People start the new businesses. People create the music and images that come streaming at us out of devices that other people create. Every new thing that gives us convenience or pleasure or productivity—be it the Palm Pilot, *Pulp Fiction,* the iPod, or the tweaks that make a chemical plant run better—can be traced to human ingenuity, to people having ideas and finding better ways of doing things. What really drove the great boom of the 1990s was not greed or even rampant venture capital and high-tech entrepreneurship, but a tremendous unleashing of human creativity of all sorts.

In a larger sense, it's always been this way: People think of something new—farming instead of hunting and gathering, building a steam engine instead of harnessing a horse—and the material and social realities follow. What's happened in recent times is that the pace and intensity of all forms of creative work have exploded. That's what produced most of our economic growth over the late twentieth century.

Perhaps the most incredible thing about the creative age is that it holds the possibility not only for economic growth and prosperity, but also for a much fuller development of human potential in general. Over the past decade, I've interviewed literally hundreds of people, from executives and engineers to secretaries and recent college graduates, who left secure jobs for something new. Very few of them were doing it for a stock-option bonanza, which they knew was a long shot, or for higher pay—usually the pay was lower. Time and again they told me they cherished the chance to do "exciting work" and to play a part in "building something new." In short, people love to do creative work; it's what we're about.

I've also visited auto factories and steel plants across the U.S. where Japanese-style continuous-improvement methods were instituted.[2] In every one of these places, workers told me that they now *enjoyed* coming to work, rather than dreading it—not because their pay was better or their job was easier but because they finally had a chance to contribute their ideas. I've seen it on the so-called lower rungs of the economic ladder as well. While unions and politicians bemoan the loss of good manufacturing jobs, such as machine-tool operators, states like Pennsylvania and Michigan have actually had a hard time filling them, even as cosmetology schools fill up with working-class kids hoping to be hairstylists. The hair salon typically pays less and offers fewer benefits than the machine shop—but it's seen as a more stimulating career option.

The point is not that we should all join start-ups or become hairstylists. It's simply that what growing numbers of Americans want today is the very same thing needed to strengthen our economy: not just financial gain but the opportunity to engage their creative faculties. The best part of this equation is that the kind of work that people love is also the work that leads to prosperity.

## The Creative Economy by the Numbers

More people than ever before are getting to do creative work for a living. The number of people in highly creative occupations—from architects to aesthetic workers, engineers and scientists to artists and writers, high-end managers, planners, and analysts to health care, finance, and law professionals—climbed dramatically in the twentieth century. In 1900, creative workers made up only about 10 percent of the U.S. workforce. By 1980, that figure had risen to nearly 20 percent. Today, almost 40 million workers—some 30 percent of the

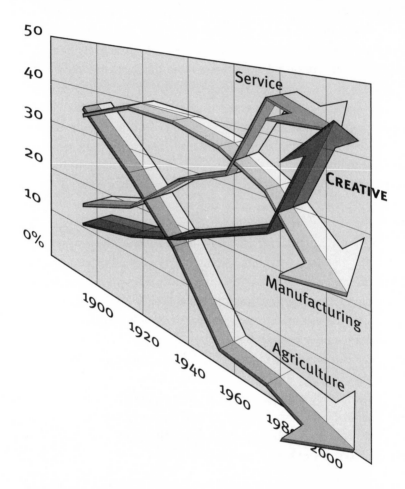

**Figure 2.1: The Growth of the Creative Economy**

The Creative Sector has been the growth engine of the U.S. economy, increasing consistently over the past century and dramatically since 1980.
Updated from: Richard Florida, *Rise of the Creative Class,* New York: Basic Books, 2002.

workforce—are employed in the creative sector. There are, in fact, more creative workers in the United States today than there are traditional blue-collar workers. The trends are similar across much of the advanced industrial world.

What's more, the creative sector accounts for the lion's share of all wealth generation. When we divide the economy into three sectors—the creative, manufacturing, and service sectors—and add up all the wages and salaries paid, the creative sector accounts for nearly half of all wage and salary income in the United States. That's nearly $2 trillion, almost as much as the manufacturing and service sectors combined.

There is broad agreement among economists and business forecasters that the growth of the overall economy will come in the creative or knowledge-based occupations and in the service sector. Fritz Malchup and Peter Drucker long ago pointed to the growth of the knowledge economy and the importance of knowledge workers.

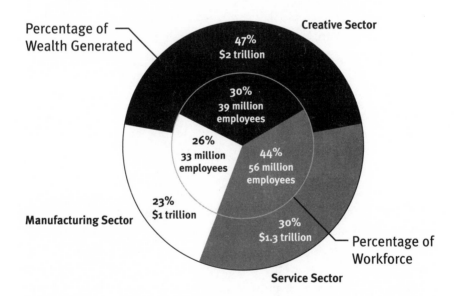

**Figure 2.2: The Economic Impact of the Creative Sector**

The creative sector of the economy accounts for 30 percent of U.S. employment and nearly half of total wages and salaries—roughly equal to the manufacturing and service sectors combined. Compiled by Kevin Stolarick from U.S. Bureau of Labor Statistics.

Writing in 1960, Herbert Simon, the Nobel Prize–winning economist who was also a leader in the fields of cognitive psychology, computer science, and robotics, predicted that while routine factory and
clerical work would be automated, new work would be created in the
fields of management, innovation, and design, predicting that: "There
will be a substantial number of men at professional levels responsible
for the design of product cut, for the design of productive processes,
and for general management." Robert Reich later called attention to
the role of "symbolic analysts," who think and manipulate symbols for
a living. The sociologists Steven Brint and Steve Barley have estimated that knowledge workers compose between 30 and 35 percent
of the workforce and are growing fast.[3] This is how several experts
summarized the trends in a May 2004 issue of the *New York Times:*

> Over the past decade the biggest employment gains came in
> occupations that rely on people skills and emotional intelli-
> gence—like nurse and lawyer—and among jobs that require
> imagination and creativity: designer, architect, and photogra-
> pher. But not all of the new jobs require advanced degrees or
> exceptional artistic talent; note the rise of employment for hair
> stylists and cosmetologists. Trying to preserve existing jobs will
> prove futile—trade and technology will transform the economy
> whether we like it or not. Americans will be better off if they
> strive to move up the hierarchy of human talents. That's where
> our future lies.[4]

A 2004 book by economists Frank Levy and Richard Murnane
looked closely at the changes that have occurred in the kinds of work
people actually do over the course of the past several decades.[5] Using
comprehensive data from the U.S. Department of Labor's *Dictionary of
Occupational Titles,* which provide painstaking detail on twelve thousand individual occupations, Levy and Murnane show how work has
split into the following types:

- *Expert thinking:* Jobs that require creativity and expert problem solving, from designing new products to diagnosing ill-

nesses to creating unique dishes from fresh ingredients. These jobs have grown rapidly since 1969, experienced considerable salary and wage gains, and are predicted to continue to grow.

- *Complex communication:* High-paying jobs in design, innovation, and motivation or management of others that require face-to-face interaction. These jobs have also grown rapidly, seen considerable wage and salary increases, and are likely to continue to do so.

- *Routine cognitive tasks:* Jobs that require mental tasks that follow well-defined logical rules, such as work in a call center or data-processing center, and also some routine aspects of software coding. These jobs have declined in the United States since 1969 and are especially vulnerable to outsourcing.

- *Routine manual tasks:* Physical-labor jobs that follow defined rules, such as blue-collar assembly-line work. These jobs have already declined and will continue to be vulnerable to automation and outsourcing.

- *Nonroutine manual tasks:* Physical-labor jobs that are difficult to automate because they require "optical recognition" and "fine muscle control," including a range of factory jobs, but also personal-service jobs such as haircutting or housecleaning. These jobs declined between 1969 and 1989 and have leveled off since then. While nonroutine factory work is vulnerable to outsourcing, personal services are not. It's hard to imagine a robot that cuts hair or gives good back massages, and impossible to contemplate how to offshore manicures.

In Levy's and Murnane's estimation, then, nearly all of the growth in jobs has come in two fields: expert thinking and complex communication. These are sectors that define the skill requirements and work profile of the creative class to a tee.

As Levy and Murnane also point out, highly educated people, particularly those in such occupations, have sucked up nearly all of the wage and salary gains over the past two decades. These gains reached record highs in the 1990s, even as the wages of high school graduates deteriorated considerably, leaving them worse off in terms of their real purchasing power than in the early 1970s. High school dropouts fared even worse. All of these trends contribute to the growing class divide we face as we traverse the creative age.

## Creative Capital

From an economic point of view, creativity is a form of capital—call it "creative capital." Economists have long thought in terms of different types of capital: physical capital (raw material), investment capital (finance), land (functional property), human capital (educated people), and social capital (the kind that comes from people acting in groups). Today's leading growth theorists argue that economies develop not so much as a result of their physical and investment capital but based on the stocks of human capital they possess. But human capital is typically measured by economists based on workers' formal educational levels.

If we use the most conventional measure of human capital—the percentage of people with a bachelor's degree—we tend to overlook extraordinary contributions made by entrepreneurs and cultural creatives who may not have completed college, people like Bill Gates, William Faulkner, or David Geffen. Plus, the human capital measurement is based on the assumption that specific skills matter and that these skills are the ones being taught by our educational institutions. This concept made sense for the industrial age, when mass production was key and skills were implanted in large numbers of the workforce. In the creative age, real economic growth requires more than a degree.

Now it is the intrinsically human ability to create new ideas, new technologies, new businesses models, new cultural forms, and whole new industries that really matters. This is what I mean by creative capital. For an economy to grow and prosper, all types of organizations—individuals, firms, cities, states, and even nations—must nurture, harness, mobilize, and invest in creativity across the board. Similarly, for economists and academics to have any success whatsoever in measuring such capital, we must find ways to take into account the full range of human creative potential. This is the reason I've moved to an occupationally based model of measurement in my work; it still doesn't go the full distance in getting at what drives creative economic growth, but I believe it's more accurate than the standard education-level measurement.

Recently, a team of Canadian economists made a significant breakthrough in quantifying creative capital, differentiating it from human capital, and demonstrating its importance to economic growth.[6] The Canadian team found that if you measure *actual skills* (similar to my occupationally based concept of creative capital) rather than simply educational qualification or degree, you get a much more powerful explanation for economic growth. As *The Economist* puts it, "educational qualifications may be relatively easy to measure, but [they] offer only a poor proxy for human capital. What one wants is a direct measure of economically relevant skills." Exactly.

Working with Statistics Canada, the research team came to two important conclusions. First, indicators that reflect a population's literacy do much better in predicting economic growth than measures based on years-in-school. This speaks to the importance of independent, creative thinking to economic growth. As crucial as a strong educational system is to a country's economic well-being, the number of days that children and young adults are required to sit in desks tells us little about how they will do as individuals—let alone how a society will do in the aggregate. It takes genuine *learning*—both in and out of our classrooms, and teaching both the fundamentals and more advanced, creative problem solving—to build an economy.

But what's even more important than the literacy measure's success as a comparatively better indicator is its more straightforward success in demonstrating a positive and significant connection to long-term economic well-being. The Canadian economists note that a 1 percent rise in literacy scores (relative to the international average) is associated with an eventual 2.5 percent rise in labor productivity and a 1.5 percent rise in per capita GDP (both also relative to the international average). Rising investments in literacy, they conclude, are closely tied to a country's subsequent GDP growth and increased productivity.

Perhaps the study's major drawback is that the necessary data (a country's results on the International Adult Literacy Survey) were available for only fourteen OECD countries: Belgium, Canada, Switzerland, Denmark, Finland, Germany, Ireland, Italy, the Netherlands, Norway, New Zealand, Sweden, the United Kingdom, and the United States. Even with this limited pool, though, a definite pattern exists: The three countries where literacy rose the fastest in the period 1960–1995 also experienced the fastest relative growth. The three countries with the least relative improvement in skills (whether because of a lack of investment or because they had already progressed further by 1960), New Zealand, Sweden, and the United States, experienced a relatively slower growth rate. "The key economic policy implication that comes out of this result," write the authors of the study, "is that . . . human capital accumulation matters for the long-run well-being of developed nations."

## Every Human Being Is Creative

One of the greatest fallacies of modern times is that creativity is limited to a small group of people with particular talents. Most people, the belief goes, don't want to be creative, couldn't do it if asked, and would be very uncomfortable in an environment where creativity was expected of them. This belief is false.

The single most overlooked—and single most important— element of my theory is the idea that *every human being is creative*. By our very nature, each and every person is endowed with an incredible capacity for innovation, a by-product of the innate human capability to evolve and adapt. Creative capital is thus a virtually limitless resource. Human beings are creative in many different ways, and in many different fields that go beyond acquired skills. Each of us has creative potential that we strive to exercise, and that can be turned to valuable ends. If we are to truly prosper, we can no longer tap and reward the creative talents of a minority; everyone's creative capabilities must be fully engaged. In my opinion, the great challenge of our time will be to spark and stoke the creative furnace inside every human being.

The creative class concept should therefore be understood as neither elitist nor exclusionary. In fact, I coined this term largely as a result of a personal and intellectual frustration with the snobbery of such concepts as "knowledge workers," "the information society," "high-tech economy," and the like. I chose "creative class" because I found it to be both more accurate in defining the real source of economic value creation and also more useful in highlighting who of our fellow workers is or is not rewarded monetarily and professionally for making use of their own inherent creativity. The real challenge of our time is to extend its membership beyond the 30 percent or so who currently are allowed in—to make the creative class a much broader and inclusive group that taps the great reservoirs of creative human energy that are already in our midst.

For creativity is the great leveler. It's a trait that can't be handed down, and it can't be owned in the traditional sense. It does not recognize the social categories that we impose upon ourselves. It defies gender, race, ethnicity, sexual orientation, and outward appearance. We cannot know in advance who the next David Ogilvy, Gwendolyn Brooks, Paul Allen, Oscar Wilde, or Barack Obama will be, or where they will come from. Yet our society continues to encourage the creative talents of a minority, neglecting the creative capacities of many more. Consider what Dave Bayless, a venture-capital investor and writer, has to say on the subject: "Even if a person doesn't happen to have the talent that is currently in demand today, that underappreciated talent could well prove to be foundational for the economy of tomorrow." For precisely this reason, it is useful to think of the vast collective pool of human creativity as an enormous ecosystem where the traits of one type of being are complementary to and symbiotic with those of another. Diversity is not merely enjoyable; it is essential. "Biologists were the first to understand the importance of diversity to a healthy ecological system," writes urbanist Don Rypkema, "but it is true of an economic system as well. . . . The competitive place won't just focus on industrial diversity, but perhaps even more importantly on human diversity."

Our society is not engaging even a fraction of the creative capital at its disposal. On the one hand, we are doing a relatively poor job of motivating the 30 percent of the workforce fortunate enough to make up the creative sector of the economy. A 2004 study of Silicon Valley workers provides some useful data with which to evaluate the issue of how much creativity employers actually tap on the job.[7] According to the study, based on personal interviews with 316 Silicon Valley workers, nearly nine in ten respondents said they were "creative" outside work: 49 percent were involved in artistically creative activities, such as playing a musical instrument, while another 38 percent said they were involved in a creative hobby. But only 40 percent of the workers surveyed said their jobs required a lot of creativity, while almost 20 percent said their jobs required "no creativity at all." Interestingly, while more than three-quarters of high-tech workers said their jobs require a "lot of creativity," less than half said that their bosses were supportive of them being "creative on the job." And this is for the high-tech elite.

On the other hand, we are systematically neglecting the creative potential of the 70 percent of the population that lies outside the creative class. As Chapter 7 will show, inequality is rising, and there are fewer and fewer rewarding job opportunities for people without college degrees. This amounts to massive creative waste, a huge inefficiency in our system for generating and harnessing creative capital. My best estimate is that we are tapping at most 10 percent of our latent creative capital. Consider the wealth, prosperity, and human betterment possible if we began to draw on even a fraction of that untapped creativity.

Put these three basic ideas together—that creativity is the most important source of wealth in the modern world, that every human being is creative, and that people everywhere place a high value on engaging creative work—and you begin to see the scope of the transformation. The last such change, the corporate-industrial transformation of the late 1800s and early 1900s, became complete only after its benefits began to accrue more broadly throughout society. Not just skilled-trades people but unskilled workers joined assembly lines and unions, and saw their wages and incomes rise. Industrialization in nineteenth- and early twentieth-century America did not remain confined to factories and power plants. Agriculture, too, became mechanized; electricity brought machines into homes, schools, stores, and offices; and everybody began to drive cars. Machines and ready power relieved much physical drudgery and so brought an incomparable improvement to people's lives.

The future of the creative economy presents an even more compelling vision. It holds out the promise to relieve the mental drudgery that now consumes a vast chunk of so many people's work and lives. Given the room and the resources to flourish, it might massively increase the wealth of society and the economic situation of the many, even as it allows us to more fully develop our unique human capabilities.

## The 3 Ts of Economic Growth

So how can creativity best be harnessed for sustained economic growth? What powers economic growth? What do we need to do to ensure prosperity for the next century? The answer lies in a formula I call the 3 Ts of economic development: Technology, Talent, and Tolerance. Economists have typically emphasized the first two Ts, but to truly prosper in the creative age, all 3 Ts, and especially the third one, tolerance, are essential.

The first of the three is also the least controversial; economists have long argued that technology is the key to growth. MIT's Robert Solow won a Nobel Prize for his work in isolating technology as the driving force of such growth. Paul Romer argues that growth is an endogenous process, based on the continuous accumulation and exploitation of human knowledge. I agree wholeheartedly that technology plays a fundamental role in economic growth. In fact, I consider it so important that I made it my first T.

Talent is the second variable in my model. Leading economists, including Nobel Prize winner Robert Lucas, have argued that growth is a consequence of human capital, a view shared by Harvard's Edward Glaeser.[8] Lucas and others have argued convincingly that more urbanized and denser urban areas realize a tremendous productivity advantage because they gain those economies of combining people's creative energy. Lucas refers to the human capital-augmenting functions of cities as "Jane Jacobs's externalities," and has gone so far as to suggest she deserves a Nobel Prize for that idea. In this view, the role of cities is to bring together and augment human capital, and since places with more human capital grow more rapidly than those with less, urbanization (and the density that accompanies it) is a key element of innovation and productivity growth. As mentioned above, I capture the role of talent by substituting a measure of creative *occupations* for the typical education-based measure of human capital, thus emphasizing what people *actually do* over past educational achievements.

This brings me to the third T, tolerance. While economists have long recognized technology and talent as key drivers of economic growth, they tend to think of them in the same way they think of more conventional factors of production, like raw materials. That is, they think of them as constituting a stock. According to this view, places are endowed with certain stocks of technology or talent and these stocks account for their different rates of innovation and economic growth. But resources like technology, knowledge, and human capital differ in a fundamental way from more traditional factors of production like land or raw materials: they are not stocks, but *flows*. People are not forever wedded to one place; they can and do move around. The technology and talent that people therefore equally bring with them are mobile factors, and accordingly flow into and out of places.

The key, then, is to understand why some places are better than others at generating, attracting, and holding on to these critical factors of production. The answer, I believe, lies in their openness, diversity, and tolerance—or lack thereof. When I say tolerance, I mean more than simply accepting different kinds of people, though of course that's an important start. But truly successful societies go out of their way to be open and inclusive, and the places most likely to mobilize the creative talents of their people are those that don't just tolerate differences but are *proactively inclusive.* Courting divergent ideas and inputs isn't about political correctness; it's an economic growth imperative. My research finds a strong correlation between, on the one hand, places open to immigrants, artists, gays, bohemians, and socio-economic and racial integration, and, on the other, places that experience high-quality economic growth. Such places gain an economic advantage in both harnessing the creative capabilities of a broader range of their own people and in capturing a disproportionate share of the flow.

My own findings on diversity and economic growth have been confirmed in several other studies. University of Toronto researchers Meric Gertler and Tara Vinodrai, working in collaboration with Gary Gates and me, found that the relationship between bohemians and high-tech growth not only held but was in fact markedly stronger among Canadian regions. Independent research by the Australian think tank National Economics discovered the relationship between gays, bohemians, and tech growth to be quite substantial in their comparative analysis of Australian regions and urban centers.[9]

The detailed econometric research by Gianmarco Ottaviano of the University of Bologna and Giovanni Peri of the University of California at Davis provides further independent confirmation of the relationship between ethnic and cultural diversity and economic growth in U.S. regions.[10] A "more multicultural urban environment," they write, "makes U.S.-born citizens more productive." They then go on to offer two reasons for these findings. First, immigrants tend to have skills that complement those of American-born people. "Even at the same level of education," they note, "problem solving, creativity, and adaptability may differ between native and foreign-born workers so that reciprocal learning may take place." For obvious reasons, this affects high-tech and creative industries positively. Second, foreign-born workers may provide valuable services not available from American workers. "An Italian stylist, a Mexican cook, and a Russian dancer," they write, "provide different services than their US-born counterparts and, because of a taste for variety, this may increase the value of total production." In an increasingly global world, everyone brings unique skill sets to the table. As a result, the potential prosperity of this age is enormous, but it will not be realized until we recognize the fact that every single human being is a source of creative energy that can lead to economic growth and increased living standards.

There's another reason openness and tolerance breed innovation and economic advancement. Thanks to the laws of physics and self-interested economics, traditional "materialist" societies are naturally organized in terms of zero-sum trade-offs. To gain something you don't have, you have to give something up—whether it's money, raw material, or manufactured product. If one person or society wins, another loses. Since materialist economics are literally based on materials, people in such societies get used to behaving as if most interactions, especially with strangers, were zero-sum trade-offs. Norms and values of these societies come to reflect this everyday economic reality, mainly by discouraging social mobility and emphasizing stability and the status quo. This slows social progress and therefore also economic growth.

The creative economy removes these material constraints and gives rise to what Ronald Inglehart has called a "postmaterialist" culture. Raw materials and possessions lose much of their potency in a society where ideas create relatively more economic value. And knowledge, as Romer says, is a nonrival and only partly excludable entity. In an open society, knowledge's nonrival nature means that a piece of new information can be used over and over again, by different people, in varying contexts, and to make new things. We can only partly exclude others from using it—through patents, for example—which further adds to its value to the society as a whole. In a truly free marketplace of ideas, one good piece of knowledge will live several lifetimes, undergo different iterations, and be put to ever more unique purposes.

In the end, the more postmaterialist, tolerant, and accepting of new ideas a place is, the more likely economic growth is. As Carnegie Mellon doctoral student Brian Knudsen puts it, economies that are full of postmaterialist social capital, with people who are typically pushing the envelope, not willing to defer to authority, and interested in self-expression and new ideas, are the ones that will most easily take advantage of the "public good" nature of knowledge. Materialist places, in contrast, are closed, and so will either not care at all about new ideas or, taken to the extreme, actually be hostile toward the existence of those ideas. In short, places with postmaterialist structures are conducive to growth, while places with materialist constitutions are not as conducive to growth, and possibly detrimental to it. Another reason tolerance is so crucial to the 3 Ts of economic growth.

## The Great Creative Class Debate

I would have never guessed when writing *The Rise of the Creative Class* that my theory relating openness to economic growth would become so controversial. At the time, I naively thought I would just let the numbers speak for themselves. With political polarization and the culture wars now escalating on all fronts, though, I suppose it shouldn't be surprising that most of the controversy revolves around the idea that cities, regions, and nations with thriving cultural climates and openness to diversity of all sorts also enjoy higher rates of innovation and high-wage economic growth. In the few short years since I advanced my original theory, I have been accused of eroding traditional family values (I don't), of promoting a gay agenda (I'm straight), and of undermining the very tenets of Judeo-Christian civilization (I'm at a loss).

Such heated rhetoric puzzles me; I harbor no hidden agendas. Over the course of a more than twenty-year academic career, my work has been concerned with one thing: identifying the key factors that drive economic growth. When I find myself in front of audiences primarily interested in arts, culture, or diversity issues, I always start with an apology: I am not a student of those subjects, I say, and I have only a cursory understanding of them. The reason I came to arts, culture, and diversity issues (rather late in my career) is simply because I found them to be fundamental to the process of economic development.

In the interest of full disclosure, I should say that I'm a political independent, fiscally conservative, socially liberal, and a believer in vigorous international competition and free trade. I'm middle-aged, white, Italian-American, single, and straight. I have voted for and served under Democrats, Republicans, and independents, working during the late 1990s with Tom Ridge, the head of Homeland Security under the Bush administration, when he was the governor of Pennsylvania.

I work closely with mayors, governors, and business, political, and civic leaders from both sides of the aisle on economic-development issues. A good deal of the time, quite honestly, I can't even tell who's a Republican and who's a Democrat—a welcome contrast to the bitterly polarized and broken-down state of our national politics. The members of my core team of colleagues and collaborators include international and American researchers, registered Democrats and Republicans (from far-left environmentalists to right-wing libertarians and staunch GOP conservatives), married and single people, recent college graduates and middle-agers, and at least two gay men, one a left-leaning Democrat and the other a moderate Republican. What binds us together is not a political agenda, but our common determination to identify the factors that drive technological innovation, spur growth, and ultimately bring about improved living standards for people from all walks of life. We make these factors our priorities, regardless of which side of the aisle (or the ocean) we happen to occupy, because we believe that if our society is to prosper, the connection between creativity and economic development must remain a nonpartisan issue.

Unfortunately, liberal and conservative critics alike have attempted to politicize these issues and cast my research in an ideological light. From the right, consider what the neoconservative Manhattan Institute has to say:[11]

> To a generation of liberal urban policymakers and politicians who favor big government, Florida's ideas offer a way to talk economic-development talk while walking the familiar big-spending walk. . . . Now comes Florida with the equivalent of an eat-all-you-want-and-still-lose-weight diet. Yes, you can create needed revenue-generating jobs without having to take

the unpalatable measures—shrinking government and cutting taxes—that appeal to old-economy businessmen, the kind with starched shirts and lodge pins in their lapels. You can bypass all that and go straight to the new economy, where the future is happening now. You can draw in Florida's creative class capitalists—ponytails, jeans, rock music, and all—by liberal, big-government means: diversity celebrations, "progressive" social legislation, and government spending on cultural amenities. Put another way, Florida's ideas are breathing new life into an old argument: that taxes, incentives, and business-friendly policies are less important in attracting jobs than social legislation and government-provided amenities.

And, from the left, the following appeared in *Blueprint,* the house organ of the Democratic Leadership Council:[12]

> Those most outspoken about such a culture- and lifestyle-based urban revival have all the heady passion of a religious movement; indeed, they've organized themselves into something called the creative class. One hundred of them—they called themselves the "Creative 100"—met in Memphis last spring to lay out their principles in a document called the Memphis Manifesto. Their mission, it reads, is to "remove barriers to creativity, such as mediocrity, intolerance, disconnectedness, sprawl, poverty, bad schools, exclusivity, and social and environmental degradation." The 1934 Soviet constitution couldn't have said it better.

In the forward to the Australian edition of *The Rise of the Creative Class,* entrepreneur Terry Cutler gets to the root of what seems to motivate this kind of reaction. He recounts a meeting of distinguished intellectuals and civic leaders to whom he presented my key ideas concerning diversity and economic growth. "Summoning my courage," he writes, "I described Florida's findings about the correlation between bohemianism and diversity in the location of high-tech firms. The palpable recoil around the room at such a radical and distasteful recipe for success left me in no doubt that these civic leaders would clearly prefer to drift into a genteel poverty."

Jane Jacobs has a word for this kind of behavior. She calls it "squelching." Jacobs believes that all cities have creative energy, and that all people are creative. What distinguishes thriving cities from those that stagnate and decline is a group of people she calls the "squelchers." Squelchers, she explains, are those political, business, and civic leaders who divert and derail human creative energy by posing roadblocks, acting as gatekeepers, and saying no to new ideas, regardless of their merit. What worries me is that even when they are wrong on the facts, my critics have continued to provide ample ammunition for such squelchers. In the interest of productive dialogue, then, it's important to address the concerns of these critics before moving on with the main themes of this book.

## Chickens-or-Eggs

Some say my theory falls victim to a classic "chicken-and-egg" problem by misunderstanding the cultural effects of economic growth as the underlying cause of that growth. What typically come first, these critics argue, are the jobs. Once a region has those, the people—as well as the amenities, lifestyle, and tolerance—will gravitate naturally. One conventional economic developer put it this way: "Create the jobs and diversity will follow."

This kind of thinking does not square with reality. My research and other recent studies have shown that place does matter; many people choose location first and *then* look for jobs in those locations. A 2002 survey of four thousand recent college graduates reported in the *Wall Street Journal,* for instance, found that three-quarters of the graduates identified location as more important than the availability of a job when selecting a place to live.[13] My own interviews and focus groups have indicated the same trend: People select locations—particular sets of cities—in which to orient their search for work, as opposed to vice versa.

We see in everyday urban life how arts, culture, and demographic diversity help to spur job creation and economic revitalization on the front end (rather than simply following behind these phenomena). Take the gentrification of inner-city neighborhoods like New York's

SoHo or San Francisco's SoMa. What came first in these places? As any sentient observer of urban affairs can attest, these neighborhoods initially lost blue-collar jobs as factories and warehouses moved out of outmoded facilities. Artists, culturally creative people, and immigrants moved in, often reclaiming the properties from ruin by way of illegal conversions and sweat equity revitalization. Gays and singles came next. Only much later—once these initial, pioneering groups had increased real-estate values—did families, professionals, yuppies, technology-based businesses, and retail shops follow.

In the end, the jobs-versus-people question is a false dichotomy. The two come together at the nexus of *place*. Real places provide the thick labor markets that match people to jobs, the mating markets that enable people to find life partners, the social markets that beget friendships, the amenities that allow people to pursue the lifestyles they wish, and the smorgasbord of daily choices that encourage people to construct and validate their identities holistically.

Roger Martin, dean of the University of Toronto Business School and competitiveness consultant for Monitor, has referred to this place-based part of my theory as its "jurisdictional advantage" component. He compares it to Harvard Business School professor Michael Porter's concept of competitive advantage. But where Porter focuses on the ways in which companies identify and leverage their internal strengths, Martin suggests these companies gain an additional advantage from the places in which they're located, particularly in their ability to attract and replenish their stocks of talented people. Because it's no longer a matter of people simply moving to jobs; people move to jobs and places as a total package, and successful places are built up as complex, multifaceted ecosystems that, like those occurring in the natural world, defy simplistic linear thinking.

## What Kind of Growth?

Another line of criticism of the creativity theory has focused on the question of what types of cities create the most jobs. "Jobs data going back 20 years, to 1983," writes one critic in the neoconservative *City*

*Journal,* "show that Florida's top ten cities as a group actually do worse, lagging behind the national economy by several percentage points, while his so-called least creative cities continue to look like economic powerhouses, expanding 60% faster than his most creative cities during that same period." If true, these assertions are intriguing. But for them to be at all useful, it is necessary to break down the numbers into more manageable—not to mention more relevant—sets of statistical analyses, to really get a handle on what *kinds* of jobs, what *kinds* of cities, and therefore what *kinds* of economic growth we are talking about.

With this aim in mind, my colleague Kevin Stolarick of Carnegie Mellon ran a slew of key economic performance indicators for two groups of regions: the eleven top performers on my updated (2004) Creativity Index versus the eleven regions with the lowest Creativity Index scores. He chose eleven regions in each group (instead of the more common "top ten" designation) because there was a tie between two of the ten lowest-ranked regions. To keep things comparable, Stolarick based his calculations on the forty-nine regions with more than 1 million people. The two groups thus represent roughly the top and bottom 20 percent of all 1-million-plus American cities. Take a look at what he found.

## BOOMING EMPLOYMENT AND POPULATION

- Between 1990 and 2000, the creativity leaders generated three times as many jobs as the lowest-ranked regions, 2.32 million versus 850,000 jobs.

- Allowing for the fact that the leading regions employ more people, the leaders still generated jobs at more than twice the rate of the others, 22 percent versus 11 percent.

- The leading creative regions continued to perform better in recent years, deflating the claim that their earlier performance was an unsustainable by-product of the tech boom.

These regions generated more than 35,000 jobs between 1999 and 2002, while the lowest-ranked regions lost nearly 400,000.

- The top-ranked regions added more than 225,000 high-paying creative sector jobs, while the lowest-ranked regions lost more than 30,000 of these jobs. They also added nearly 500,000 people between 1990 and 2000, compared to 125,000 for the lowest-ranked regions, a growth rate of 23 percent versus 9.27 percent.

## Robust Wage and Salary Growth

Considering job creation alone can be misleading. A region may well create lots of jobs, but the quality of those jobs—the wealth they generate and the salaries they pay—also matters.

- According to Stolarick's analysis, the leading Creativity Index regions added more than $100 billion in total wages between 1999 and 2002. That's more than five times the $20 billion added by the lowest ranked.

- Workers in the leading creative regions averaged over $5,000 more in wages and salaries than those in the lowest-ranked regions, $40,091 versus $34,383.

- Wages in the top-performing regions grew at almost double the rate (5.1 percent) of the laggards (2.8 percent). This translates into a far better "raise" for workers in creative cities, who took home 37 percent more money than their counterparts in lower-scoring regions, $5,125 versus $3,129.

## Explosive Innovation and High-Technology

Leading creative centers were also far more inventive, and accounted for far more jobs in high-wage, high-tech fields than low-scoring regions. It's only fair to note that high-tech industry and patents are included in the Creativity Index (along with several other indicators) and thus by definition my highly ranked regions perform better on these measures. Still, these are key economic outputs that many cities are aiming for, so it's worth looking at how the two groups of regions stack up.

- In 2001, the eleven top-ranked regions accounted for eight times the number of high-tech jobs held by the eleven lowest-ranked regions (248,000 versus 61,000).

- The top-ranked regions generated nearly 100,000 more patents than the lowest-ranked regions between 1990 and 1999.

- Even taking into account the larger average size of the highest-ranked regions, they increased their rate of invention (or patenting) at more than double the rate of the laggards—12 percent versus 5 percent.

Given these trends, which city would you put your money on to be an economic powerhouse fifty years from now: Las Vegas, a city typically held up as a model of recent growth by my critics, but that could easily go the way of post-1920s Atlantic City; or San Francisco, which boasts Stanford, Berkeley, and a long legacy of technological and cultural innovation? It's true that between 1990 and 2000, Las Vegas ranked first in population growth and third in job growth. But in per capita income growth, it ranked a lowly 294th out of some 315 U.S. Metropolitan Statistical Areas.

Right-wing critics also challenge my work on the grounds that it doesn't deal adequately with the issue of entrepreneurship and new-firm formation. This happens to be an area in which I've conducted a fair amount of research with colleagues Zoltan Acs, a leading expert in the field, and Sam Youl Lee, a doctoral student at Carnegie Mellon. Our work, supported by the Ewing and Marion Kauffman Foundation, shows that rates of new-firm formation are considerably higher in creative regions, and that entrepreneurship is closely correlated with the Creativity Index.[14]

But the Manhattan Institute crowd is not actually interested in the numbers; it has a much bigger ideological ax to grind. "Liberal policymakers and politicians," it contends, "have latched on to [Florida's] theories so enthusiastically" because "to them, an expanding government is always more interesting than an expanding economy." Now we have it: The real goal here is to denigrate all forms of public policy while promoting the traditional right-wing mantra that tax cuts, privatization, and unfettered free markets will not only generate economic growth, but will also solve all that ails us. While these right-wing prescriptions fuel the flames of conservative ideology, their claims are contradicted by almost everything that serious urban and regional economists have to say on the subject. The broad consensus in the field is that tax rates have at best a minor effect and that real growth stems from the improved productivity and higher rates of innovation produced by concentrations of skilled human capital.

My view is no paean for more government spending. It unequivocally states that large, top-down government development projects are a major part of the problem. I roundly criticize public boondoggles like stadium-building efforts and large-scale downtown revitalization plans. In almost all of my public speaking, I've called for a moratorium on such government megaprojects. Like Jane Jacobs, I argue that real economic development is people-oriented, organic, and community-based.

## The Great Suburban Utopia?

Recently, a related line of thinking has surfaced among urban analysts who argue that the combined effects of the dot-com bust and September 11, 2001, have shifted the engine of regional innovation and growth away from urban centers and back toward the exurbs flung out along highway exits. *New York Times* columnist and conservative cultural critic David Brooks is perhaps the denizen of the new suburban/exurban booster crowd, though admittedly he does a much better job of acknowledging that cities are still tremendously important to a nation's economic life. But Brooks, who like these others once posed his cappuccino-swilling urban-oriented "bobos" as the replacement for 1950s-style organization men, now sees the future as revolving around a new exurban archetype, "patio man." In a *New York Times Magazine* article, "Our Sprawling, Supersized Utopia," Brooks writes:

> The geography, the very landscape of life, is new and unparalleled. In the first place, there are no centers, no recognizable borders to shape a sense of geographic identity. . . . Robert Lang, a demographer at Virginia Tech, compares these new sprawling exurbs to the dark matter in the universe: stuff that is very hard to define but somehow accounts for more mass than all the planets, stars and moons put together. . . . Suburban America is a bourgeois place, but unlike some other bourgeois places, it is also a transcendent place infused with everyday utopianism. That's why you meet so many boring-looking people who see themselves on some technological frontier, dreaming of this innovation or that management technique that will elevate the world.[15]

According to the *Boston Globe,* Edward Glaeser, whose work I greatly admire, agrees that "people want to live in sunny, dry climates and—to the horror of smart-growth advocates everywhere—they actually like car-centered cities. In place of Florida's 'Technology, Talent, and Tolerance,' Glaeser proposes a different recipe, 'Skills, Sun, and Sprawl.' "[16]

Let me start by saying that Glaeser and I have much we agree on. He is, in my mind, the leading scholar of urban and regional economics at work today, and has almost single-handedly revitalized that field. We have shared data, he has given my students solid advice and comments on their work, and he wrote an astute review of *The Rise of the Creative Class.* I agree that the suburbs are the source of much growth. No reasonable observer would suggest that Silicon Valley or the Route 128 area around Boston do not exist. But these innovative peripheries must be understood within a broader regional context, and in relation to the thriving urban centers and the open and tolerant cultures in which they are embedded. I have been consistently clear on the point that the most successful regions offer many options, including flourishing suburbs with affordable housing, safe streets, and good schools.

My real concern, then, is only that the new suburban boosters go overboard with their claims. Much innovation—technological, business, and cultural—continues to occur in cities, and despite the claims of fanatics, the suburbs are no utopia. A report by Jay Greene and Greg Forster (also of the Manhattan Institute)—utilizing data from the National Longitudinal Study of Adolescent Health—found that suburban teens experienced rates of drug and alcohol abuse, drunk driving, cigarette smoking, sexual activity, and delinquent behavior (including stealing and fighting) comparable to, or *exceeding,* those of urban teens. On nearly every score (save for teen pregnancy), their study concluded, the suburbs share many of the social problems we have long assumed to be the province of racially diverse urban centers.[17] In positive ways, too, the suburbs are beginning to look a lot more like our cities as they mature. They are, for instance, much more ethnically and culturally diverse than we commonly believe. A 2001 Brookings Institution report by the demographer William Frey found that the suburbs became much more diverse between 1990 and 2000, with minorities making up more than a quarter (27 percent) of the total suburban population. In fact, in large metropolitan areas such as Chicago, it is the suburbs, and not the central cities, that serve as the ports of entry for increasing numbers of immigrants.[18]

Nonetheless, nearly all of the literature on regional economics emphasizes that cities are based on urbanization economies. This compacting of people is what gives cities their ability to innovate, generate productivity, and grow. Without such urbanization economies, high-cost cities like New York, Chicago, London, Tokyo, or San Francisco simply wouldn't exist. Jane Jacobs noted long ago that cities are key incubators of innovation: "It may be romantic to search for the salves of society's ills in slow-moving rustic surroundings, or among innocent, unspoiled provincials," wrote Jacobs in her classic *The Death and Life of Great American Cities,* "but it is a waste of time. Does anyone suppose that, in real life, answers to any of the great questions that worry us today are going to come out of homogeneous settlements?"[19] Even the great chronicler of 1950s suburban life and author of *The Organization Man,* William H. Whyte, grew to see the suburbs as bland, uninnovative places and spent the later part of his life researching and writing on the creative potential of dense urban centers.

Research by Brian Knudsen demonstrates the powerful effects that density has on economic growth. In a detailed analysis of some three hundred regions, Knudsen found that patenting and high-tech industry are strongly correlated with high population density—especially the concentration of creative people like scientists, engineers, artists, and musicians. The equally detailed research by economists Dora Costa and Matthew Hahn on the location of "power couples" finds that such high-skill, high-earning couples are disproportionately concentrated in larger, denser, higher-amenity urban areas (as opposed to suburbs). In other words, places where people are not sprawled out so thinly tend to have more creative economic activity.[20]

While many people think of the sun—and the Sunbelt—as synonymous with economic growth, most studies have found that neither sunnier weather nor warmer climates are systematically associated with regional growth. Detailed research by the University of Chicago sociologist Terry Clark finds that natural amenities, including sun and temperature, are not associated with the location decisions of high human capital individuals.[21] Such individuals are far more likely to be drawn to cities that offer what he calls "constructed amenities," from arts and culture to high-quality restaurants. Cities from Minneapolis and Chicago to Boston, Seattle, and Toronto have enjoyed long-run economic success despite their frequent cold temperatures, gray skies, and rainy weather. Most systematic studies have concluded that climate has little, if any, effect on regional growth.

I agree wholeheartedly with Glaeser and other economists on the importance of human capital. But as I said earlier, I think there is an important difference between creativity and educational qualifications. Where economists tend to use education as the key measure of human capital, we try to gauge creativity by using occupations—what people actually do. In reality, these two measures are highly correlated. But, as the independent research of the statistician Robert Cushing of the University of Texas at Austin found, my creative capital measure performs better than the educationally based human capital measure at predicting innovation and growth. This measure of creative occupations has the added advantage of being a better tool (than simply counting the number of people with bachelor's degrees) for allowing nations and regions to assess and capitalize on their particular talent assets.

Overall, though, I agree with Glaeser that talent, or human capital, is the primary driver of economic growth for both regions and nations; I say so in *The Rise of the Creative Class.*[22] But my theory differs from the conventional theory of growth in one important way. While I concur that talent drives growth, my theory goes a step further, to ask: *Why* are some places better than others to harness and attract this human, creative capital? The answer lies in the third T: Tolerance.

That's right—tolerance. In my view, it's not amenities—nor bohemians, nor even gays—that give places the ability to grow and prosper, though they can all signal that ability. What accounts for why places grow is a more fundamental characteristic: simply put, their openness, or what I refer to as "low barriers to entry" for talent. It is important to understand exactly how tolerance and diversity act on talent and in turn on economic growth. In my view, tolerance acts indirectly, giving places the underlying creative capacity to grow. Tolerant, open places have an edge in attracting varied talent from across the entire demographic spectrum. This ability to attract talent in turn bolsters their ability to build and mobilize creative capital, which in turn leads to the ability to innovate, create new business, attract other companies, and ultimately to create new wealth and prosperity.[23]

Finally, there is the issue of what cities and regions should actually *do* with all of this information. The point I need to reemphasize here is that there are no silver-bullet solutions. In fact, I have publicly taken issue with simplistic schemes that try to bolster a city's ability to compete for talent by building latte bars, ultimate Frisbee fields, or music venues. What cities and regions really need to do is figure out where they fall on each of the 3 Ts and make strategic investments in them, especially where they are weak. For cities and regions that are weak on technology or talent, it means bolstering the capabilities in those areas. For regions that are weak on tolerance, it means becoming more open. To be successful, regions need to do all 3 Ts well and to offer people lots of options. Our demography is changing, regardless of whether we agree with the social implications of the changes or not. Fewer people are married; fewer live in nuclear families. There are more and more singles, power couples, dual-income-no-kids families, and gays. All of these groups need options.

Of course, superb suburbs with excellent schools and low crime are essential. But so are other kinds of neighborhoods and communities. Jacobs long ago said that regions are federations of neighborhoods or communities. This is what regions like Boston, San Francisco, and New York provide: lots of options that appeal to lots of different contributors of talent. And cities need to do all of this in a way that taps the energy of their people. Top-down planning approaches, Jacobs argued, almost always bring higher costs and more problems than they are worth.

The way for cities and regions to create a balanced approach with lots of options is to allow it to happen organically, by finding ways to unleash the creative energy of lots of different groups trying lots of different things, some of which will make little difference and some of which will be successful. Here, all those concerned with the future of cities would do well to remember the financial writer's James Surowiecki's powerful insight about the "wisdom of crowds" in coming up with aggregate solutions to complex problems.[24] They don't do so by all toeing the same moderate line, but rather by making independent and diversified guesses that can then be in some sense compiled. The natural variation that different human beings with different needs and desires bring to the table may, in this respect, be the most powerful tool we have for improving communities, regions, and nations.

## All in the Family

But diversity, I've learned, is not an easy sell. Certain critics predictably blanch at the connection between gays and bohemians and growth. They argue not only that sprawling, sunny suburbs are key, but that another part of the growth equation is a place's connection to family values. Urbanist Joel Kotkin believes my theory mistakes cities that cater to "singles, young people, homosexuals, sophistos, and trendoids" as the driving force of economic growth, when in fact the real engine lies in the outer rings of a city's solar system.

This line of criticism implies that a place must either be family-friendly or gay-and-bohemian-friendly, suburbs-driven or city-oriented—but can't be both. Politically, this is divisive thinking; worse, it's economically inaccurate. Kotkin himself cites McAllen, Texas, and the California cities of Fresno and Riverside as fast-growing, family-friendly cities. Among the 331 metro areas in the United States, McAllen ranks first in the percentage of households with children headed by gay parents, while Fresno and Riverside rank eighth and twenty-first, according to Gary Gates of the Urban Institute. Apparently, "family" means more in these places than just Ward, June, Wally, and the Beaver.

Likewise, various lists of America's most family- or child-friendly places turn out to be loaded with cities that also score high as homes for gays and artists. I cited one such list in *The Rise of the Creative Class.* The top five child-friendly major metros were Portland (Oregon), Seattle, Minneapolis, New York, and San Francisco. All but one of those top five regions ranked well above average on the Gay Index. All five were among the top seven on the Bohemian Index. According to a *Boston Globe* report, Kotkin says he was "startled" when the leaders of older Midwestern communities began soliciting his advice on how to lure "25-year-old gay college graduates to the regions." "What to you mean?" he replied. "You don't have a snowball's chance in hell." Not only does this assumption smack of arrogance and elitism, it also blindly ignores the fact that many of these people *already* live in places like St. Louis.

The most successful regions welcome all kinds of people. They offer a range of habitation choices, from nice suburbs with single-family housing to hip urban districts for the unattached. *Why* do they offer all of the above? Simple: because they have to. Like it or not, only 23.5 percent of Americans now live in a standard nuclear family with two parents and children at home. According to the 2000 Census, there are 95.7 million single Americans, a number representing an astounding 43 percent of U.S. residents age fifteen and over. Increasingly, young people are delaying marriage and child rearing. More and more adults are separating or divorcing. Many of us live in some sort of alternative personal arrangement. Appealing only to traditional families and bashing everyone else may make good propaganda for the culture wars, but as a development strategy, it's a pretty narrow approach—and any region or politician that implements that approach stands to alienate a lot of talented people.

Yet these black-or-white-only critics continue to drive a wedge. "The new mantra advocates an urban strategy that focuses on being 'hip' and 'cool' rather than straightforward and practical," write Kotkin and his colleague Fred Siegel, preferring to tackle a straw-man caricature of my ideas rather than address the facts at hand. "Cities that will win the new competition," they continue, "will be those that pour their resources into the arts and other cultural institutions that attract young, 'with-it' people who constitute, for them, the contemporary version of the anointed. Call them latte cities." This is not at all what I say on the subject. They forget that in *The Rise of the Creative Class,* I explicitly discuss the necessity for cities to build diverse climates that appeal to various groups: gays, straights, young people, retirees, families, and more.

It's worth noting how significantly Kotkin has changed his tune in a very short time. Consider this passage from his 2001 book, *The New Geography,* where he lavishes praise on the new denizens of the Internet age, clustered in gentrifying urban centers, as the economic motor force of what he then referred to as a digitally driven "knowledge-value revolution":

> New urbanites are not, for the most part, drawn from the typical American middle class family . . . but from two distinct groups largely outside the mainstream. One group is recent immigrants. . . . The second group . . . consists largely of childless people—aging boomers, childless couples, gays, 'empty nesters,' and singles. . . . These often-unattached new urbanites constitute the critical fuel for the post-industrial urban economy. Companies, wherever they might be located, rely increasingly on skilled urban professionals in fields from fashion design, entertainment, and Internet commerce to international trade, investment, specialized retail, banking, and other business services.[25]

Changing theories with the oscillations of the business and political cycles, we are expected to believe that in just four years' time the whole of what propels economic advantage has shifted to an entirely new set of low-cost suburban centers. The problem is, cultural climates and business cycles ebb and flow. The important thing remains to identify enduring economic and social trends.

In attempting to debunk the ideas behind *The Rise of the Creative Class,* such critics tend to misrepresent my work in other ways as well. At one point, they criticize the "latte Index—the density of Starbucks" in a given area, which, implicitly, my team and I use "as a measure of urban success." Huh? Not once do my collaborators or I ever reference such a ludicrous measure. In fact, my book points to the major pitfall of trying to correlate amenities (whether coffee shops or symphony halls) to either talent or economic growth: These measures are necessarily based on crude, biased, and unreliable data. This is precisely why we developed measures such as the Bohemian Index, which attempt to capture the actual concentration—what we refer to as "revealed locational preferences"—of creative people.

These criticisms compare my measures (suggesting them to be inferior) to the "New Economy Index" developed by Robert Atkinson of the Progressive Policy Institute. Atkinson and I have long been colleagues. I know his work well and respect it. My team collaborated closely with Atkinson in the development of this index; we exchanged data, and I advised and commented extensively on it. There are great similarities between the two measures: Both make use of basic data on technology, talent, and other factors, and they are rather closely correlated to each other. Even more strangely, the measure of high-tech industry we use in the Creativity Index is the same one developed and used by the Milken Institute, with which Kotkin is closely affiliated. As my book notes, it was graciously provided to me by his Milken Institute colleague Ross de Vol. So much for divisive rhetoric.

## Gays and Growth: What's Really at Stake

I'm tempted to believe that *the* key concern from which all other critiques flow is a visceral abhorrence of the idea that gay populations could possibly have a positive impact on their communities—and, indeed, their country. While we've not planned it this way, our findings have an eerie resonance in contemporary American society's impassioned debate over gay marriage. Massachusetts, the first state to attempt to legalize gay marriage, ranks first both on my Creativity Index and on the Milken Institute's most recent ranking of high-tech states, while San Francisco and Seattle, perennial leaders on almost every listing of high-tech hot spots, boast the same distinction. States and cities that have already or are currently trying to restrict gay rights tend to rank at the very bottom of such lists.

Several critics have brought up the success story of Silicon Valley: Isn't it a staid, boring place—a "nerdistan," to use Kotkin's vocabulary— that appeals mainly to conventional engineering types who want to *avoid* artists, bohemians, and gays? My book argues that, on the contrary, Silicon Valley can be understood only in relation to the adventurous culture and great research universities of the *entire* Bay Area, a place where early hippie-entrepreneurs like Steve Jobs and Steve Wozniak were not merely tolerated, but actually *financed* by venture capitalists. Imagine the long-haired, bearded, sandal-wearing Jobs and Wozniak, à la 1972, showing up at Mellon Bank in Pittsburgh with their new invention, the personal computer, in tow; would they have made it past the security guards at the front door?

Furthermore, in our analysis of the connection between tolerance and technology, Gates and I went to great lengths to control for the special circumstance of the San Francisco Bay Area. As my book reports, we even removed it from our analysis to ensure that it was not skewing the results. As I recount there, "the influence of the Gay Index on high-tech industry was strengthened when San Francisco was removed from the analysis."

In his 2003 book, *The City as Entertainment Machine,* University of Chicago sociologist Terry Clark offers a more reasoned and nuanced critique of our findings on gays and high-tech location. Clark reexamines this relationship using detailed information from thousands of U.S. counties. His findings lead him to conclude that "gay relations with jobs appear strong in large metro areas, but fall in smaller metro areas." Gates and I have no quarrel with Clark's county-level results. In Chapter 14 of *The Rise of the Creative Class,* I explicitly state that gays and bohemians are much more strongly associated with high-tech and job growth in larger metropolitan regions, while immigrants tend to drive growth in small- and medium-size regions.

But I go on to note that it is precisely the result for large metro regions that warrants attention. Using counties as the basic measurement unit masks the true relationship between gays and high-tech location, since people (both gays and straights) can, and do, commute relatively long distances to work. In actuality, gays and urban singles commute from San Francisco to work in Silicon Valley, while family-oriented professionals live in Silicon Valley suburbs and work in downtown San Francisco. What gives the Bay Area its advantage is that it has something for everyone.

Nonetheless, it's amazing how many times people misconstrue what Gates and I have to say on this score. Many in both academe and the general public seem to think we are positing a direct connection between being gay and being in high-tech industry. Not once do we imply that gays literally *cause* high-tech growth. Rather, we see a strong and vibrant gay community as a solid *leading indicator* of a place that is open to many different kinds of people. Ronald Inglehart, a political scientist who has studied the relationship between culture and economic growth for some four decades, has noted that the lack of societal acceptance of gays is the most significant remaining bastion of intolerance and discrimination around the world. Accordingly, places that accept gays are also likely to be accepting of all different types of people, and those places therefore open themselves up to innovation and entrepreneurship from a wide range of human sources.

Whatever pundits might say about our findings, business and civic leadership in city after city has taken them to heart. In Cincinnati, for example, Procter & Gamble joined with civic and gay activists to overturn Article 12, which forbade the city from passing antidiscrimination legislation that would apply to gays and lesbians. Why did they go to such great lengths to fight on behalf of the gay and lesbian community? Because they found it discouraged both talented people and companies from relocating there.

As *BusinessWeek* columnist Chris Farrell points out, workplace sexual-orientation discrimination is on the run. "Politicians without a significant challenge in the next election (most of the gerrymandered Congress) can take extreme positions on gay marriage or homosexuality," he writes, "but there's no doubt that discrimination against gays is out in Corporate America." As proof, Farrell offers up the case of Wal-Mart, the nation's largest employer and perhaps the most powerful symbol of Middle America. Wal-Mart has joined the majority of the nation's largest companies by including sexual orientation in its nondiscrimination policies. Farrell goes on to outline a "virtuous circle," where diversity is "good for creativity and creativity encourages diversity." Both of these, he adds, "are good for the profit and loss statement." [26]

Nonetheless, in September 2004, two socially conservative groups, Focus on the Family and the American Family Association, urged their members and conservatives around the country to boycott Procter & Gamble products such as Crest and Tide. Toothpaste and detergent? Why? Because of—you guessed it!—the company's opposition to the antigay-rights Article 12. "For Procter & Gamble to align itself with radical groups committed to redefining marriage in our country is an affront to its customers," said James Dobson of Focus on the Family. It's not just a matter of burning academics at the stake (that has apparently become played out enough that it's not fun anymore); these people would sacrifice even leading American companies in pursuit of their myopic social agenda.

## It's Not the New Economy, Stupid

The creativity thesis has also come under fire from the left. Writing in *The Baffler,* a journal devoted mainly to postmodern culture studies, one literary critic paints me as a vapid elitist and a starry-eyed huckster for creativity and flexibility who continues to plug the New Economy while failing to see how the real economy exploits the masses.

That strikes me as strange, to say the least. In fact, my work has always taken aim at 1990s New Economy fantasies, and has little to do with making cities yuppie-friendly, though leftist critics have tried to frame it that way. In the preface to *The Rise of the Creative Class,* I decry "the naïve optimism of the so-called New Economy." The first chapter notes that "not all is rosy" for workers today: "With no big company to provide security, we bear much more risk. . . . [We suffer] high levels of mental and emotional stress. . . . We crave flexibility but have less time. . . . The technologies that were supposed to liberate us have invaded our lives." Later, I write, "flexibility does not mean the end of long hours. . . . In fact, the long trajectory of modern capitalism has involved the relentless extension of the working day across time and space." A chapter called "The Time Warp" describes the many "insidious factors" that lead to overwork and stress. Moreover, "the real losers, in terms of overwork, are those holding two full-time minimum-wage jobs to support a family. . . . [They] are a modern-day equivalent of the nineteenth century's burned-out factory laborers."

It should be obvious even from these brief excerpts that my theory is no homage to the so-called New Economy and the Internet age.

*The Rise of the Creative Class* opens with the time-traveler example—the whole point of which is to say that the truly big changes of our time are social, not technological. I wrote the book to point out the weaknesses—indeed the silliness—of the "technology will save us" mentality that dominated the 1990s. I tried to focus on the bigger, long-running, and still-evolving changes in our economy and society. In my travels around the country, I do not find people strapping on suits and ties and going back to organization man–style work in big corporations. People are still striving to be themselves, to find meaningful work, and to live in communities that let them validate their identities and live as complete human beings.

Nonetheless, some critics dismiss the advantage of places like San Francisco, Boston, Seattle, and Austin as mere flash-in-the-pan products of the 1990s dot-com bubble. But these places have been experiencing quality growth for decades, building solid new industries that have helped to strengthen our economy and change the world. Much has been made of the fact that several of these 1990s growth centers are losing population. While it's true that people are moving out of these and other places, though, the simple fact of net outmigration (in most cases minimal) misses a bigger point. What's much more informative is to look at the kinds of people and jobs that are moving into or out of regions. Suffice it to say for now that the creative centers continue to attract the high-wage, highly skilled workers even as they lose other jobs.

And while it's certainly true that some higher-skill, creative people are leaving creative meccas for less expensive places, where they can purchase nice homes and live less expensive lifestyles, it's also true that they are not always happy with what they find. Consider this e-mail, which I received from a former Austinite who left for Baton Rouge, Louisiana.

> Diversity is a way of life in Austin. It's always been cool to go one's own way. Risk is more than tolerated, it's respected. Artists are valued. . . . But it's true: the city has cooled—which is part of the reason why my husband and I left. The blur of traffic, bitter once-overpaid techies complaining over lattes—it got to be

too much. Housing prices shot through the roof. The city lost its soul. . . .

Perspective, however, is everything. And living 3 years in a conservative town in the Deep South [Baton Rouge] that "says" it wants to evolve but does everything to stop it—has provided me with a new frame of reference for my Austin. Now when I think of the "real" Austin, my mind ventures deep into South Austin—where artists live side-by-side with recent immigrants. Or just north of campus at the winter holidays—when a whole neighborhood of artists, techies, and others create a kitschy drive-through light display. Or the site of old cars covered in hula grass and green plastic dinosaurs—which seems perfectly reasonable in context.

If nothing else, Austin serves as model of what can go right and wrong with the whole "city of ideas" notion. And if anyone was let down, it was the city herself—her assets were promoted and put on display by many locals in a gratuitous way with no thought to the ramifications or concern for her future. Former Mayor Kirk Watson tried to set the city back on track (bless him), but new conservative energy in federal, state and local government is out to "punish" Texas's liberal oasis for its wanton success. We'll see who wins. I'm betting on the real Austin. Or maybe that's just wishful thinking.

As far as the implication that I don't fully grasp the value of the common workingman and woman, I can only respond that I am intimately aware of both the all-too-common plight and, more importantly, the immense creative potential of blue-collar workers. I learned about these things not only from books and academic life, but firsthand—from my father, who worked for more than four decades in a factory, until it was mismanaged into ruin. My entire theory emphasizes the incredible talents of both factory and service workers, and argues that harnessing the creative energy of people currently ignored and misused is crucial to our long-run economic prosperity.

If social conservatives can't turn back the moral clock to a time when every family resembled the Cleavers, neither can the left magically restore a time when 40 percent of the workforce toiled in blue-collar factory jobs and real bohemians sported black berets and lived in artists' enclaves. The creative economy is not going away, and my advice to my colleagues on the left is simple: Deal with it. They might even discover that the devil they don't know is a lot more benign than the devil they do.

## Completing the System

People often ask me what I have learned since writing *The Rise of the Creative Class.* The short answer is: a lot. But more than anything else, I have come to conclude that the creative economy is no panacea for the myriad social and economic troubles that confront us. No matter how much free-market champions wish that economic inequality, unaffordable housing, the trade deficit, or any one of a number of these problems will somehow magically go away as a result of unmediated economic growth, they won't. Left to its devices, the creative economy, like economic systems before it, will both exacerbate existing social problems and create new ones. The shift from an agricultural to a capitalist industrial economy generated incredible disruption and social turmoil—huge flows of people from the farm to the factory, from rural outposts to great centers—and brought social problems ranging from workplace injury to crime, congestion, and disease.

We are going through a similar period of turmoil and transformation today. Inequality is rising. Housing has become unaffordable in many of the leading creative centers. People are more mobile. We're postponing marriage, and our family structures are morphing. Stress and anxiety are everywhere rising as creativity and mental labor have become the key forces of production. These are all externalities of the creative age—and they are just beginning to be felt. Without any concerted action they will doubtless both continue and worsen into the foreseeable future. We will need to respond to these externalities to enable the creative economy to emerge and to prosper.

Of course, we are currently in the very early stages, the infancy, of

the creative economy. At this point, it is close to impossible for anyone to predict what these institutions and systems can or will look
like in advance. It will take a long time to figure them out—lots of
experiments, lots of on-the-ground work. But one thing is for certain: It will not be enough simply to invest in the creative economy.
That may well be a first step. But the creative economy generates all
sorts of social and economic problems that will need to be addressed
before its benefits can be fully felt.

As with most national challenges, though, the roots of this one
cannot be confronted without first understanding the larger global
economic system in which we operate. It is this system that will increasingly be the source of our country's biggest headaches—and also
its best potential solutions. Our own history serves as the best teacher
of that lesson.

# 3

# The Open Society

*Remember, remember always, that all of us . . . are descended from immigrants and revolutionists.* —FRANKLIN D. ROOSEVELT

The Summer 2004 Olympics in Athens, Greece, captivated more than just the usual crowd of sports enthusiasts and history buffs. Economists, too, got in on the Games. Two "teams" in particular—one at PricewaterhouseCoopers and the other a duo of economics professors—garnered much public attention for creating medal-count predictors based on economic indicators for the participating countries. When the races were run, the national anthems played, and all was said and done, both models did a decent—though not terribly impressive—job of predicting which countries would walk away with how much gold, silver, and bronze.

But the most interesting analysis of the athletic successes and failures of the summer of 2004 came from Daniel Gross, a writer for

*Slate* magazine. Gross argued that if these economists *really* wanted to hit their medal predictions on the head in 2008, they would look beyond the usual indicators of national GDP and aggregate rates of development to the most important economic factor of all: "a nation's openness to human capital." "Some nations have comparative advantages when it comes to certain sports (the Americans in basketball, the Norwegians in cross-country skiing) and comparative disadvantages in others (the Austrians in beach volleyball and the Jamaicans in bobsledding)," noted Gross, "but the free movement of people can alter the dynamics of sports." He went on to cite a dozen examples in which immigrants from Jamaica had won sprinting medals for Slovenia, former Soviet Union Jewish exiles had won wrestling medals for Israel, and so on. Perhaps not surprisingly, the United States was the country that benefited most from this talent exchange, boasting a Cuban-born gymnast, Eritrean-born marathon runner, former Soviet swimmer, and the second-generation daughter of Indian immigrants. Each of these competitors brought home an Olympic medal—and the reputational and economic rewards that come with it—to their adoptive country. And they are only a handful of such Olympic-sports success stories.

Closer to home, we need look no further than the New York Yankees to see how global talent competition has benefited the United States. What would the modern-day Yanks be without the pitching of Orlando Hernandez ("El Duque"), who defected from Cuba in 1997? Or how about three-hundred-save reliever Mariano Rivera, who hails from Panama City? Hitting hero Hideki Matsui, originally from Japan? One thing is certain: These are no longer the Yankees of only Babe Ruth, Lou Gehrig, and Mickey Mantle. As great as those teams of yesteryear may have been, on the *new* Yanks' roster there seems to be a player whom kids from each and every nationality and ethnicity can root for. And, crass as it may sound to reduce our multicultural heroes to dollars-and-cents symbols, an inspired crowd is an inspired economy. Here again, the sports metaphor is not simply a metaphor; it represents in very real terms how the United States benefits economically from the free flow of talented people across global boundaries.

What made America the world's greatest power was not just our technology, market size, or natural resources; the fundamental cause lies in one thing: our amazing ability to attract the world's greatest scientists, engineers, and cultural entrepreneurs. Those who settled America came here to escape religious and social intolerance, bringing with them their talents and intellectual capital to lay the foundations of one of history's greatest economic growth machines.

## Openness and Economic Growth

Openness is the real motor force of economic growth. Recognizing this means we have to rethink the way that culture affects economics. Social and economic theorists from Max Weber to Edward Banfield and Daniel Bell have argued that culture effects economic growth by producing incentives that promote effort, thrift, and hard work. Weber's classic work, *The Protestant Ethic and the Spirit of Capitalism,* published at the turn of the last century, argued that Protestantism, specifically Calvinism, helped to usher in modern capitalism by sanctioning a code of everyday behavior that emphasized hard work, honesty, thrift, and the productive use of one's time. This Protestant ethic, according to Weber, did not directly propel capitalist accumulation; it did so indirectly. Protestant values gave rise to a new kind of "economic man," one whose underlying values compelled him to live and work a certain way. It was this way of life that was the driver; capital accumulation, wealth, and increased productive potential were the important by-products.[1]

Culture, according to this view, motivates economic growth by focusing human energy and effort on work, and away from the pull of nonwork activities such as leisure, play, sexuality, or other forms of enjoyment. Human beings are seen as undisciplined agents in need of rules and constraint. Left to their own devices, humans would defer work in favor of other more enjoyable activities. Bell went so far as to identify culture as the core contradiction of modern capitalism, seeing the rise of a more open, expressive, and hedonistic culture during the 1960s as undermining the effort, social incentives, and discipline that power innovation, entrepreneurship, and economic growth.

Similarly, Nathan Glazer and Daniel Moynihan pegged the unique aspect of American culture that propelled its development as its capacity to absorb and assimilate immigrants, its melting-pot mentality.[2] This melting pot obliged immigrants to relinquish aspects of their national identities and foreign tongues for English and the promise of upward mobility. The melting-pot mentality was much more than an academic theory; it was deeply ingrained in immigrants. I know the feeling well. My grandparents all came from southern Italy during the great wave of immigration of the turn of the last century. We were a melting-pot family. My parents named their two boys Robert and Richard. They did not speak Italian in the home. My father would tell us stories of how he and his brothers preferred Sinatra and other crooners to the Italian opera that his father played. And he would regret how he and his siblings gave away an entire stash of Caruso 78s, which they thought were too "Italian."

Samuel Huntington is another influential scholar—a distinguished Harvard professor, director of its Center for International Affairs, and editor of *Foreign Policy*—with a long-standing interest in the connection between culture, democracy, and human progress.[3] In his 2004 book, *Who Are We?: The Challenges to America's National Identity,* Huntington argues that America's economic and political success has rested centrally on a "founding culture" of Anglo-Protestant values. Among the key elements of this founding culture, he writes, "are the English language; Christianity; religious commitment; English concepts of the rule of law; the responsibility of the rulers and the rights of individuals; and dissenting Protestant values of individualism, the work ethic, and the belief that humans have the ability and duty to try to create heaven on earth, a 'city on a hill.' " According to Huntington, his book is primarily about the "salience and substance of national identity"—which he defines as the importance Americans attach to their national identity compared to the many other identities they have. Huntington contends that the salience of national identity has waxed and waned over the past centuries, largely in accordance with real or perceived foreign threats. Before the Civil War, of course, national identity ranked low, but in its aftermath America became a nation. In the late twentieth century, this sense of national self ebbed again with the end of the Cold War and the onset of soaring economic prosperity. The attack of September 11, Huntington contends, made America a "nation" again.

Where his previous book, *The Clash of Civilizations,* was mainly concerned with external threats to American power—most notably, the rise of some eight or nine regional civilizations and especially the Islamic Middle East—*Who Are We?* views the main challenge as internal. At the same time that our core culture has become ever more important to ensure a national unity of purpose, it has broken down under the assault of rampant immigration, Huntington argues. He is particularly concerned about a perceived failure of Mexican-American immigrants to assimilate, and the naive worldview of a "cosmopolitan elite" of globally oriented business leaders and multi-culturist academics and apologists. Mexicans and Latin Americans in general, he argues, are unique in this failure—not as well educated and less likely to make English their "first" language, to apply for citizenship, or to intermarry as frequently as other groups.

Many others have effectively taken Huntington to task for his misguided views on Mexican immigration, and I have little to add to their critiques. But I will offer up one anecdote for consideration. In 2003, I was the guest of Iowa governor Thomas Vilsack at a major conference on the future of the state's economy. A key theme of the conference was Iowa's need for immigration. Indeed, Vilsack had first made a name for himself in some political circles by establishing a controversial program to revitalize Iowa's economy by making the state "the Ellis Island of the Midwest." As is often the case, much of the conversation at the economic conference revolved around the need for Iowa to attract high-skill immigrants—Indian software developers, Chinese engineers, and European biotechnologists. At one point, a young man raised his hand and rose from the audience.

Governor, political leaders, distinguished guests, with all due respect, I'm not so sure about all of this talk of attracting "high-skill" immigrants. Those skills are important, we know. But, in my experience, it's not such an easy distinction to make, between high-skilled and low-skilled. Especially over time. Low-skill immigrants often turn into high-skill immigrants. Maybe not always in a single lifetime. But over the lifetime of a family, or a community. Take my example. I'm the son of Mexican immigrants, both low-skilled. I'm also a recent graduate of Grinnell College [one of the most respected small liberal-arts colleges in the country]. Of my graduating class, only five of us have decided to stay in the state of Iowa. Just five. And you know what? *All five* were the sons and daughters of so-called low-skilled immigrant families. We stayed in this state, and in our communities, because these were places that gave so much opportunity to us, and to our families. We relish the chance to give back.

The young man sat back down to roaring applause.

The parallels between this story and another immigrant tale that many people know well by now are striking. Mike Bezos was fifteen years old when he escaped from the repressive grip of Cuban communism and fled—alone—to the United States. He worked his way through the University of Albuquerque and eventually did well enough for himself that he was able to marry a young woman who was already the mother of one. Bezos took seriously the responsibility for raising his stepson. He fostered a strong entrepreneurialism in the young boy and, several years down the road, was one of the first investors in and strongest supporters of his stepson's bold new business. The elder Bezos even gave his stepson, Jeff, a 1998 Chevy Blazer. As Jeff's wife, Mackenzie, drove that truck across the country to Seattle, Jeff Bezos typed the business plan for Amazon.com that would become a part of entrepreneurial start-up history. Not bad for a first-generation immigrant escapee who came to the United States with nothing and left to his stepson the ideas, energy, and support that would help to grow the entire field of e-commerce in the early days of the Internet.

Samuel Huntington, like others before him, falls victim to the view that the main function of culture—in this case, what he sees as the Anglo-Protestant "core" culture of the United States—is to constrain and limit people. As Daniel Lazare put it, Huntington believes that America must "return to its roots by restricting immigration, protecting the English language, and turning its back on liberal secularism." But as the examples of Jeff Bezos and the young Iowan illustrate, it will be a moral shame—and an economic disaster—if views such as Huntington's ever succeed in keeping the children of Mexican immigrants or any other ethnic group from getting a college education in the U.S. because their parents' English is not perfect.

My theory sees a very different role for culture. The economic importance of culture, in my view, lies in its ability to absorb and harness human talent. Since every human being has creative potential, the key role for culture is to create a society where that talent can be attracted, mobilized, and unleashed. All of this turns on an expansive, open, and proactively inclusive culture—one that does not discriminate, does not force people into boxes, and does allow them to be themselves and to validate their varied identities. In my theory, culture operates not by constraining the range of human creative possibilities but by facilitating and mobilizing them. Another word for this is "freedom." Freedom, as we all know, means much more than being able to cast a vote; it means the ability to be yourself and to follow your dreams. Open culture is a spur to innovation, entrepreneurship, and economic development. Historically, it's exactly this kind of openness and freedom that the United States in general, and its great cities in particular, have been especially good at encouraging.

Although scholars like Huntington, Bell, Christopher Lasch, and others view the cultural explosion of the 1960s with derision and condescension, the great social movements of that decade promoted this underlying ideal of openness. Until the Republican revolution anyway, most social liberals had taken it for granted that they'd won that battle—or at least incorporated many of its core values into the larger system. Unfortunately, old wounds from that era are continually reopened by both sides, as Vietnam, women's rights, and the social welfare state are dragged out of the past for judgment and revision.

Like it or not, though, the 1960s undoubtedly expanded the

boundaries of political and social freedom to include equal opportunity for racial minorities and women. Our landscape will never be the same. Recall that before that time, to be different was to be labeled a rebel, not an innovator. Women were homemakers; nonwhites were semicitizens; gays were stigmatized. The expanded freedoms of expression ushered in by the 1960s allowed new art forms—from rock music to independent publishing to digital media—to flourish. They allowed artistic and technical creativity to commingle. People found ways to become themselves, to self-actualize to an extent that had never before been possible. And, as *The Rise of the Creative Class* showed, these social movements laid the groundwork for the rise of Silicon Valley and its modern high-tech culture, in turn the cause of much of our innovative capability and subsequent economic growth. The result was a sustained outpouring of human creative activity, in every form imaginable, from popular music and film to industry-defining breakthroughs in high-tech fields from software to biotech. In this sense, the 1960s still serve as a poignant reminder of what can go right when tremendous amounts of human creativity are unleashed in an open culture.

The most conclusive support for the relationship between open culture and economic growth comes from Ronald Inglehart. With his comprehensive surveys of cultural values in more than seventy countries over four decades, Inglehart successfully dismisses the idea that culture spurs economic growth by constraining people's choices. On the contrary, he finds a particularly powerful connection between openness and tolerance, especially tolerance toward gays, and both economic growth and political democracy. Countries where gays are frowned upon, and where a woman's place is deemed to be in the home, Inglehart finds, tend to be economically backward and ruled by authoritarian regimes.[4] "Today," Inglehart writes, "relatively few people express overt hostility toward other classes, races, or religions, but rejection of homosexuals is widespread." The countries where more than nine in ten people reject homosexuality include Egypt, Bangladesh, Iran, and China. In advanced industrial democracies like Britain, Germany, and Canada, just a quarter of the population rejects gays. Within the United States, the figure is 32 percent.

My work with Gary Gates has found this same connection. A 2004 study by Gates examined the effect of diversity on economic growth in more than three hundred metropolitan regions across the United States. Gates's research employed several alternative measures of diversity, including the presence of ethnic and racial minorities, the percentage of the population made up by gays and immigrants, and the level of integration. He also examined the effects of two kinds of social capital originally identified as important to community cohesion by Harvard's Robert Putnam: "bonding," or within-group social capital, and "bridging" social capital, the strength of ties *between* different ethnic, racial, or social groups. In every measure Gates applied, he found diversity to be significantly related to economic growth. Particularly, he found that communities with higher levels of diversity in the form of ethnic and racial minorities, gays, immigrants, higher levels of integration, and higher levels of bridging social capital tended to have better growth rates.[5]

The point, in the end, is to get beyond diversity as just a cultural or moral issue. It's inevitable that different people, raised as they are in different environments, will never completely agree on what defines the fabric or character of a nation—especially one of nearly 300 million inhabitants. But the need for diversity and tolerance is an economic issue, too, and in that sense affects each and every American. To discard something that has been, is, and will be such a clear contributor to economic growth would be foolhardy, even for the staunchest cultural conservatives.

## Beyond Greed

Economists have long argued that growth is powered mainly by economic incentives. In a way, this emphasis on greed as the motivator of human effort is the crude bastard child, if you will, of the Protestant work ethic. Perhaps the only argument that has enjoyed more attention as a universal explanation for economic growth than the culture-as-economic-discipliner line of reasoning is the "greed is good" school of thought. According to this viewpoint, it's the chance to make money, the chance to get rich and acquire material goods that powers economic growth. It is greed that drives people to work hard, greed that drives entrepreneurs, and greed that drives our economy. It's part of our economic dogma.

During the 1990s, many otherwise astute commentators came to believe that personal greed would power a literally endless technology boom. A similar idea, expressed only a bit less crassly, is well enshrined in free-market economic theory: Each person, maximizing his or her own utility, contributes to the efficient functioning of the market and thus to the optimal economic outcome for society as a whole. Greed, in other words, is the sine qua non of the creation of wealth, the fuel that drives our economic engine.

But this has always been only partly true, and it constitutes a crucial misunderstanding of the reasons people work. To understand the economics of our emerging age, we need to move past the tired debate about greed as vice and virtue, and recognize the role of other motivations. The insistence on seeing greed as the primary economic driver is a consequence of an outmoded conservative morality. Commentators on the right, who are unable or unwilling to see factors like openness, tolerance, and self-expression as sources of economic growth, keep insisting that the combination of family values and greed will bring us prosperity. Those who recoil from this suggestion tacitly admit its basic assumption and are reduced to arguing that we should accept less economic growth as a price of discouraging greed. My years of research suggest that just the opposite will result.

Start with the easy arguments: It's a no-brainer to find examples of greed that do societies and economies no good at all. Bernie Ebbers, Jeffrey Skilling, and Dennis Kozlowski (of WorldCom, Enron, and Tyco respectively) were all deeply engaged in maximizing their utility at the expense of their shareholders, employees, bankers, and others. But were these scandals merely exceptions? Carl Schramm, president of the Ewing Marion Kauffman Foundation, argues that they are not. Throughout the business, banking, and accounting world, he says, monetary concerns have grown so dominant over naive and old-fashioned values like honesty, ethics, and even good taste that they have created a widespread atmosphere of distrust. The economic effects of this culture of distrust are largely negative. According to his analysis, the years 2000–2003 were the first years since the Great Depression period when start-ups actually declined. The reason, Schramm believes, is that entrepreneurs, accountants, venture capitalists, bankers, and others can no longer be sure of the others' intentions: whether they actually plan to build a business or are just hoping to strike it rich with smoke-and-mirrors tactics and get out, leaving the others in the lurch. As a result, fewer people with ideas try to turn them into businesses, less money gets invested in start-ups, fewer of those new ideas get off the ground, and growth suffers. Here the famous invisible hand works against the common good: The belief that others are out to maximize their gains is a brake on the economy as a whole.

Intelligent economists have always known that the desire for profit or for tangible material gain is not the only thing that drives an economy. The assumption that it is was always an oversimplification employed to keep the equations under control. Greed alone, no matter how urgent, cannot innovate. Consider just a small sampling of some of the major innovations that have shaped our modern world: The airplane was invented one hundred years ago by Wilbur and Orville Wright, who were by no means out to make a buck. These two young brothers were motivated by the dream of manned flight, and in fact routinely neglected their bicycle-shop business to chase that dream. The telephone was invented by a man who had to hide his experiments from his financial backers. The men behind Alexander Graham Bell were looking for big returns fast, and were paying him to deliver a practical invention related to Morse-code telegraph systems, not to play around with anything so far-fetched as a system for transmitting voices.

The personal computer was developed three decades ago by a ragtag group of hippies from the San Francisco Bay Area who called themselves the Homebrew Club. These counterculture geeks were pursuing an idea that most businessmen of the time thought absurd: the notion that people could be empowered by having their own little computers. Then there's my personal favorite, rock and roll, the most commercially potent musical form in history. Rock and its many derivatives now compose a multibillion-dollar global industry and help to drive profits in many other industries. But this musical form was developed in the black ghettos and country backwaters of America, by musicians tinkering with chords and rhythms for sheer creative expression and enjoyment.

To simply assume that creative people are motivated mainly by the chance to get rich is, to put it bluntly, inaccurate. The majority of research on the subject finds that intrinsic rewards are far more effective in motivating creative people than money alone. From decades of study, the Harvard psychologist Teresa Amabile has found that extrinsic rewards are actually counterproductive in motivating creative people, whose motivation comes from within. Economist Scott Stern has found that academic scientists actually *pay* to do basic research. On average, they forgo about a quarter of what they could earn in the private sector for greater freedom to pursue the questions that interest them.

In surveys of information-technology workers, *Information Week* found that the job qualities most highly valued by the greatest numbers of workers were "challenge" and "responsibility." Base pay ranked third and financial incentives such as bonuses and stock options far below that, even below quality-of-life factors like commuting distance. There is no denying that many people got very rich in the 1990s doing creative work. But to conclude from this fact that greed was their primary motivation is to deeply misunderstand both the choices these people made and the way the economy operates. If we don't appreciate the underlying motivations of creative people, we can't think intelligently about work, period.

Often we see that greed—the desire to maximize gain, to focus on getting ahead—only gets in the way. It fuels our often-unsustainable, 24/7, always-on pace of life. No wonder stress, anxiety, burnout, self-medication, and other forms of psychological injury have replaced on-the-job physical injuries as the workplace hazards of the creative age. I'm not saying capitalism has got to go. Far from it: What I argue for is a new kind of market-based society, one that fosters human creativity more broadly, more directly, and across all social and demographic strata. The society that can build the most productive and efficient mechanisms for harnessing human creative energy will move ahead of those continuing to make a fetish of the greed motive. Is America still the best place in the world for such an economic paradigm shift to occur? That depends on whether or not we look at the relevant pages from our own historical playbook.

## The Real Roots of American Greatness

De Tocqueville and others long ago argued that America is a unique place, and it's been common to do so since—though, of course, in the American tradition, always with a different argument in mind. I would argue that the crucial factor that has made America unique among nations has little to do with greed and less to do with some vague commitment to a core of Anglo-Protestant values. Rather, its uniqueness—and success—spring from its ability to attract people from far and wide, assimilate and aggregate their talents, and motivate and reward their efforts. Few sentient observers would argue that American culture today is the same as it was during the founding of the republic, after the Civil War, at the dawn of the Industrial Revolution, or even as late as the 1950s. The core strength of our culture has not been its reliance on a static set of beliefs, but rather its dynamic adaptability, its skill at mutating to accommodate new people and new economic realities.

As Huntington himself once believed, rather than an "ethnic state," the United States is an "ideological state" based on an American Creed of liberty and justice for all. "The more culturally pluralistic the nation becomes," he wrote in 1981, "the more essential the *political values* [my emphasis] of the Creed become in defining what it is Americans have in common." Does Huntington really believe that Mexicans don't desire the same economic and political freedoms that his imagined natives strive for? Can't a person who doesn't speak perfect English still believe in democracy? How is he or she any different from the multitudes who've come to our shores from other countries in search of economic opportunity and a better life?

Certainly in contrast to the rest of the world, the United States has been a relatively open country since its inception. We must remember, however, that the United States' commitment to openness has waxed and waned over time, largely in response to economic conditions. There is also our past reliance on that most brutal of all economic arrangements, slavery, to be reckoned with. But, since the mid-1960s, the United States has been an extraordinarily open and tolerant country.[6] This is at least in part because the United States was originally conceived as an immigrant nation; most of our earliest settlers came here to avoid religious and political persecution. As such, even in times of great darkness and abuse, there are always our founding ideals to appeal to, to shoot for, and to improve upon.

The first great wave of immigration came between 1820 and 1880, when some 10 million German, Irish, English, Scandinavian, and other, mainly Northern and Western European immigrants, came to America. While some were entrepreneurs, the great majority provided a ready source of labor for the emerging American system of manufacturing. After the Civil War, Congress passed the Act to Encourage Immigration, establishing the first federal bureau of immigration and allowing immigrants to deduct the cost of getting to the United States from their wages.

The success of the American Industrial Revolution spurred the second great wave of immigration, of which there were two similar parts. The first was the entrepreneurial migration of leading industry and corporation builders such as John Kluge, the German-born media tycoon; Andrew Carnegie, the Scottish steel magnate; Adolphus Busch, the German-born brewer; and Joseph Pulitzer, the Hungarian newspaper giant, to name just a few. The second was the throngs of low-skilled newcomers who worked to feed the voracious demand created by the booming industry these immigrant entrepreneurs created.

Beginning in the 1880s, the floodgates opened to a huge influx of these low-skilled immigrants, and in turn they powered American factories. Between 1881 and 1930, 27.6 million immigrants came to the United States from Italy, Austro-Hungary, Russia, and Eastern Europe, among other countries. From 1870 to 1910, immigrants made up roughly 14 percent of the U.S. population. In 1890, immigrants made up more than 40 percent of the population in eight of America's fifty largest cities: Fall River, Massachusetts (51 percent), Lowell, Massachusetts (45 percent), New York City (42 percent), San Francisco (42 percent), Chicago (41 percent), Detroit (40 percent), St. Paul, Minnesota (40 percent), and Paterson, New Jersey (40 percent). In another fifteen cities, that number was more than 30 percent.

Immigration ebbed from the early 1900s through the Great Depression. A series of measures after World War I imposed new restrictions, including literacy requirements, prohibitions on Asian immigration, and set ceilings for European immigrants. The economic recovery following the end of the World War II encouraged the softening of this immigration policy, and the 1952 Immigration Act eliminated restrictions based on race or ethnicity but retained quotas based on national origin. The landmark 1965 Immigration Act liberalized our policy further, among other things replacing the national quotas with an annual cap on admissions on immigrants from seven broad segments of the world. By 1978, roughly 600,000 immigrants were entering the United States each year.

Of course, in the late 1970s and early 1980s, America's economy hit a crisis point, with record unemployment, stagnant productivity, a rusting industrial base, and an oil crisis that highlighted a dangerous dependence upon raw materials whose supply we could not necessarily guarantee. Business leaders grew gravely concerned. So much so, in fact, that new organizations such as the Council on Competitiveness were formed to spur public-private cooperation around innovation and economic growth.

Beneath the surface, though, some interesting things were happening. Previous investments in scientific research by both government and industry were yielding new technologies, from inexpensive computer chips to biotechnology to fiber optics. New financial instruments and practices were making capital more available for innovative ventures. American film, television, and music were finding new export markets. Foreign investment was rising and new factories were built in the industrial heartland. U.S. corporations, spurred by competition from Japan and guided by best-selling books like Tom Peters's *In Search of Excellence,* responded powerfully and restructured their operations, pushing decision making down the chain of command and into the hands of factory workers.

In the late 1980s and early 1990s, I witnessed this resurgence first-hand during my visits to revitalized Midwestern factories, where workers were made part of the innovation system of the factory. I recall the plant manager of I/N Tek—a state-of-the-art continuous steel cold-rolling mill in Indiana—telling me how his factory had been transformed into a "living laboratory," based on the knowledge, intelligence, and creativity of its workforce. Everywhere, economists and managers were talking about the need for more knowledge work, increased science and technology, and better education. But a key (though less noticed) dimension of this transformation was driven by our ability to attract and absorb foreign talent.

Since the 1965 Immigration Act, the United States has witnessed one of the greatest periods of immigration since its founding. The immigrant share of the population grew steadily from 4.7 percent in 1970 to 6.2 percent in 1980, and then 7.9 percent in 1990. In 2000, it hit 10.4 percent. Even more than the wave of immigration that helped to power the industrial age, this newest arrival fueled the engine of the emerging creative age, bringing leading scientists, technologists, entrepreneurs, artists, and the energy of millions of creative new people to our shores.

The 13 million new immigrants between 1990 and 2000 constituted the greatest single wave of immigration in U.S. history, substantially outpacing even that of the 1890–1910 period. During that decade, immigrants accounted for nearly half of the increase in the overall labor force, and nearly two-thirds of the growth in the male labor force. The number of immigrants living in the U.S. has more than tripled in the last thirty years, from a little less than 10 million in 1970 to 31.1 million in 2000, the largest absolute number in U.S. history. Another 2 million immigrants came to the United States between 2000 and 2003, accounting for nearly 60 percent of all labor-force growth in this period.[7] Today, immigrants make up 12 percent of our population, a figure just slightly less than that of the late nineteenth and early twentieth centuries, and more than double that of 1970.

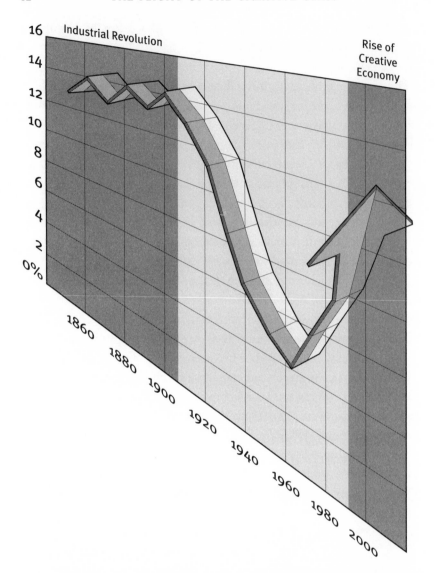

**Figure 3.1:  Immigration in America, 1860–2000**

In the creative age as in the Industrial Revolution, immigrants have con-
tributed mightily to American prosperity. Immigration surged during the
Industrial Revolution and again with the rise of the creative economy.
U.S. Census Bureau, "Profile of the Foreign-born Population in the United
States: 2000," Washington, D.C.: U.S. Government Printing Office, 2001.

Not only are the absolute numbers impressive; immigrants have a powerful effect on reshaping American society. Immigration has nearly single-handedly driven population growth in recent decades, accounting for more than 40 percent of total growth over the 1990s. Current demographic trends suggest that as our own population's birth rate dips below the level needed for repopulation (around 1.7 children per family), the economic burdens of our economy (not to mention our Social Security system) will of necessity fall on the shoulders of our society's newest members.

Many, including Huntington, suggest that this third wave of immigration is distinguished largely by a flood of low-skilled, and often illegal, Hispanic immigrants. That view is mistaken. This most recent wave of immigration is in fact distinguished from other such waves by its abundance of high-skilled workers. A systematic study of recent U.S. immigration by William Carrigan and Enrica Detragiache concludes that, in contrast to the conventional wisdom, the numbers for individuals with no more than a primary education are quite small— about 500,000 out of 7 million, or 7 percent.[8] The largest group of immigrants to the United States, some 3.7 million people, is made up of high-school-educated workers from Mexico and Central America. The second largest group, totaling almost 1.5 million people, draws on highly educated populations from Asia and the Pacific Rim.

A separate survey of new legal immigrants to the United States found that one in five has at least seventeen years of education, implying some level of study beyond college. Of the 1 million people from India living in the United States, more than three-quarters of those of working age have a bachelor's degree or more. The United States has even attracted a lion's share of talented people from Mexico and the Caribbean. Lindsay Lowell of the Pew Hispanic Center found that 12 percent of Mexico's population with college education is in the United States, as is a whopping 75 percent of Jamaica's. Canada, until recently, also lost many of its highly educated people to the United States; for years the Canadian press was littered with stories bemoaning the brain drain south. Carrigan and Detragiache conclude that "migrants to the United States tend to be better educated than the average person in their home (that is sending) country, and the proportion of very highly educated people who migrate is particularly high." Or as *The Economist* puts it: "America, the world biggest skills-magnet, absorbs large portions of the most educated people from neighboring countries."[9]

High-skilled immigrants have added immeasurably to our scientific, technological, and entrepreneurial success. Low-skilled immigrants, meanwhile, have helped revitalize old industries and communities throughout this country, providing new sources of talent and energy in manufacturing, service, and agricultural industries. And, as the Grinnell graduate's example illustrates, low-skill immigrants frequently turn into high-skill immigrants as first-generation American parents invest in their children's education.

This influx of talent has conferred huge economic benefits upon the United States. Those benefits are hard to quantify, precisely because they're so far-ranging and drawn from such a wide geographic sweep. As we put different pieces together, though, we begin to get a sense of their scope. A systematic study by researchers at Harvard University and Queens University in Canada, for instance, found that the movement of talented people from India to the United States during the 1990s represented a financial transfer to the United States equivalent to "one-third of current Indian individual tax receipts."[10] Though concern over the outsourcing of American jobs is the political hot potato of the day, Peter Drucker estimates that the United States imports two or even three jobs for every job it exports. And, according to a ranking that controls for inflation across time by standardizing wealth as a percentage of the GDP, five of the ten richest Americans of all time have been immigrants.

Immigration has further accounted for much of the resurgence of urban economies in recent decades. Immigrants have made up for the net losses of the domestic population in major cities like New York and Chicago. New York alone is home to 2.9 million immigrants, Los Angeles 1.5 million, and Miami 1.1 million (a staggering 50 percent of the city-proper's total population).

Largely as a result of immigration, our major cities and metropolitan regions have become much more diverse places. A 2004 Brookings Institution study of America's ten largest metropolitan areas found that fewer Americans in these large cities today live in homogeneous, white neighborhoods. Overall, the number of predominantly white neighborhoods fell by 30 percent in these regions (which include both their central cities and extensive suburban rings) between 1990 and 2000, while the number of mixed-race neighborhoods rose by 14 percent. All told, nine in ten regions saw an increase in mixed-race neighborhoods, and fully half the neighborhoods in the ten regions could be classified as "mixed race." [11]

More recently, sociologists and anthropologists have begun to note

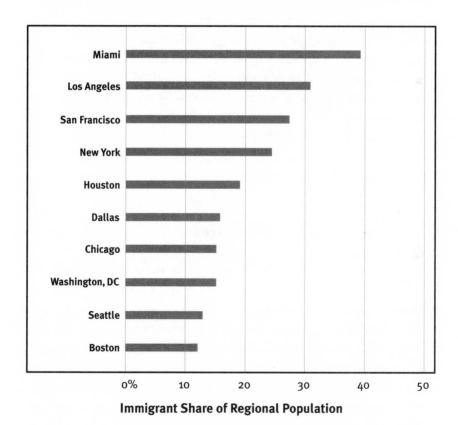

**Immigrant Share of Regional Population**

**Figure 3.2 Foreign-born Residents in U.S. Regions, 2004**

Steven Camarota, *Economy Slowed, But Immigration Didn't: The Foreign-born Population, 2000–2004,* Washington, D.C.: Center for Immigration Studies, November 2004.

the growing attraction of the suburbs and smaller cities to immigrant families. My own research with Kevin Stolarick and Gary Gates, as well as that of others, has shown that immigrants are key even more to economic growth in small- to medium-size regions than in major metropolises. This can be partly attributed to the fact that such communities are, generally speaking, more tolerant of immigrants than they are of gays, bohemians, or other socially marginalized but economically crucial groups. In this way, we are beginning to see immigrants pave the way for the eventual inclusion of these other groups, yet another economic benefit.

This much is clear: Immigration is the lifeblood of the creative economy. The key to America's success has been the same thing all along: openness to new ideas and new people from all over the world. Our ability to take in immigrants and utilize their talents has had a huge impact on creativity and American economic growth from the dawn of the Industrial Revolution to the high-tech growth engine of Silicon Valley. And just as they shaped the American Dream of the twentieth century, so will immigrants play an ever-increasing part in the new dream of the twenty-first.

## A New Dream

What do most people think about when they hear the phrase *the American Dream*? My parents and grandparents knew what this meant: You got a decent job, worked hard, learned and taught your kids, made sure they got a good education. You saved your money, bought a nice home in a nice community with good schools. That, in a nutshell, was the old dream. It was a curious and for its time powerful blending of the economic view that greed powers economic growth and culturalist notions of the Protestant ethic and the melting pot. As great as it was, its days are over.

Today, we are seeing the rise of a new dream in America and across the world that promises much more. "The most remarkable feature of the modern workplace has nothing to do with computers, automation or globalization," writes Alain de Botton. "Rather it lies in the Western world's widely held belief that work should make us happy." [12] Botton rightly notes that, though work has always been a defining and central element to a nation's or a culture's identity, now for the first time in world history job searches are predicated on the idea that one's work ought to be "fulfilling," to use the parlance of the time.

Behind this shift in the way people work and what we expect to get out of our jobs again lies the rise of the creative economy. A new dream has emerged. It's not just an American Dream, either, but the dream of people across the world. If the old dream was to have a job with which to feed your family and a nice house in a safe neighborhood to shelter them, the new dream is a job you love, doing work you enjoy, and living in a community where you can be yourself.

Was the old dream ever really sufficient? For the times in which it was born, it probably was. But in the years just after World War II, millions of people, first in the U.S. and eventually in the other advanced industrial nations, quickly acquired a steady job, a car, and a new house—and then quickly grew bored. They read books like *The Organization Man* and *The Lonely Crowd,* recognizing in these works their own stifling monotonous lifestyles. They idolized James Dean and Marlon Brando, and dreamed of being a *Rebel Without a Cause* or *The Wild One.* Soon, the British jumped on the counterculture bandwagon with the much-celebrated British invasion of the Beatles, the Rolling Stones, the Who, the Kinks, and countless others. They stuck to the grind for the sake of their children, only to have those children become hippies and reject this "higher standard of living" in favor of more creative lifestyles.

As that new generation and its children matured and entered the workforce, they sought a new and expanded dream of their own. I grew up with that old dream. My parents believed in it and lived it. They invested all of themselves in their children's education; they worked constantly and never took a day off. When we were young, they encouraged my brother and me to learn instruments—guitar in my case, drums for my brother—and to form a rock-and-roll band. Once we graduated college, though, it was a different story. We cut our hair and got real jobs; we conformed. It was, after all, what was expected.

My father knew this well. He was in many ways a victim of it. On Saturdays, on the way home from visiting his factory or from my guitar lessons, he would drive me past a beauty parlor, what we would now call a women's hair salon. He would stop and say, "Richard, look at that place. I could have owned it. That could have been mine." He would go on to say how his two older sisters had owned and run that beauty shop. But when his sister Mary moved to California with her husband and family, they had to give it up. My father was a creative person, a talented amateur artist who had a knack for cutting hair and frequently cut my brother's and mine. He even helped my mom color and set hers. His sisters wanted to turn the business over to my father, and he, deep down, wanted to run it. But he couldn't accept their offer. "Richard," he would say, "I would have loved to own that place and do that work. But I couldn't take it on. How would it look for a man of my generation to give up work in a factory to be a lady's hairdresser."

Even a few supporters have poked fun at the machine-shop-versus-hair-salon anecdote in *The Rise of the Creative Class*. But work in the figurative hair salon can be both rewarding and lucrative. In Cleveland, I met Albert Ratner, the real-estate giant of Forrest City Enterprises. He called me into his office and introduced me to two young people; "Now, guys, tell Richard the story of your father." Their father owned a beauty salon in Cleveland. One day he noticed that it took a long time to apply fake eyelashes on women, going one lash at a time. So he developed the basic technology for press-on eyelashes. Later, he noticed the damage hair products did to women's hair. He developed a less-damaging line of products, called Matrix. He sold the business for hundreds of millions of dollars. His two children later endowed the entrepreneurship program at a local university in his honor.

In the tumultuous time from the late 1960s through the 1970s, the old dream began to erode. From Woodstock to Silicon Valley, from the high-tech start-up to the artist's studio, from the university classroom and dormitory to the research laboratory, people were resisting the constraints of established society in different ways. Of course, during these early days, before the full-blown emergence of the creative economy, there weren't really many places to go. You had fun during your college years, but then you needed to get serious. Then the options became more limited. You could go into a university to teach. You could be a beatnik or a bohemian (not a lot of great career advancement in that one). You could go to work in a research laboratory. Or, eventually, you could make the pilgrimage to Silicon Valley or perhaps the Route 128 area around Boston and join a start-up, trading security for freedom and a hell of a lot of risk. Smart, talented people may already have been cringing at the prospects of an organization-man future, but it would take the full-blown rise of the creative economy during the 1980s and 1990s to give them the options they were looking for.

What I've described here is of course a history that pertains only to some of us. Not everyone grew up in the suburbs, and certainly not everyone was involved with the counterculture revolt of the 1960s. Today, though, whether they realize it or not, and regardless of their own personal or familial story, more and more people are living this new dream—engaging in work that pays well, is challenging, and that they love. This is naturally upsetting for those who hold a vested interest in the more traditional vision. It threatens the existing hierarchy of control and the established status order. But the new dream continues to spread despite these protestations. As observers from Ronald Inglehart to Nobel Prize–winning economist Robert Fogel have pointed out, such is the effect of living in a postmaterialist society, where self-fulfillment has replaced subsistence or even financial gain as the primary motivator, where increasing numbers of people have come to value intrinsic or creative opportunity over the ability to make money.

Consider for a moment an archetypal story of modern-day popular culture. From hardscrabble Eminem in *8 Mile* to aspiring rock journalist William Miller in *Almost Famous,* why do young people from the ghetto to the suburbs dream of being rappers, rock stars, and writers? It's not just because they're rebellious, or because it provides their best shot at big money. Most stand a far better chance of earning an academic or athletic scholarship than a recording contract—and even big-money athletes apparently want to be rappers. It's because being a musician is creative. It's not a kind of creativity that someone from my generation always understands, to be sure, but I imagine it's stimulating in a way that a routine desk job never will be.

Should our economic goal be to enable every young person to earn a living as a singer or a scribe? Of course not. But, conceptually, it's in the right ballpark. Recognizing and tapping creative talents, whatever those talents may be, is a good starting point for a serious debate on how to realize the full creative potential of our economy. It's not the work ethic. It's not the greed. It's not the same old dream. It's the openness—to new people, new ideas, and new dreams. We'd do ourselves quite a bit of economic good to . . . well, open up to that idea.

**Part II**

# The Global Competition for Talent

# 4

# The Closing of America?

*In times of shrinking expectations . . . everyone feels like a victim and pushes away outsiders to defend his own corner.* —OSCAR HANDLIN

It was a gorgeous early-spring evening in 2004, and I was eating dinner at the residence of the president of a small Midwestern liberal-arts college. The home, situated on the periphery of the college, was lovely and the guests were an interesting mix—the head of an innovative community foundation, the newly recruited editor of the excellent local newspaper, and several university types. I sat down at my table with the president's wife and, to my delight, a group of the college's students. They were a remarkable lot, intelligent, engaged, and ever ready to ask a probing question or provide a useful comment. They hailed from various parts of the country—two from small, rural Midwestern towns; a young African-American woman from Columbus, Ohio; and another young woman from New En-

gland. Some majored in arts or dance, while others were pursuing political science or economics.

I like students, and always find instructive their perspectives as
young people entering the labor market and searching for places to
live and work. I casually mentioned that I had just returned from Australia and one of the students immediately chimed in. "Professor
Florida," he said, "when I graduate, I'm seriously considering Australia. I did my junior year of study there and it's a fabulous place. I'm
not sure if I'll get a job, or just hang around for a while and see things,
or go there for graduate school." Before he could finish, a second student piped in: "I'm thinking about Europe. I studied for some time in
Spain. I loved it there. I met a girl and had a wonderful time. Maybe
I'll go to graduate school there." One of the young women jumped
in: "I'm thinking of Europe, too. I like Dublin. Or maybe somewhere
in Canada. Maybe Toronto."

I was astounded. When all was said and done, three of the five students were seriously considering moving outside the United States
after graduation. Such a thing was unthinkable when I graduated
Rutgers College some twenty-five years ago. Few of my friends
moved outside the New York–New Jersey metropolitan area, let
alone out of the country. Here, a majority of the students at our table
were considering doing just that. "It's so easy," one of the young men
said. "Many of my friends are considering it. Lots of us have been
overseas to study. We have friends there. There's work and scholarships, good graduate schools. Most of us know people there. Some
people have significant others who are over there or from there."

Here's the rub. All of these students were looking for and finding
in other countries something I had come to believe this nation's leading creative centers had in abundance: economic opportunity, careers
and education, and most importantly vibrant cities filled with challenging opportunities, exciting people, and great things to do. I had
been to all the places they mentioned; now that I thought about it in
this context, I realized that they met the needs of creative people.
They had what these students, and tens of thousands just like them,
were looking for.

That's when it really hit me: All that I'd written about in *The Rise of the Creative Class* was occurring not just on the national scene, but on a truly global scale. This dinner conversation was not just an intriguing occurrence, but the reflection of a basic modern-day reality. For decades, Americans have taken it for granted that talented and creative people—the world's best and brightest—would, if given the choice, come here. But in front of me sat three out of five highly educated young people who wanted not only to study, but to actually live and work abroad.

The more I probed the issue, the more concerned I became. These young people were only the tip of the iceberg. Not just for them, but for established scientists and engineers, for entrepreneurs and inventors, for artists and cultural mavens, America was no longer the only place to be. This was doubly true of foreign-born students, on whom we depend to help build our scientific enterprises, and of immigrant inventors and entrepreneurs, who power so much of our growth. The balance of the world's creative brainpower was shifting, becoming less one-sidedly American and more global in character. I came to think that this country might for the first time in its history risk losing its advantage in attracting global talent. But why?

## Outsourcing: The First Pincer of the Claw

These days, the public conversation about jobs in the United States revolves around the issue of outsourcing. Thanks to pandering politicians and overzealous journalists, the nation is apoplectic about foreign labor taking "our" jobs. The great fear is that outsourcing, which has thus far threatened mostly lower-skill jobs in fields like data processing, is beginning to move upstream to threaten higher-wage, high-skill jobs—the jobs upon which American prosperity and many citizens' American dreams are based. There was a great hubbub when the *New York Times* reported in June 2004 that Microsoft had shifted a number of high-paying software-architect and software-development jobs to India. Surely, it was the beginning of the end.

While estimates vary, the most reliable figures suggest that between 1 and 2 million jobs were moved abroad in the early 2000s. Forrester

Research predicted that between 3 and 5 million additional jobs would be moved abroad by the year 2010. In the end, though, outsourcing is far less threatening to the U.S. economy than the deindustrialization of manufacturing industries, which destroyed millions of jobs in the industrial Midwest during the 1980s. At worst, outsourcing threatens but a fraction of this country's 140 million or so jobs.

A June 2004 report by the Bureau of Labor Statistics put the issue in perspective. Outsourcing, it pointed out, accounted for just 2 percent of the roughly 240,000 people laid off during the first quarter of 2004. The report found that a total of 16,000 layoffs were the result of the relocation of work. Of those, 6 of 10 were moved to another part of the United States. Of the 4,633 jobs moved outside the U.S., the report found that two-thirds were moved within the same company to a new location abroad, while just one-third (1,500 or so jobs) were outsourced to another company. A June 2004 study by Charles Schultze, the distinguished Brookings Institution economist, reached much the same conclusion, finding the overall effect of outsourcing on U.S. jobs to be minimal.[1]

Most international economists concur that the outsourcing of work has at most a minimal effect on the U.S. labor market. The vast majority of job reductions, they argue, are traceable not to outsourcing or globalization but are the consequence of labor-saving technology. Of course, the evolution of the world economy and increasing competitive pressure will inevitably lead to more jobs being moved offshore in the future. And that's an understandably difficult fact to face for many of us who, maybe for the first time in our lives, feel pressure from abroad to shape up or get shipped out. This is why N. Gregory Mankiw, chairman of the Bush administration's Council of Economic Advisors, was publicly skewered for his comment that the movement of these jobs overseas was "probably a plus for the economy in the long run," even though it was largely accurate.

But even among economists, there is not total consensus that globalization and outsourcing will ultimately be beneficial, if somewhat painful, developments for advanced economies. In their 2000 book, *Global Trade and Conflicting National Interests,* renowned economist

William Baumol and Ralph Gomory, former IBM executive and current president of the Alfred P. Sloan Foundation, looked carefully at what happens when lower-wage economies begin trading more extensively with higher-wage ones. In contrast to the widely held assumption that such trade generates win-win benefits for both kinds of economies, their models led them to conclude that both sides benefit only if the wage differential between the two countries is "sufficiently large." There is the possibility that less developed countries can rapidly develop, take away more and better jobs, and ultimately gain at the expense of more developed ones.

In a widely cited article published in the *Journal of Economic Perspectives* in summer 2004, Nobel laureate and MIT professor Paul Samuelson zeroed in on the question of outsourcing. Samuelson called into question the "polemical untruth" perpetuated by most economists that this movement of jobs is a win-win situation for the United States and the countries on the receiving end. He issued a powerful warning that, as a low-wage economic powerhouse such as China improves its technology, educates its people, and gains geopolitical influence, it also increases its own chances to completely change the terms of trade with the U.S. and other advanced nations. Economics heavyweight Jagdish Bhagwati countered that Samuelson's models are more useful in the high-technology sectors, where the U.S. has held a traditional lead that is now eroding, than across the economy broadly.

Samuelson himself emphasizes, and I would do the same here, that his views are not to be taken as calls—or justifications—for the U.S. to implement protectionist measures to restrict the free flow of goods, services, or people. Such measures will only make matters worse. Rather, they are meant to temper the influence of the gung-ho free marketeers who tend to forget the real and everyday impact not just on blue-collar veterans of the outsourcing game or even on white-collar newcomers, but on the American economy more generally.

My own view is that outsourcing is a natural consequence of economic evolution, and that it alone poses at best a minor threat to American jobs and living standards. It's when outsourcing is taken together with the new global competition for talent coming from countries such as Sweden, Finland, Canada, Australia, New Zealand, and others that America's real competitive challenge becomes clear.[2]

## The Second Pincer of the Claw

The reality is that outsourcing is just the first step—or, if you will, the first pincer of the claw. The more routinizable aspects of what we consider brainwork—writing computer code, analyzing X-rays—are being lured away by countries such as India and Romania, which have lower labor costs and educated workforces large enough to do the job. Though such outsourcing is socially alarming and economically disruptive, history teaches us that it is manageable if we are able to substitute a new tier of jobs derived from the cutting-edge technologies and ideas coming out of our creative centers.

What should really alarm us is that our capacity to create these necessary new technologies and industries is being eroded by a different kind of competition—competition for higher-skilled, more highly educated global talent. At the same time that the United States is becoming more restrictive, other nations and regions are upping their ability to attract global talent. I'll describe in more depth exactly what is happening in these places in Chapters 5 and 6. For now, though, suffice it to say that these places are doing precisely the kinds of things the United States ought to be: They're increasing their spending on research and development, bolstering their universities, and opening their borders. Consequently, they're attracting global creative talent, including ours. The sort of high-end, high-margin creative industries that used to be the United States' province and a crucial source of our prosperity have thus begun to move overseas.

The key to U.S. success over the past decade has been our own ability to *in-source* talent. Our historical reliance on immigrants will only increase as the talent we need in critical fields of science, technology, engineering, and entrepreneurship becomes scarcer. This is not to say that we should forget about the average American and devote all our resources to talent importation. Just that importing this talent allows us to keep our economic engine well oiled, enables us to close the looming talent gap and hold a leadership position in cutting edge high-tech industries, which in turn maintains and creates more jobs and more economic opportunity for Americans and foreigners alike. Consider the following:

- Foreign-born scientists and engineers made up nearly a quarter of the science and engineering workforce (22 percent) in 2000, up from 14 percent in 1990. Foreign-born engineers make up about 40 percent of all U.S. engineering professors.

- Between 1990 and 2000, the percentage of international students among all bachelor's-degree holders in the U.S. increased from 11 to 17 percent; the percentage with a master's degree from 19 to 29 percent; and PhDs from 24 to 38 percent.

- By the early 2000s, nearly a third of all graduate students in science and engineering were from outside the United States, including more than half of all PhDs in engineering, computer science, life sciences, and the physical sciences.

- The number of foreign-born scientists and engineers on permanent visas increased more than threefold from 10,000 in 1988 to nearly 35,000 in 2001. Foreign students with permanent visas earned roughly 25 percent of scientific and engineering degrees in the 1990s, more than double the rate in the late 1970s.

- Temporary-visa holders make up half of all graduate enrollment in engineering mathematics and computer science. From 1985 to 2001, U.S. colleges and universities awarded about 150,000 doctorates, 350,000 master's degrees, and 270,000 bachelor's degrees in science and engineering fields to temporary-visa holders.

Beyond just enormous economic and research contributions, a substantial percentage of foreign students who earn doctoral degrees from U.S. universities stay in this country, shoring up our sagging indigenous talent base in key science and technology fields. A 2001 study found that roughly half of all doctoral-degree recipients in 1994–1995 and nearly two-thirds (63 percent) of those who received doctoral degrees in 1997 were still in the United States in 1999. Between those specializing in computer science and computer and electrical engineering, more than three-quarters of computer scientists who received PhDs in 1997 also stayed. Chinese and Indian students were the most likely to stay—with "stay rates" of 91 percent and 87 percent respectively. Taiwanese, Japanese, and Koreans (with stay rates of 42 percent, 27 percent, and 15 percent, respectively) were more likely to return home. Still, compare this to the fact that 69 percent of Chinese doctoral students and 95 percent of Taiwanese doctoral students who graduated in the UK returned home in 1998.[3] This influx of foreign talent was absolutely critical to the 1990s tech boom in the U.S.

Economists Sharon Levin and Paula Stephan shed additional light on the extraordinary contributions made by foreign-born scientists

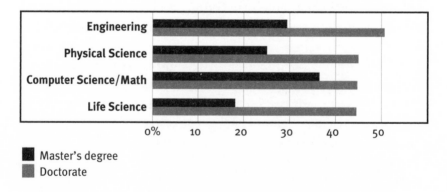

**Master's degree**
**Doctorate**

### Figure 4.1: U.S. Science and Technology Depends on Immigrants

In both master's degree and doctoral programs in the United States, foreign-born students account for a large share of science and engineering students. National Science Board, *Science and Engineering Indicators, 2004,* Washington, D.C.: U.S. Government Printing Office, 2003.

and engineers.[4] In a 1998 study, Levin and Stephan looked in detail at the role of foreign scientists in making exceptional contributions to U.S. science in the form of influential publications, important patents, and membership in prestigious scientific organizations. Since only 6 percent of all publishing scientists write 50 percent of all published scientific papers—a phenomenon known as "Lotka's Law"—this is an important question. Their findings overwhelmingly indicate that foreign-born talent accounts for both a disproportionate share of the most influential scientists and engineers and also the most significant contributions to the scientific literature.

Foreign-born engineers made up roughly one in five members (19 percent) of the National Academy of Engineering and nearly a quarter (24 percent) of the National Academy of Science, significantly greater than their overall share of the scientific and engineering workforce. Foreign-born scientists accounted for nearly three in ten of the authors of classic papers overall, and more than half (56 percent) of the classic papers in the physical sciences. They were more likely to be "outstanding" authors of the most cited "hot" papers, and the inventors on "highly-cited patents" in the life sciences.

The Nobel Prize is considered by many the beacon of scientific excellence. Between 1985 and 1999, foreign-born scientists made up a third (32 percent) of U.S. Nobel Prize winners in chemistry. Three of the four winners of the 1999 Nobel Prize in science, for example—Günter Blobel for medicine, Ahmed Zewail in chemistry, and Martinus Veltman in physics—were born in other countries but spent huge chunks of their professional careers in the United States. Blobel studied at Rockefeller University, Zewail at the California Institute of Technology, and Veltman at the University of Michigan.

The United States has long creamed the best talent from top foreign universities. According to Columbia University economist Jagdish Bhagwati, graduates of India's prestigious Indian Institute of Technology accounted for 78 percent of U.S. engineering PhDs granted to Indians. Nearly two-thirds of Korean students awarded U.S. science and engineering Ph.D.s went first to Seoul National University, the country's top school. Roughly half of all Taiwanese students receiving U.S. engineering doctorates had attended two top institutions: the National Taiwan University and the National Cheng Kung University. The numbers were similar for Beijing University and Tsinghua University, the top schools in China.[5]

For years, I've been involved in debates over American science policy, working with groups such as the President's Office on Science and Technology Policy, the Council on Competitiveness, Harvard's Center for Science, Technology and Public Policy and others. For a time, I served on the U.S. Committee for Science, Engineering and Public Policy. Before issues of homeland security came to dominate the discussion, many of these conversations revolved around the stay rates of foreign-born scientists and engineers. My American colleagues would frequently complain when foreign scientists and engineers returned home to work after their education.

My view of the matter has always been very different. Foreign-born scientists and engineers, from the time they are graduate students, are doing important work to advance the scientific enterprise in America—which can only be good for our country. There is nothing wrong with their wanting to return home to develop research projects of their own, start companies, or develop collaborative projects with American universities or companies. What's more, I reminded my colleagues, this inflow of foreign talent was highly subsidized by their home countries. Isn't it somewhat unbelievable, I would say, that the scientific and engineering establishment in what is arguably the richest country in the world is being underwritten by the people of some of the poorest countries, who spend enormous resources investing in this talent so that talent can come to American universities?

But consider the ironic turn of events: Now that terrorism and national security dominate the discussion, we are in effect telling them not to come, or to get out once they have their degrees. And this is where the other pincer of the claw is really beginning to clamp down. "If you don't want them," the rest of the world is saying, "by all means send them our way."

## The Coming Talent Squeeze

When you add up all these factors, it becomes clear that the employment issue of the future goes far beyond outsourcing. A far graver concern on the minds of leading thinkers, from former Treasury Secretary and Harvard University President Larry Summers to labor-market expert Edward Montgomery, is the looming talent shortage likely to confront key fields of the economy.

The market for skilled and talented people is already tight. In July 2004, the unemployment rate for workers with a bachelor's degree or above was a meager 2.7 percent (a level that barely accounts for friction and turnover in the labor market), compared to 5.1 percent for workers with only high school degrees, and 8.3 percent for those lacking a high school diploma. College-educated workers in 2004 earned 74 percent more than workers with just a high school education—a differential that has doubled since 1979. A National Association of Manufacturers' report forecasts a skilled-worker gap beginning in 2005 and growing to 5.3 million workers by 2010 and 14 million by 2020. According to the report's author, the labor-market expert Anthony Carnevale, the shortages that high-tech companies' experienced in the halcyon days of 1999 and 2000 will look like a "mild irritation" in comparison.

The cause of this labor squeeze is simple: the incontrovertible nature of demography. Baby boomers, the largest generation in American history, dominate the labor market, currently constituting about 60 percent of our prime-age workforce—that is, workers between the ages of 25 and 54. During this decade and the next, this generation will exit the workforce in equally massive numbers, and the cohorts following behind are too small to make up for that loss. Even setting aside issues of skills and competitiveness, there simply aren't enough available warm bodies in the U.S. to plug the hole. The basic rules of biology indicate that, in the next twenty years, the U.S. is going to experience a lack of available workers that hasn't been seen for the past fifty years. What we saw happen in the information technology markets of the late nineties was only a warm-up for what's coming.[6]

While the coming talent shortage will hit the economy as a whole, it will hit much harder at the cutting edges of scientific and technological creativity. The talent gap is likely to reach epic proportions by 2010. Employment in the scientific and engineering segment of the workforce has grown four times faster than overall employment since 1980. While we have produced a growing number of scientists and engineers, we have produced them at a much slower rate than our economy has produced jobs in these fields.

These trends are projected to continue. According to the Bureau of Labor Statistics, scientific and engineering occupations are projected to grow at three times the rate of the overall workforce—adding 2.2 million new jobs by 2010, a nearly 50 percent increase. At the same time, the average age of the scientific and technological workforce is rising. More than half of those in the scientific workforce are 40 years old or older, and the 40–44 age group is nearly four times as large as the 60–64 age group. Obviously, many of these people will retire over the next two decades.

The National Science Board saw this threat as so serious that it issued a special addendum to its biannual publication, *Science and Engineering Indicators*, outlining looming talent crisis in science and technology.

If the trends . . . continue undeterred, three things will happen. The number of jobs in the U.S. economy that require science and engineering training will grow; the number of U.S. citizens prepared for those jobs will, at best, be level; and the availability of people from other countries who have science and engineering training will decline, either because of limits to entry imposed by U.S. national security restrictions or because of intense global competition for people with these skills.

## Replacement People

You don't have to be a rocket scientist to figure out that there is one particularly effective way to fill this gap: foreign talent. In a sense, the

U.S. has already been cheating for decades with this strategy; instead of growing our own creative population, an expensive and time-consuming endeavor, we've been importing our talent from elsewhere. According to Kenneth Prewitt, the political scientist who oversaw the 2000 U.S. Census, immigrants in the United States and increasingly across the advanced capitalist world play the crucial role of "replacement people."[7] A 2000 United Nations report showed the critical dependence of the world's most advanced economies on these replacement people, defining them as "the international migration that would be needed to offset declines in the size of the population, the declines in the population of working age, as well as to offset the overall aging of a population."

Writing in the 2002 edition of the *Brookings Review,* Prewitt summed up our dependence on foreign talent this way:

> The UN projects negative population growth for 31 European nations, with especially dramatic declines for the working-age cohort. For example, under current (median) UN projections, in the next half-century Italy's population will drop from 57 million to 41 million and the Russian federation's from 147 million to 121 million—respectively, 28% and 18%. The replacement migration numbers get very high. To maintain Italy's working-age population, for example, would require some 370,000 new migrants each year; Germany's, just short of a half-million (Germany is now debating whether to grant 30,000 or only 20,000 temporary visas for immigrant workers). Population is declining not only in Europe but also in the advanced economies of the Far East, such as South Korea, Hong Kong, and Japan. Japan, for example, expects to drop from 127 million people to 105 million in the first half of the 21st century.

The United States, according to Prewitt, has offset this problem through immigration. Although our "native stock" has similarly stopped reproducing at a sufficient replacement level, our adjustment in immigration has allowed us so far to skirt the problem. Prewitt estimates that immigration plus "higher-than-replacement fertility among the foreign-born" added nearly 33 million people to our country's population in the last ten years alone. This population growth has been highly concentrated among the working-age demographic and, even more encouragingly, has been spread out across low-skilled and high-skilled industries, as service, agriculture, and high-tech jobs have all drawn many new Americans. The question is: How long can this continue?

## The New Immigrant Entrepreneurs

Our ability to in-source the best and the brightest extends far beyond scientists and engineers, bringing in everyone from high-ranking business executives and artistic and cultural luminaries to superstar baseball and basketball players. But the United States has in-sourced its greatest leads at the cutting edge of high-tech innovation and entrepreneurship.

According to the systematic studies of AnnaLee Saxenian, foreign-born entrepreneurs make up a huge share of Silicon Valley's core innovative and entrepreneurial engine, which has powered this country's move to unquestioned leadership in the creative age. It is the technological and entrepreneurial benchmark for the United States and the rest of world. Saxenian's study, *Silicon Valley's New Immigrant Entrepreneurs,* is based on extensive and detailed research. She and her team plowed through census data on immigrants' educations, occupations, and earnings. They used a customized database provided by Dun & Bradstreet, the company that tracks company performance and credit ratings, to distill immigrant-run companies from the nearly twelve thousand Silicon Valley high-tech companies founded between 1980 and 1998. Saxenian herself conducted more than one hundred in-depth interviews with immigrant entrepreneurs, venture capitalists, and others connected to the Silicon Valley high-tech scene. She conducted dozens more interviews with investors, entrepreneurs, and technologists in Taiwan and India.[8]

Her findings provide an in-depth look at the importance of immigrant talent to America's innovative and entrepreneurial growth machine. "Well-known technology companies like Yahoo and Hotmail, which have immigrant founders, represent the tip of a significantly larger iceberg," she reminds us. According to her research, fifty-nine public technology firms in Silicon Valley were founded or run by Chinese or Indians in the late 1990s. By the end of the 1990s, Chi-

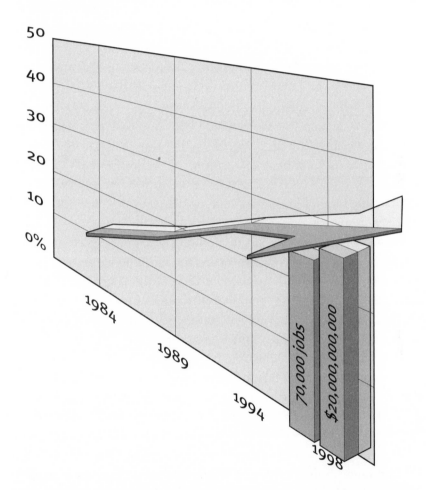

**Figure 4.2: Immigrant Entrepreneurs Power Silicon Valley**

The percentage of Silicon Valley companies started by immigrants rose steadily between 1984 and 2000. These companies generated a total of 70,000 jobs and $20 billion in annual revenue.

AnnaLee Saxenian, *Silicon Valley's New Immigrant Entrepreneurs,* San Francisco: Public Policy Institute of California, 1999.

nese and Indian engineers were running nearly 30 percent of Silicon Valley's high-tech companies.

In 2000 alone, nine foreign-born American were added to the Forbes 400 list of the richest Americans. All made their fortunes in high-tech fields. Among them were Gururaj Deshpande of Sycamore Networks ($7.6 billion), Pradeep Sindhu of Juniper Networks ($2.5 billion), Romesh Wadhwani of Aspect Development ($1.3 billion), and Taiwanese entrepreneurs Jing Jong Pan ($1.8 billion), Theresa Pan ($1.7 billion), and JoMei Chang ($825 million). Saxenian estimated that the Silicon Valley companies started by Indian- and Chinese-born entrepreneurs alone accounted for nearly $20 billion in sales and more than seventy thousand jobs. And Saxenian believes her numbers are, if anything, conservative. Because she was only able to use the Dun & Bradstreet data to identify companies with a current Chinese or Indian chief executive, she thinks her findings likely "understate the scale of immigrant entrepreneurship" in Silicon Valley.

Even more intriguingly, Saxenian's research finds that the open flow of people is a win-win situation for the United States and other nations. Her follow-up studies of Indian and Chinese entrepreneurs in Silicon Valley show that many of these technologists and business founders participate in "transnational professional and social networks" that enable them to start businesses and contribute to economic growth both in the United States and back home.

Such is the case of Milin Wu, who received his doctorate in electrical engineering from Stanford University in 1976. While a student, he saw little use for his skills in Taiwan and chose to remain in the United States after graduation, taking positions at Intel and Siliconix. By the mid-1980s, the Taiwanese economy began to improve, developing semiconductor manufacturing capability. In 1989, Wu founded one of Taiwan's first important semiconductor companies, Macronix Co., in the Hsinchu Science–based Industrial Park. Macronix went public on the Taiwan Stock Exchange in 1995 and became the first Taiwanese company to list on the NASDAQ in 1996. By 2004, according to Saxenian, Macronix became the sixth largest semiconductor company in Taiwan, with more than $300 million in sales and some 2,800 employees. Wu later established an advanced design and engineering center in Silicon Valley, and remains an active participant in Silicon Valley's Monet Jade Science and Technology Association, building professional, social, and business connections that benefit high-tech industry in both Taiwan and Silicon Valley, and especially between the two.

By establishing high-tech companies back home, returning immigrants bring modern business techniques and cultural practices to their home countries. As in the United States and elsewhere, this causes much chafing on the part of established social and economic interests. But it's hard to see how economic and therefore human development can take place without it. My colleagues from India tell me that new software firms in Bangalore are helping to break down the old castelike system of social relations and establish more democratic and egalitarian business and social cultures. Hence Saxenian's claim that the old zero-sum view of immigration is outmoded. "In some parts of the world," she writes, "the old dynamic of 'brain drain' is giving way to . . . 'brain circulation.' Most people instinctively assume that movement of skill and talent must benefit one country at the expense of another. But thanks to brain circulation, high-skilled immigration increasingly benefits both sides."

I couldn't agree more. Open flows of people to and from the United States benefit all, increasing the economic opportunities open to foreign-born people, creating wealth in U.S. communities, and contributing to much-needed economic development and cultural change in countries on both sides of the exchange.

## Voting with Their Feet

Unfortunately, increasing U.S. impediments to immigration threaten to break the cycle. As one expert put it, immigrant scientists and engineers, especially students, are "starting to vote with their feet," pursuing alternative options in other countries.[9] When foreign students cannot get into U.S. universities or professionals are denied visas to work here, the win-win cycle is stopped before it has begun: Both sides stand to lose a great deal.

A growing number of people are staring to take notice. After a trip to Silicon Valley in early spring 2004, columnist Thomas Friedman warned of the impending threat.

> Executives complained bitterly that the Department of Homeland Security is making it so hard for legitimate foreigners to get visas to study or work in America that many have given up the age-old dream of coming here. Instead, they are studying in England and other Western European nations, and even China. This is leading to a twofold disaster. . . . First, one of America's greatest assets—its ability to skim the cream off the first-round intellectual draft choices from around the world and bring them to our shores to innovate—will be diminished, and that in turn will shrink our talent pool. And second, we could lose a whole generation of foreigners who would normally come here to study, and then would take American ideas and American relationships back home. In a decade we will feel that loss in America's standing around the world.[10]

Alan Weber, founder of *Fast Company,* put it this way:

> Until recently, if Americans heard the words "brain drain," they knew clearly what that meant: Bright, talented scientists, engineers and other techies from all over the world were migrating to the United States. They were drawn here by the world's best universities, the most dynamic companies, the freest economic and social environment and the highest standard of living. Today, while many of these conditions still apply, Americans are starting to hear a new term: "reverse brain drain." What it suggests is the United States is pursuing government and private-sector policies that, over the long run, could lead to a significant shift in the world's balance of brainpower.[11]

Not everyone agrees that things are so bad. Writing in the *Washington Post*, science expert Daniel Greenberg pointed out that: "The alarmists of scientific shortage have been warning for decades that a homeward exodus of foreign scientists will someday occur. But, contrary to this expectation, the 'stay' rates of foreign doctoral students have actually increased, according to the National Science Foundation, which reports that 71% of foreign citizens who received their PhDs in 1999 were still in the United States two years later—up from 49% in 1987." The problem with citing this particular statistic, of course, is that it fails to take into account the post-9/11 political landscape—which is precisely the reason so many leading businesspeople, academics, scientists, and commentators are concerned.

My own take on the matter is twofold. First off, when we talk about losing brain- and people-power, we should remember that it doesn't have to be many brains or people to have a serious effect; the loss of just a few leading inventors, entrepreneurs, or venture capitalists can hurt a great deal. Second, while all is not yet lost, the writing is certainly on the wall. For the first time in a long time, we're plainly losing foreign talent. The evidence, as we've seen, is everywhere.

- The total number of visiting scholars declined in the 2002–2003 academic year for the first time in almost a decade, according to a January 2004 report in *Nature*. In 2003, the number of foreign researchers at the five largest research institutes of the National Institutes of Health outside Washington, D.C., fell for the first time in the nine years such records have been kept. The number of visas issued to foreign-born scientists and engineers dropped by roughly 55 percent between 2001 and 2002 from 166,000 to 74,000, according to figures from the National Science Board. That adds up to a one-year decline of more than 80,000 researchers.

- Visa applications for students fell by 74,000 between 2001 and 2003, from 400,000 to 326,000, while high-skilled visas fell by nearly 50,000 from 248,000 to 200,000 over that period.[12] This mirrors more general trends. Between 2000 and 2003, the total number of U.S. visas applied for declined by more than 40 percent—from 6.3 million to 3.7 million people, while applications for student visas fell by almost 100,000 over the same period.

- Finally, fewer of those students who do apply are getting in. The rejection rate for H–1B visas (also called "high-skilled visas"), which allow professionals who are not U.S. citizens to work in the country for up to six years, increased from 9.5 to 17.8 percent between 2001 and 2003.

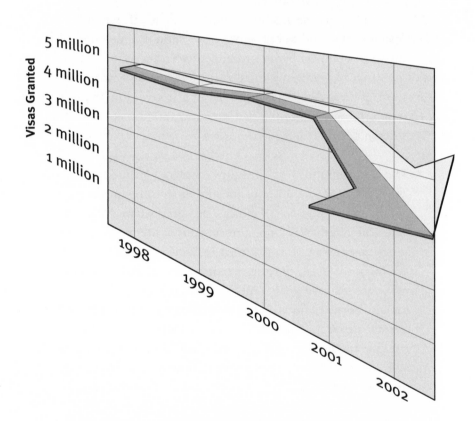

**Figure 4.3: Visas Decline for Foreign Students**

Since 2001, there has been a dramatic decline in the number of visas granted to foreign students applying to study in the United States.
National Science Board, *Science and Engineering Indicators, 2004,* Washington, D.C.: U.S. Government Printing Office, 2003.

More and more people, including our future technological leaders and budding entrepreneurs, are being denied entry. Between 2001 and 2003, the rejection rate rose in almost all categories of high-skilled visas. Rejection rates for the cultural exchange visa (used by many foreign medical students), for example, rose from 5.1 percent in 2001 to 7.8 percent in 2003. For exchange visitors on J-1 visas, rejections rose from 7.8 to 15.9 percent, and the rate for other high-skilled visas increased from 9.5 to 17.8 percent. In 2003, the number of student visas issued by the United States dropped 8 percent—after already falling 20 percent in 2002. These were the two largest-percentage decreases since government began to track student statistics in 1952. As *BusinessWeek* put it in October 2004, "Immigrants with the most to offer the U.S. are having the hardest time getting in."

More disturbingly, fewer foreign students are choosing to come to the United States to study. Overall, American colleges saw the smallest increase in the enrollment of international students in 2003 in a decade, less than 1 percent (0.6 percent) compared to 6.4 percent in each of the two previous years. Several studies show the precipitous a drop in applications from foreign students. To cite just a few:

- A February 2004 study by a consortium of higher-education organizations found that applications for graduate study by foreign students declined at nearly half (47 percent) of all colleges and universities and 36 percent reported decline in undergraduate applications.[13] In addition to this, nearly 60 percent of doctoral research institutions reported a decline in applications from foreign students. The downswing in foreign-student applications was much more pronounced at the nineteen universities with the largest international enrollments. All of them reported declines of at least 10 percent among graduate students and nine saw a drop of at least 30 percent.

- Overall, U.S. graduate schools saw a 28 percent decline in applications from foreign students and an 18 percent drop in admissions, according to a September 2004 report by the Council of Graduate Schools.[14] Nearly nine in ten of the responding graduate schools experienced a decline. Engineering applications fell by 36 percent, and the number of actual admissions to engineering graduate schools dropped 24 percent. Applications fell the most from the countries that have traditionally sent the most students. More than half of all foreign-born graduate students hail from Asia, including 14 percent from India and 10 percent from China. Applications from Chinese, Indian, and Korean students dropped 45 percent, 28 percent, and 14 percent; while the number of admitted students from China dropped 34 percent, from India 19 percent, and from Korea 12 percent.[15]

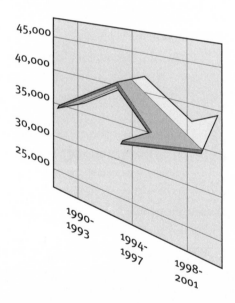

**Figure 4.4: Declining Foreign Student Enrollment in Key Science and Technology Fields**

Foreign-student enrollment in scientific and engineering graduate programs has declined steadily since the mid-1990s.

National Science Board, *Science and Engineering Indicators, 2004,* Washington, D.C.: U.S. Government Printing Office, 2003.

- One-third fewer international students applied to take the Graduate Record Exam, or GRE, in 2004, according to the Educational Testing Service. There was a precipitous decline in students taking the GREs from China and other Asian countries: Chinese test takers were down 50 percent, Taiwanese 43 percent, Indians 37 percent, and Koreans 15 percent.

## The Climate Chills

Why would talented foreigners avoid the United States? In part because other countries are simply doing a better, more aggressive job of recruiting them. But having talked to hundreds of talented professionals in a half-dozen countries over the past year, I'm convinced that the biggest reason has to do with the changed political and policy landscape in Washington. In the 1990s, the federal government focused on expanding America's human capital and interconnectedness to the world—crafting international trade agreements, investing in cutting edge R&D, subsidizing higher education and public access to the Internet, and encouraging immigration. But in recent years, the government's attention and resources have shifted to older sectors of the economy, with tariff protection and subsidies to extractive industries. Meanwhile, Washington has stunned scientists across the world with its disregard for consensus scientific views when those views conflict with the interests of favored sectors (as has been the case with the issue of global climate change). Most of all, in the wake of 9/11, Washington has inspired the fury of the world, especially of its educated classes, with its "my way or the highway" foreign policy. In effect, for the first time in our history, we're saying to highly mobile and very finicky global talent, "You don't belong here."

While we like to view ourselves as an open nation, international relations experts John Paden and Peter Singer report that, among other things, the Patriot Act of 2001 has created restrictions on the vetting and monitoring of foreign visitors—including students and scholars attending or visiting American universities—that exceed in scope those in any other Western democracy.[16] The Patriot Act, along with the Border Security and Visa Reform Act of 2002, significantly tightened the requirements and the enforcement of entry procedures for foreign visitors. Together, these bills have significantly affected the ability of universities and colleges to attract foreign students. Under these measures, universities are required to provide the State Department with electronic background data before issuing student or scholar visas.

An electronic surveillance system known as the Student Exchange and Visitor Information Service, or SEVIS, was set up to allow officials to maintain up-to-date information on foreign students and exchange visitors to the United States. Students and scholars working in "sensitive" areas listed on the government's "Technology Alert List" face even greater security checks by the Visa Mantis program, which was designed to prevent transfers of sensitive technologies. All visitors and green-card holders are required to report any changes of address to the INS. And all male visitors between the ages of sixteen and forty-five are required to register with the INS, even if they already registered when first entering the country. INS officials are required to physically visit and certify every American university and college that accepts foreign students.

Visitors and students from Muslim states face even more arduous procedures, including the selective registration of Muslim males, according to Paden and Singer. As they note, these policies have created massive resentment in many countries. "Nearly every Muslim ambassador to the United States has raised the matter with the State Department," they write. "The foreign ministers of Bangladesh, Indonesia, and Pakistan have all traveled to Washington, D.C., to personally protest the measures, which they saw as an affront." The result, Paden and Singer conclude, is "long-term damage" to American ideals. "By burning American bridges with the next generation of business and political leaders, Washington will undercut its ability to encourage progress aboard. . . . The humiliating sting of being forced to stand in line for days only to be rejected for a visa will not be salved by a glossy brochure or radio program."

Obviously, these restrictions are justified to some extent, deriving as they do from understandable and important security concerns. But the logistics of creating such a massive database, gathering and entering information, and registering students and scholars have—beyond just offending potential foreign talent, of course—created huge bureaucratic snafus and institutional coordination problems. The unintended consequence has been significant delays in processing visas and substantial frustration on the part of universities and foreign scholars and students alike. A November 2003 survey of three hundred universities and colleges by the Association of International Educators found that the number of international students whose start dates were delayed by visa problems was nearly 50 percent (48 percent) higher in 2003 than at the start of the previous year; the increase for younger scholars and postdoctoral researchers was 76 percent. In July 2003, the American Institute of Physics reported that nearly a quarter of foreign students who applied to study for physics Ph.D.s in the United States were initially denied a visa. More than three-quarters of the delayed students were in the critical fields of the physical sciences, biological sciences, and engineering. A Government Accountability Office study of seventy-one scholars and students found that it took an average of sixty-seven days for a visa requiring "Visa Mantis" review.[17]

By 2003, antiterrorism measures had begun to catch up not just with visa applications but also with requests for more permanent U.S. residence. Thanks to delays in the processing of green-card applications, only 705,827 people became legal permanent residents that year, down from 1.06 million in 2002. This decline is the steepest since 1953, when Joseph McCarthy stoked fears that Communists were invading the government and the general population. Nearly half those affected by the government slowdown in 2003 were foreign students, workers, and others already residing in the U.S. and hoping to become permanent residents. Such figures may understate the extent of the problem, because they do not include pending green-card applications—which were backlogged to more than 6 million by the end of fiscal year 2003. Of these over 6 million people whose legal lives as residents were put on hold, roughly 3.6 million have had applications pending for more than six months.

The practical, everyday implications of such a wait can be exasperating. Without a green card, many immigrants are prohibited from traveling, denied the benefit of in-state tuition rates, or even put at risk for job loss and deportation if the wait goes on too long. These risks accrue not only to individuals and families but to the businesses that hire them and need their skills. The *Washington Post* put a more human face on this situation when it described the situation of Alba Salgado, a hotel housekeeper living in Alexandria, Virginia. Salgado holds a work permit and was sponsored for a green card by her father over ten years ago. Even though she's in the U.S. legally, she hasn't been able to leave the country in that whole time. Every summer, she sends her children, ages thirteen and six, to El Salvador to visit with family. Salgado is prohibited from joining them. Worse, just after authorities informed Salgado last year that she would soon receive residency, her file was lost when immigration services was folded into the new Department of Homeland Security. Salgado had to resubmit many of her documents. She puts it succinctly: "It's a long time saying, 'Maybe this year, maybe this year.' "

It's difficult to understand who benefits from this kind of stagnant waiting game. And more and more are losing out. In December 2004, Professor Tariq Ramadan, a leading scholar of Islamic studies, resigned his tenured position at the Notre Dame University when he was unable to get his visa renewed. The details behind his "prudential revocation" remain confidential. What we do know is that, post-9/11, Ramadan called on Muslims around the world to condemn terrorism as a betrayal of Islamic principles. He also taught classics and peace studies at one of America's most prestigious universities. Said one Notre Dame official: "This is an opportunity lost." For students, for scholarship, and certainly for the United States.

Well, respond skeptics of calls for efficient immigration processing, that's the price you pay for hitching your wagon to the most powerful economy in the world. And it's true that many of the world's people still jump at the chance to have even a shot at permanent U.S. residency. But we forget when we make statements like this that one of the primary drivers of this economy are those very wagons we sometimes treat so incredulously. Immigration to the United States is a mutually beneficial arrangement for newcomer and host country alike, and we would do well to start seeing it that way.

Such long delays in both temporary and permanent status, a study by the American Association of the Advancement of Science concludes, discourage many from ever coming to the United States again. "We're slapping these people in the face," is how William Wulf, president of the National Academy of Engineering put it, and "the long-term cost in good will will be enormous." According to Debra Stewart, president of the Council of Graduate Schools, the effect of these measures is likely to be lasting: "The problem is not this fall [semester]. . . . The real problem is long term." Adds Michael Crow, president of Arizona State University, where the number of foreign students fell 7 percent over the course of 2004, "It's a major issue for us, and it's going to get worse." While American students tend to go into business, economics, or law, fields in science and engineering are increasingly filled by foreigners, where, according to Crow, "our pool of talent is going down."

The students and scholars I have spoken to report not only encountering delays, but a general failure to get information on what is causing the delays. This restrictive climate has engendered growing frustration and resentment on the part of leading foreign scholars who resent not just the delays but being treated like potential criminals. The following are a small sampling of such unfortunate incidents.

In November 2003, two Chinese students studying at the University of Toronto were prevented from attending a scientific conference at the University of Texas at Austin, even though they had applied for visas, were invited by the conference organizers to present their work, and had attended the same conference a year earlier. It took three months to process the security and background checks on the students. By this time, the conference was long over.

Heng Zhu, a genomics fellow at Yale University, was denied entry back into the United States for more than ten months, according to a *Wall Street Journal* report. Zhu was forced to return to China when his visa went overdue and was told he needed to return to China to get a new one. Zhu's three-year fellowship from the Damon Runyon Cancer Research Foundation was cut off as a result of the delay, derailing his efforts to map the yeast genome and hurting the work of his research group.[18]

In early 2002, a Chinese doctoral student at the University of Wisconsin, Madison, was denied reentry into the United States for almost nine months, despite having proof of enrollment, details of his course, a letter from his department, and U.S. government forms confirming his immigrant status. He was forced to take up work in a Chinese shipping company to make ends meet while he was delayed.

Olexei Motrunich, a Ukrainian physicist who has worked in the United States since the early 1990s, was stranded in his home country for months in 2003 and early 2004, leaving him unable to assume his postdoctoral position at the University of California at Santa Barbara. He told *Nature* magazine: "I have been telling my friends how great America is, how one does not feel foreign in this country. Now I have to explain to the same people why, after more than eight years of doing science in the United States, I have a hard time receiving a visa to continue my work."[19]

In October 2002, a prominent University of Toronto professor canceled a scientific visit to the United States, so flabbergasted was he by the fact that he had to be fingerprinted, photographed, and questioned even though he was a Canadian citizen (he was born in Iran). This might not seem so strange—except the professor had been invited to chair a major meeting by the main scientific arm of the U.S. government, the National Science Foundation.[20] A top minister in the Canadian government, also a Canadian citizen but born in Egypt, told me he encounters similar hassles when traveling to the United States for high-level meetings at the White House or cabinet-level agencies. As a result, he no longer travels to the U.S., except when he absolutely has to, and has taken to rerouting all of his foreign travel to avoid U.S. connections.

The altered flow of talent is already beginning to show signs of crimping America's long-standing role as the global crossroads of science and technology. "We can't hold scientific meetings here anymore because foreign scientists can't get visas," a top oceanographer at the University of California at San Diego told me. Another added that it may be time for academics in that part of the country to "have our scientific meetings in Tijuana," because at least there international experts can get in. The International Astronomical Union decided to hold its 2009 general assembly in Brazil rather than Hawaii. Not surprisingly, they cited potential visa concerns.

Unintended or not, for the first time in modern memory—perhaps in the history of our country—top scientists and intellectuals from elsewhere are choosing not to come here. The foreign students I have taught at Ohio State, Harvard, MIT, and Carnegie Mellon have always been among the first to point out the benefits of studying and doing research in the United States. But their impressions have changed dramatically over the past two years. They now complain of being hounded by the immigration agencies as potential threats to security, and worry that America is abandoning its top standing as an open society. Many are thinking of leaving for foreign schools, and they tell me that their friends and colleagues back home are no longer interested in coming to the U.S. for their education, instead seeking out universities in Canada, Europe, and elsewhere. A spring 2003 survey of 1,700 foreign students and scholars at the University of California at Berkeley found a "general climate of anxiety and alarm at what international students felt was a very unfriendly attitude of the U.S. government." Sixty percent of the respondents felt they had to endure "unreasonable delays" in obtaining visas. A large number of others reported feeling "humiliated" by being fingerprinted, photographed, or otherwise harassed by U.S. immigration officials.[21] While some may say, "Well, this is a small price to pay for coming to school in the United States," the fact of the matter is that it is causing these students to go elsewhere and to tell their friends and colleagues to do the same.

And this talent does indeed stop coming when it doesn't feel welcome. Sun Zhi, a top student from a leading Chinese university, decided simply to quit trying after he was twice denied a visa to the United States despite being admitted and having been granted a scholarship from a renowned U.S. university. Zhi told the *Chronicle of Higher Education* that he "gave up his dream of studying in America" after the second denial. "Many of my classmates have changed their plans to go to American universities," he added; "since it has become so difficult [to enter], we think it is a waste of time to apply." In July 2003, the *New York Times* reported that Brazilian students, long a source of talent for U.S. MBA programs, were increasingly choosing European business schools. An eminent Oxford University professor told me that he had never seen such impressive applications for graduate study, and that most of the improvement had come from international students who were choosing Oxford instead of top American universities.

Many pundits and politicians have suggested that current dissatisfaction with the United States extends little beyond the particular administration currently at the helm of American foreign policy. They point to a summer 2004 worldwide survey in which a large majority of respondents said they would prefer Democratic challenger John Kerry to Republican incumbent George W. Bush. Indeed, there is growing dissatisfaction around the globe with the Bush administration's unilateralist bent. But placing the blame only on the Bush administration keeps us from examining the broader trends in global trade and economic insecurity. The real problems are structural, and so far few national-level politicians have coupled the economic comprehension with the political savvy necessary to bridge the global divide.

## The Costs

What will the effects of such an altered talent landscape mean to the U.S. economy? While it is impossible to fully quantify the effects of lost brainpower, other evidence, much of it collected by the U.S. business community, suggests the U.S. may be seriously losing out—in real dollars and cents—on the talents of a wide range of foreign scientists, engineers, inventors, and other professionals. Visa delays alone have cost U.S. businesses roughly $30 billion in two years, according to a June 2004 study commissioned by the Santangelo Group, a consortium of leading U.S. industry groups ranging from the Aerospace Industries Council and the National Foreign Trade Council to the Association for Manufacturing Technologies.[22] The study was based on a survey of 734 companies belonging to the group's eight trade associations. Of the 141 companies that responded, 73 percent reported having had problems processing business visas since 2002, and the average financial impact per company was nearly a million dollars ($925,816). Thirty-eight percent of respondents said that visa delays caused projects to be postponed, 42 percent said the delays made them unable to bring foreign employees to the United States, and 20 percent said training events had to be relocated outside the country.

The direct-sale giant Amway, for instance, chose to hold a 2004 convention for its eight thousand South Korean distributors in China rather than in Los Angeles or Hawaii because the United States would require each visitor to go though an individual interview with a consular official. Amway estimated that the attendees would have spent, on average, $1,250—translating to a $10 million loss for the potential host city. Gary Shapiro, president and CEO of the Consumer Electronics Association, confided that his group was having trouble with its annual meeting in Las Vegas because fellow associations and

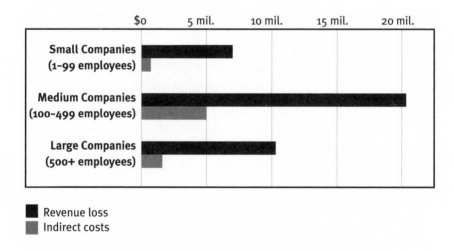

**Figure 4.5: Restrictions on Foreign Talent Cost Business Millions**

Between July 2002 and March 2004, small and large businesses alike suffered millions of dollars in losses due to the denial or delay of business-travel visas. The Santangelo Group, *Do Visa Delays Hurt U.S. Business?*, June 2004.

companies from Europe and Asia "no longer want to go through the hassle." And why would they, when they can attend the equivalent meetings now springing up around the globe? Colleagues from abroad used to rib Shapiro for stealing all their best people with better opportunities in the United States; "nobody says that anymore."

Foreign professionals already working in U.S. firms aren't having an easy time of it, either. Processing times for renewing green cards and travel documents have skyrocketed. It now takes an average of nineteen months to replace a lost green card. It takes seven months for legal workers in the U.S. whose green cards are pending to get travel papers—and during that time, the applicants cannot leave the country or they risk not being able to reenter. Meanwhile, the number of pending green-card applications has jumped by nearly 60 percent since 2001 because one thousand agents who once issued documents have been reassigned to do "extensive security checks of every applicant instead."

This leaves U.S. business in quite a bind. If the foreign talent cannot get into the United States or faces considerable delays in doing so, companies are in effect forced to go overseas to get it. The consequences are already coming into view as leading companies, particularly those in key high-tech industries, are taking steps to diversify their talent portfolio and mitigate risks by opening foreign laboratories and technical facilities. A 2004 Cendant Mobility report shows that, across the board, companies worldwide are increasingly instituting policies to reduce long-term expatriate transfers and staff instead with local talent. As companies increase their global reach, it becomes easier to tap into local talent where it already is, instead of moving talent around. The consequences of a more restrictive climate exacerbate this trend. Today, U.S. companies are being forced to go offshore not just to get access to lower-cost talent, but to get access to talent they previously would have employed here, including top foreign talent studying at our leading universities. So, for example, if Microsoft wants to recruit a Chinese-born computer scientist from MIT but for some reason cannot get him or her a postgraduation visa, it can put that person at its Beijing research facility. Instead of that person and that job going to

Redmond, they go overseas. By restricting talent flows into this country, the U.S. government ensures that both pincers of the claw of offshoring simultaneously tighten their grip on our economy.

This climate is also negatively affecting America's culture and entertainment industries, which add billions to our national income and are the mainstay of America's soft power. A host of international music groups have canceled American tours recently. In February 2004, Bulgarian soprano Alexeandrina Pendatchanska was denied a visa to enter the U.S. to perform with the Pittsburgh Opera when a government Homeland Security computer couldn't handle the spelling of her name and her proposed stay in the United States was incorrectly listed as "Feb. 2004–June 2003." [23] Cuban musicians Sierra Maestra were denied a visa when the FBI failed to complete background checks fast enough to meet INS deadlines. South African singer and guitarist Vusi Mahlasela and the Bogotá-based electronica collective Sidestepper had to cancel their American tours because they were refused visas. The problem extends beyond technical complications and bureaucratic blunders, too. Growing numbers of musicians are refusing to come to the U.S. simply because of its restrictive posture and unilateral foreign policy. Youssou N'Dour, perhaps the single most famous global-music artist, canceled his largest-ever U.S. tour last spring to protest the invasion of Iraq. If ever there was a doubt about the intersection of geopolitics and art, this controversy put that question to rest. It also put to rest what promised to be an extremely rich—and lucrative—cultural experience for the U.S.

Add to the list of casualties the way American companies and brands are viewed around the world. A survey by RoperASW of some thirty thousand consumers in thirty countries, published in the journal *American Demographics,* found that foreigners' opinions of American companies and brands have sunk to historic lows. When consumers were asked to rate their trust in leading companies worldwide, American companies were clustered at the very bottom of the list. While Islamic countries, not surprisingly, had the greatest increase in negative opinions toward the United States, the survey found that the number of Russians who saw U.S. companies in a favorable light fell by 25 percent, while the share of French, Germans, and Italians with a positive view sank by 20 percent, 16 percent, and 10 percent, respectively.[24] So much for McWorld.

## Reverse Brain Drain

Worse yet, for the first time in a very long time, our very own best and brightest, established scientists, intellectuals, and even some entrepreneurs, are starting to look elsewhere. Like stem-cell researcher Roger Pedersen, who left his position at the University of California, San Francisco, to take up residency at the Centre for Stem Cell Biology Medicine at Cambridge University in the United Kingdom. Pedersen's departure illustrates on a small scale how the macrolevel creative economy is being reshaped—both by our global competitors' increasing savvy and by our own apparent cluelessness. Pedersen bolted because of aggressive recruitment on the part of the British government, and also because of the heavy restrictions placed on stem-cell research by our own government. "I have a soft spot in my heart for America," he told *Wired* magazine, "but the U.K. is much better for this research . . . more working capital." He continued: "They haven't made such a political football out of stem cells."[25]

Stem cells are vital to the body because of their ability to develop into any kind of tissue. Scientists play a similar intellectual and economic role; their discoveries (silicon circuitry, gene splicing) are the source of most big new industries (personal computers, biotechnology), often adapting as the times demand.

Unfortunately, Roger Pedersen is not alone. "Over the last few years, as the conservative movement in the U.S. has become more entrenched, many people I know are looking for better lives in Canada, Europe, and Australia," a noted entomologist at the University of Illinois e-mailed me in 2003. "From bloggers and programmers to members of the National Academy I have spoken with, all find the *zeitgeist* alien and even threatening. My friend says it is like trying to research and do business in the 21st century in a culture that wants to

live in the 19th—empires, bibles, and all. There is an E.U. fellowship
through the European Molecular Biology Laboratory in Amsterdam
that everyone and their mother is trying to get."

That's a little stronger than most people would put it. But that
doesn't mean there aren't plenty of others thinking similar thoughts.
On the day President Bush won reelection in November 2004, the
number of U.S. citizens visiting Canada's main immigration site shot
up sixfold from its usual daily total—from about 20,000 to 115,000.
But this increasing displeasure with American society is not tethered
to one particular ideology or time period. In late 2003 and early 2004
alone, I received a spate of e-mails from techies, artists, and recent immigrants from across the United States. Here's a small sampling.

A middle-aged high-tech entrepreneur from New York wrote:

> I am one of those of who you have written about. I am a senior
> Information Technology specialist in my early fifties. And my
> dedication to my career has led me to become one of the true
> seniors in the industry. . . . However, with the decline of the
> American economy coinciding with the incompetent policies
> of the administration my wife and I are now looking to leave
> the States to make our home in Austria, a country that we have
> come to love in the last ten years for its peacefulness and beauty.
> This year I hope to open a small software business over the In-
> ternet. Yet with the declining value of the U.S. dollar the finan-
> cial basis for my company will be based on the Euro, again in
> Austria.

An English as a Second Language (ESL) instructor from Houston:

> My students are European and Asian geophysicists who work
> for the major oil companies in their countries. They usually stay
> in Houston for 4 years only . . . [now] they are all frightened by
> the possibility of having Bush for 4 more years. I've been an
> ESL instructor for almost 25 years and never . . . have I seen my
> foreign students so insecure and confused. Sometimes I hear

comments like: "It's beyond me to see that this country is actually living way back in the dark ages. Where did the age of reason go? . . . I was in the Netherlands in June and was in extreme awe. One can definitely see creativity in every corner. Went to Den Hague, Scheveningen, Delft, and Amsterdam. Every single street had something related to creativity. Art everywhere! High tech couldn't be more obvious. . . . Coming back to Houston, I felt sadness. The people here focus on nothing else but sports. The city keeps building stadiums, we have four new ones.

From a techie back from business travel in Europe:

Having just been in six countries in Europe, I have to report that the biggest hassles came in two places. The first was leaving the U.S. and the second was reentering the U.S. And, all of this was as a U.S. citizen with a valid U.S. passport. Completely ridiculous. I entered and left countries without anyone even asking for my passport or caring at all. But, it literally took over an hour on each end to both get on the plane to get out of this country and return. We talked with several people in Europe who basically said they just wouldn't come to the U.S. I now understand why.

An artist in Spokane, Washington:

We spoke some time ago of the creative and international centers moving out of America. I originally noticed this several years ago in casual discussions with friends over which country to move to. More recently it has become concrete. Friends have taken jobs in Australia while others have relocated to Europe, I personally have bought a cabin in Canada, partially for pleasure, partially in consideration of a temporary relocation out of America. . . . I have come to avoid flying for the sense of criminalization it now involves, feeling unwelcome when returning from Canada.

From a Chinese PhD student in one of America's top electrical and computer engineering programs in the country:

> Having already spent more than 7 years in the U.S., I find myself thinking mostly in English and favoring a career in America. However, I am now considering having a career elsewhere. With the stringent post 9-11 immigration policies/procedures, it's harder to find employers that are willing to sponsor employees with international status. And I would have to be close to 40 if I do get my green card; by th[at] time my ambition would have worn out and my American dream will probably reduce to just a 30-year mortgage.

From an aspiring young author struggling to get a visa to stay in this country:

> I grew up in Casablanca, Morocco and went to a private American school. . . . After graduation I enrolled at Middlebury College in Vermont where I majored in Economics and graduated in 2003. . . . Because I am a native Arabic speaker, I took 6 months to write an instructional Arabic book which will be published by Random House in early 2005. In early 2004 I began working at a private investment firm on Wall Street. Everything was going smoothly until my immigration attorney informed me that there were no more work Visas going around and that I had to go back to my country. I love this country. . . . I think the U.S. is as close to a meritocracy as possible and I want to contribute to its greatness. But now I find myself in a situation where I'm not able to work lawfully in the U.S. . . . I am deeply concerned about this country's immigration policy (especially under this administration) and I'm determined to do everything that I can so that I and others can live the American dream.

A creative class member in New Mexico:

> Albuquerque is my last stand in America. If I don't feel insulated enough here from the White House's harsh ignorance and

blatant disregard for scientific inquiry, then I'm gone. Outta here. And in fact, I'm already exploring the options with a vacation to Vancouver and research on Sydney. Once upon a time, America was large enough to hold a beautiful multiplicity of opinions but that's no longer true . . . Soon this country will shrink small enough that there's no room left for me.

## The Death and Life of Great American Advantages

Think about what a heartbreaking statement that is: *Once upon a time, America was large enough to hold a beautiful multiplicity of opinions but that's no longer true.* Is it accurate? Not entirely, but the fact is that an increasing number of America's citizens are beginning to *feel* there is no place for them here. As a result, they're looking elsewhere. And this is not just the result of one U.S. administration, as many left-wingers would like to claim. There are deeper problems, inherent in the fabric of American life, at work.

Mancur Olson noted long ago that powerful or hegemonic nations like America tend to get trapped by their own success. In his classic *Rise and Decline of Nations,* he argued that these nations become so dominant that they get fooled into thinking they know best.[26] Their social and political institutions tend to get locked in place, becoming "rigid" or "sclerotic" and making it hard for them to respond to changing economic conditions. This in turn leaves the door cracked open for new nations to stick their feet in—nations that have taken a few notes and can more readily respond to and deal with new conditions.

There are many ways this plays out, and certainly there is still time to reverse course. But we need to move fast. Leadership in the creative age is not assured; advantages shift in the blink of an eye. New countries that invest in research and development, put resources into higher education, and open themselves up to foreign-born talent can quickly move up the scale. And countries that disinvest, restrict their scientific enterprise, and institute more restrictive policies can just as easily plummet.

I know this well. For seventeen years of my life, I lived in Pittsburgh, Pennsylvania. A century ago, Pittsburgh was a center of industrial innovation and entrepreneurship and a huge cauldron for immigrant talent. Immigrants like Andrew Carnegie built the region's steel industry. The Pittsburgh of the late nineteenth and twentieth century was one of the most innovative, open, and immigrant-rich regions in the world—attracting scores of Italians, Poles, and Eastern Europeans. In 1910, Pittsburgh was home to 535,000 people, making it the eighth largest city in America, behind New York, Chicago, Philadelphia, St. Louis, Boston, Cleveland, and Baltimore. Roughly a third of its people were immigrants.

But by the mid to latter part of the twentieth century, Pittsburgh lost its spark. Not only did its innovative and entrepreneurial energy damp down; it became a closed and hierarchical place. Immigrants stopped coming, save for the inflow into the region's great universities. The immigrant share of the population declined from a high point of 32.3 percent of the population in 1870 to 9.7 percent in 1950 before bottoming out at 3.7 percent in 2000, the lowest share of any major American region. Many of the most talented of their offspring left, including the region's greatest artist, Andy Warhol, the son of Eastern European immigrants (family name, Warhola). The city lost more than 150,000 jobs in the 1980s. Its population declined from a high of more than 750,000 to 330,000, where it hovers today. Its great export, local residents like to say, is no longer steel, but its young people, the very talent it invests so much in creating. In 2004, the city lapsed into bankruptcy, unable to support its own services and upkeep on the backs of a steadily declining population.

I saw firsthand what being a less open and tolerant society led by squelchers did to Pittsburgh's economy. I fear this may well be a microcosm for what is now beginning to happen to our entire country. Yet our loss of access to high-level foreign talent hasn't drawn much attention from political leaders and the media, for understandable reasons. We seem to have the bigger, more immediate problems, from the war on terrorism to the outsourcing of jobs to China and India, to deal with. But just as our obsession with the Soviet Union in the last years of the Cold War caused us to miss the emerging economic challenge of Japan, our eyes may not be on the biggest threat to our economic well-being. Less forgivably, we're so used to thinking that the world's leading creative minds, like the world's best basketball and baseball players, always want to come to the States, while our people go overseas only if they are second rate or washed up, that it's hard to imagine it could ever be otherwise. And it's still true that because of our country's size, its dynamism, its many great universities, and its large government research budgets, we're the Yankees of science.

But, like the Yankees, we've been losing some of our best players—worse, we're not cultivating enough of our young minor leaguers to take over in coming seasons. Even great teams can go into slumps. And, as Michael Lewis showed us in *Moneyball,* even low-budget, low-profile teams like the Oakland A's can become world champions when they strategically recruit just the right mix of talent. In today's global economy, that's exactly what's happening.

# 5

# The New Competitors

*It is not the strongest of the species that survive, nor the most intelligent, but the one most responsive to change.* —CHARLES DARWIN

Most of the talks I've given in the last few years have been in the United States, and the great majority have been addresses to economic and civic groups in small- and medium-size towns. So it was with great relish that I accepted an invitation to speak at the International Fashion Festival in Melbourne, Australia. It would be my first visit to a country I had always wanted to see. And what a time to go. Melbourne was the kind of place that exemplified many of my creative economy arguments, bringing together leading fashion designers, business leaders, and top government officials

When my speech ended, an audience member informed me that there were some three hundred students from the fashion and design program at the local college who had been unable to get into the main ballroom and had watched my speech remotely on a large screen in a room just down the hall. Being a college professor with a keen interest in student feedback, I found my way down the hall and went onstage to show my gratitude to the still-assembled group. After making a couple of remarks about the importance of fashion and design, I asked if there were any questions.

Almost immediately, a young woman in the back of the room shot up her hand and jumped from her seat. She was probably nineteen or twenty years old, roughly five-two with dark hair, dressed in the streetwise manner that bespeaks an aspiring fashion designer. She was of Asian descent, though I couldn't place her country of origin. She spoke North American English, without any trace of an Australian accent.

"Professor Florida," she said, "I'm the child of immigrants who moved to Canada. I'm a Canadian. I live in a country where we welcome people from all countries and all societies. We accept immigrants. We welcome gay people, and we allow them to get married, while your country wants to ban their ability to do that. In Canada, we consider our society a mosaic, which allows you to come from anywhere in the world and be a part of our society." She looked me directly in the eye and said, "How does it feel, Professor Florida, to live next door to a free, open, and democratic country?"

Needless to say, the bubble I'd been floating on was burst. I was flabbergasted by her comment—though, when I thought about it, less as a result of her critique of American society and more by her pride in being Canadian. Here was a young, well-educated woman, standing up in a foreign setting, surrounded by Australian peers, outwardly boasting of her parents' adopted country. How many teenage Americans or Europeans today, or for that matter how many young people over the past twenty or thirty years, could I imagine doing what she just did, announcing such open national pride in a foreign land? However many would consider such a display, the number could only be decreasing on the heels of the age of empire. At the same time, around the world, the creative class is growing. Its awareness of what makes for an open, welcoming, and economically successful nation is growing, too. And not just among the fashionistas of Melbourne.

## Tracking the Global Creative Class

Over the past several years, I've worked with Irene Tinagli to define
and track the world's creative class. While it's impossible to meticu-
lously map the creative class in every nook and cranny of the globe,
Tinagli and I have used detailed statistics from the International
Labour Organisation (ILO), an international organization that tracks
the worldwide workforce, to estimate the creative class in forty-five of
the world's most advanced nations, including the United States. The
ILO collects the most detailed available data on occupations, breaking
the workforce down into job categories like scientists and engineers,
artists, musicians, architects, engineers, managers, professionals, and so
forth. While the ILO categories differ somewhat from the U.S-based
statistics my team and I used in *The Rise of the Creative Class,* they are
the best available measures of the extent and growth of creative occupations worldwide.

It's worth noting, though, that because of variations in the way different nations treat the category of "technicians," we quantify the creative class in two ways. The broad definition includes scientists,
engineers, artists, cultural creatives, managers, professionals, and technicians; the narrow definition excludes technicians. For the most part,
I will use the narrow definition in my discussion of the global creative
class because of significant discrepancies in the way countries classify
their technicians. In Germany, for example, the creative class accounts
for just slightly more than 20 percent of the workforce without technicians, but more than 40 percent with them.

The creative class numbers between 100 and 150 million workers
in the thirty-nine nations for which comparable data are obtained.
The United States has the greatest absolute number of those creative
class workers, between 30 and 35 million. It also accounts for the
greatest share of creative class workers—between 20 and 30 percent
of the world's total—again, depending on whether or not technicians
are included. But the creative class already accounts for a greater percentage of the workforce in several other well-established and
up-and-coming nations. The United States ranks eleventh globally on

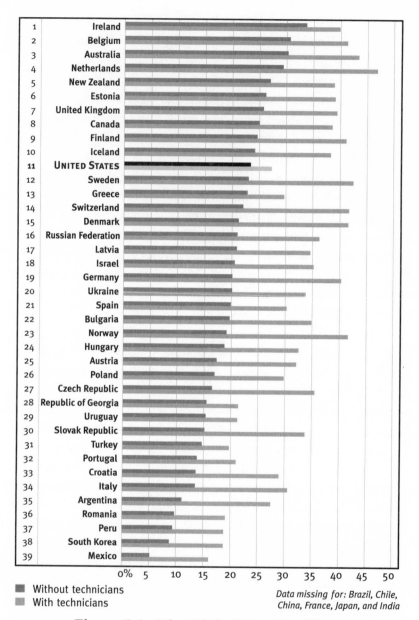

**Figure 5.1: The Global Creative Class**

The creative class makes up a sizable percentage of the workforce in countries across the globe. The United States ranks eleventh worldwide in the percentage of its workforce employed in creative sector jobs.

Based on International Labour Organisation statistics—see Appendix A.

the narrow definition and thirty-first of thirty-nine countries on the broad definition of the creative class. Even taking into account differences in how occupations are classified across countries, this is troubling.

The creative class, according the narrow definition, accounts for more than 30 percent of the workforce in three countries: Ireland (34 percent), Belgium (30 percent), and Australia (30 percent), and for more between 25 percent and 30 percent in five others: the Netherlands (29.5 percent), New Zealand (27 percent), Estonia (26 percent), the United Kingdom (26 percent), and the United States. When technicians are factored into the equation, the creative class accounts for more than 40 percent of the workforce in nine countries: the Netherlands (47 percent); Australia (43 percent); Sweden, Switzerland, Denmark, Norway (all 42 percent); Belgium, Finland (both 41 percent); and Germany (40 percent). It accounts for between 25 percent and 40 percent of the workforce of another twenty-five nations.

Economic transformation—in this case, the shift from the industrial to the creative economy—is a dynamic process, and can therefore happen surprisingly quickly. Like the earlier shift from a farm-based to a factory-driven economy, it can just as quickly bring new competitors to the fore. There is no preordained reason why the established powers should or will emerge on top. Ireland is perhaps the best example of an upstart nation leaping first off the starting block: It has seen the highest rate of creative class employment growth by far, averaging 7.6 percent between 1995 and 2002. Of the advanced industrial nations, only Sweden posted an annual growth rate of more than 2.5 percent. The United States has actually had a negative growth rate over this period.

## America's Technological Edge

Leading students of economic growth from Karl Marx and Joseph Schumpeter to Robert Solow and Paul Romer have long noted the role of technology as the motor force of economic growth. If anything, technology is even more important today. Nations with strong innovation capacity and strong high-tech industrial sectors enjoy a considerable advantage in generating new commercial products, new wealth, and new jobs while sustaining their growth.

The United States remains the world technology leader on our Global Technology Index, which employs two conventional measures

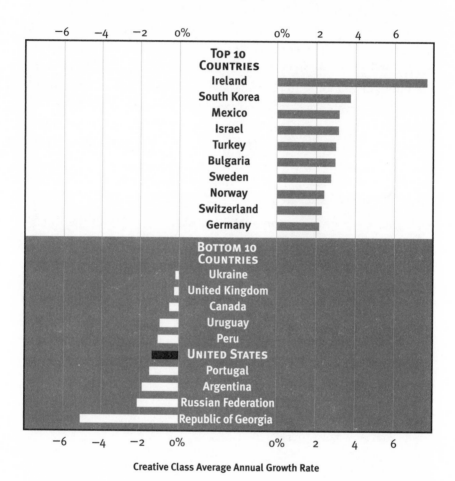

Creative Class Average Annual Growth Rate

**Figure 5.2: Growth of the Creative Class Worldwide**

Since 1995, the percentage of the U.S. workforce employed in the creative class has declined as other countries have increased their percentages.
Note: Measurements for all countries are from 1995 or the earliest year for which data is available.
Based on International Labour Organisation statistics—see Appendix A.

of technological competitiveness—an R&D Index (based on research-and-development expenditures as a percentage of gross domestic product) and an Innovation Index (the number of patent applications per million population). The United States is followed very closely by Sweden. Japan, Ireland, Finland, and Switzerland also show considerable strength in technology.

India and China do reasonably well in terms of technology, ranking twenty-third and twenty-eight respectively—putting them right on

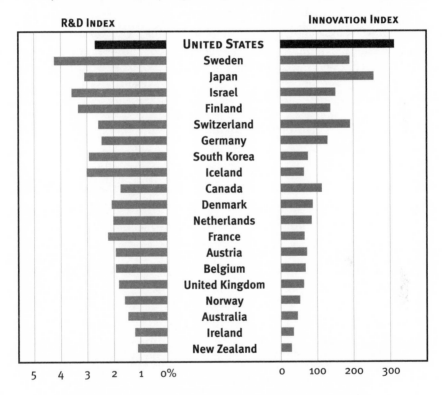

### Figure 5.3: The Global Technology Index

The United States ranks first overall on the Global Technology Index. To the left, the R&D Index shows the percentage of each country's gross domestic product that is invested in research and development. To the right, the Innovation Index shows the number of patent applications per million people.

Based on data from the World Bank, 1999–2000, and the U.S. Patent and Trademark Office, 2001—see Appendix A.

the doorstep of seemingly more advanced nations like Italy (twenty-first). Both spend in excess of 1 percent of their growing GDP—quite considerable for a developing nation and even more significant given the size and growth of their national output. Peter Drucker says of the former: "India is becoming a powerhouse very fast. The medical school in New Delhi is now perhaps the best in the world. And the technical graduates of the Institute of Technology in Bangalore are as good as any in the world." Both India and China are beginning to leverage their large university populations into technology-based development. China ranked first, the United States second, and India third in the 2004 *Economist* magazine survey of the leading countries for global R&D investment. When 104 company executives were asked by *The Economist* where they would spend the most on R&D over the next three years, China ranked first with 39 percent and India third with 28 percent of respondents, just slightly behind the United States' 29 percent.

But even the U.S. position in technology may be vulnerable. As I've said before, while the conventional wisdom among the American populace is that the U.S. is the world's single superpower and holds unassailable leads in technology, R&D, innovation, scientific publications, and patents, the reality is more complicated. For most of the post-WWII period, the U.S. was in fact unrivaled in its scientific and technological prowess. In the last five to ten years, this once-predominant position has begun to decay, and in some places rapidly. In 1999, the U.S. Council on Competitiveness warned that the U.S. could not rest on its laurels, since "other nations are accelerating their own efforts" as America's "innovation infrastructure" begins to show signs of decay. Since 1999, things have only gotten worse.

In 1990, I published *The Breakthrough Illusion* with Martin Kenney, in which we argued, like many other experts at the time, that U.S. competitiveness was under fire because while we continued to make the breakthroughs, other countries were eroding our ability to follow through and produce the kinds of products the world's consumer wants to buy.[1] Today, it seems it is our breakthrough capability that's under fire. The U.S. has seen its once-unquestioned lead erode in technology after technology, from automobiles and semiconductors to high-tech electronics and flat-panel displays. The only high-tech areas where the U.S. continues to dominate are software and biotechnology—and even there this country is highly dependent on foreign talent.

A key source of U.S. advantage on our Technology Index comes from its huge lead in patents. But I fear this may be an artifact of the data. The patent figures are based on patents filed in the United States. This lead disappears when data from the other patent offices (such as the European Patent Office or World Patent Office) are used. And the U.S. has also recorded very low rates of growth in patented innovations. According to my research with Tinagli, the United States ranks fourteenth out of fifteen in growth rate for patented innovations compared to European nations. Six nations outperform the United States on R&D effort as a percent of GDP: Sweden (4.3 percent), Israel (3.6 percent), Finland (3.4 percent), Japan (3.1 percent), Iceland (3.0 percent), and Korea (2.9 percent).

Furthermore, foreign-owned companies and foreign-born inventors account today for nearly half (47.2 percent) of all patents granted in the United States. In May 2004, the *New York Times* summed up the situation this way: "One area of international competition involves patents. Americans still win large numbers of them, but the percentage is falling as foreigners, especially Asians, have become more active and in some fields have seized the innovation lead. The United States' share of its own industrial patents has fallen steadily over the decades." In 2001, of the ten top patenting companies in the United States, only one was American, IBM.[2]

Not all patents are created equal. Some are far more important than others, and most never really amount to anything. But some patents are building blocks for many subsequent inventions and commercial products. One way to gauge the significance of patents is to look at how frequently they are cited by other patents. Foreign inventors have an increasing share of important patents, measured by the extent to which they are cited in other patents According to a study by CHI Research, a consulting firm that tracks global patenting, researchers in Japan, Taiwan, and South Korea account for more than a quarter of all United States industrial patents, and their growth rates have been rapid. "It's not just lots of patents," the *Times* quoted CHI's president, Francis Narin, as saying. "It's lots of good patents that have a high impact."

It's also worth noting that different countries excel at different kinds of patents. According to the U.S. Patent and Trademark Office, U.S. companies led in high-tech fields such as computers, software, and multicellular organisms, but also in areas such as "wells" and

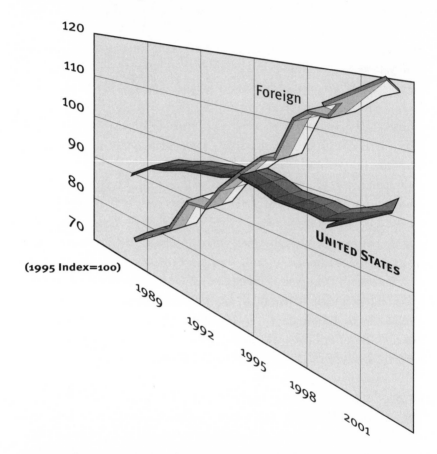

**Figure 5.4: Foreign Scientific Publications Accelerate**

From 1989 to 2001, the number of articles published in leading scientific journals by foreign authors increased much faster than the number published by U.S. authors.

National Science Board, *Science and Engineering Indicators, 2004,* Washington, D.C.: U.S. Government Printing Office, 2003.

"earth-penetrating apparatus." Japanese patents were highly concentrated in high-tech electronic fields like photography, photocopying, liquid-crystal cells, television-signal processing, optical systems, and computing technology, while German patents were concentrated in automotive technologies, advanced materials, and manufacturing technologies. Taiwanese and South Korean companies earned patents in communication and computer technology.

Publications are another widely used indicator of scientific creativity. And here, too, the U.S. lead has eroded considerably. In 1988, the U.S. accounted for roughly 40 percent (38.1 percent) of all scientific and engineering publications worldwide—undisputed first place. U.S. scientists produced 178,000 scientific papers compared to 34,000 for Japan, and roughly 7,000 for China, South Korea, Singapore, and Taiwan. However, by the mid-1990s, the European Union nations had surpassed the United States as the largest producers of scientific literature. In 2001, Western Europe researchers generated 229,000 articles compared to 201,000 for the U.S., 57,400 in Japan, and 42,700 in the rest of Asia. In physics, the U.S. lead fell from 61 percent of all publications in 1983 to 29 percent in 2003, according to *Physical Review,* a series of top physics journals.

The Nobel Prize is the icon of scientific excellence. There was a time when U.S. scientists took home most of them. But as the *New York Times* reported, "The American share, after peaking from the 1960s through the 1990s, has fallen in the to about half, 51%. The rest went to Britain, Japan, Russia, Germany, Sweden, Switzerland and New Zealand." Again, not the end of the world. But perhaps the beginnings of a new creative world order.

## Global Talent Trends

As we've seen, it's well established by now that economic growth is spurred by human capital in some form or another. Students of science, technology, and innovation add that innovation and growth depend crucially on levels of scientific and technical talent. To capture these effects, our Global Talent Index includes the conventional measures of human capital (percentage of the population age twenty-five to sixty-four with a bachelor's or professional degree) and scientific talent (the number of research scientists and engineers per million people) alongside our own creative class rankings.

The United States ranks ninth on the Global Talent Index behind

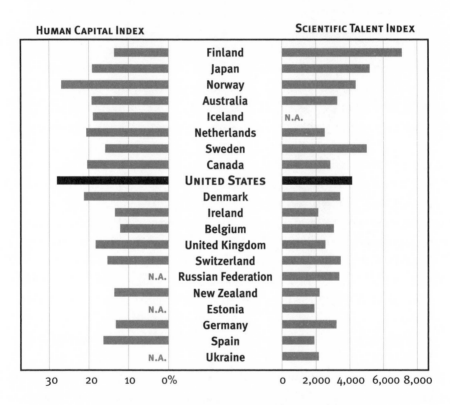

**Figure 5.5: The Global Talent Index**

The United States ranks ninth overall on the Global Talent Index. To the left, the Human Capital Index shows the percentage of a country's population between the ages of 25 and 64 that holds a bachelor's or professional degree. To the right, the Scientific Talent Index shows the number of research scientists and engineers per million people.

Based on data from the International Labour Organisation, the Organization for Economic Cooperation and Development, and UNESCO—see Appendix A.

Finland, Japan, Norway, Australia, Iceland, the Netherlands, Sweden, and Canada. A host of established powers, including the United Kingdom (thirteenth), Germany (eighteenth), France (twenty-second), and Italy (thirty-third), rank further down the list. The United States leads in the percentage of its population with a bachelor's degree or above, but Finland, Japan, Sweden, and Norway all have greater concentrations of scientific talent.

While the Western press is obsessed with the threat posed by China and India, our rankings suggest that such concerns may be overblown, certainly in the short run. China and India rank last and second to last, respectively, on our list, behind Brazil, Romania, Peru, Mexico, Chile, and many others. Both countries, of course, benefit from their large size and will continue to have cost advantages and increasingly well-educated populations to draw from. By themselves, though, it's unlikely that either will pose a short-run threat to the United States or other leading talent-magnet nations. It's only when we consider them in tandem with our other competitors—the Nordic and Scandinavian countries, Australia, and Canada, and other up-and-comers such as Ireland, New Zealand, and Israel—that the real dimensions of the global competition for talent can be seen.

## The Global Competition for Talent Heats Up

As we saw at the beginning of Chapter 4, the fundamental factors that fueled the movement of people between U.S. regions—that allowed Austin to overtake Pittsburgh or Seattle to overtake Cincinnati—operate now on a truly global scale. Talented people are a global factor of production, able to choose among economically vibrant and attractive regions the world over. My interviews, discussions, and focus groups with creative class people in not just the United States, but in Canada, Europe, and Asia, too, convince me that what they have in common more than anything else is the view that the labor market for their skills and services operates on a global scale. They search for work locations across borders, and will go to places that offer abundant economic opportunity, exciting cultural and social environments, world-class amenities, and the freedom to be themselves and realize their dreams. The competition for global talent now stretches across every field and continues to heat up.

As a result, a growing number of countries are increasing their efforts not just to retain their own talent, but to in-source economic advantage from around the globe. Immigrants already make up roughly a quarter of the high-skilled workforce in Australia and roughly 20 percent in Canada—considerably greater numbers than the United States.[3] The United Kingdom, Australia, and New Zealand all boast initiatives to attract foreign talent. Canada has initiated an extensive program of Research Chairs, in part to attract top foreign academic talent and pay them at world-market rates. The province of Quebec offers income-tax holidays to attract foreign academics in key high-tech fields. Germany launched a "green-card" effort in 2002 to attract skilled IT workers, mainly from Eastern Europe, and is aggressively courting foreign students with fellowships and grants to its elite universities. Ireland has extended its success in bringing back expatriates to go after foreign IT workers from Canada, India, South Africa, and Eastern Europe. Singapore is trying to plug its own IT-worker shortage by attracting talent from China and Malaysia.

China and India, meanwhile, have also made aggressive moves to retain homegrown talent and bring ex-pats back home.[4] Consider the case of Raymond Yang, a Chinese native who worked in the United States for twenty years. In 2003, Yang went back and became the CEO of a Shanghai-based cell-phone start-up company. He said of China: "There are a lot of opportunities for people to fulfill their dreams here. China will get stronger and stronger." He's not the only one newly invigorated by the opportunities in his home country; with each succeeding generation, the sense of possibility only grows. China is also becoming an increasingly attractive option for students from Asian countries, especially in the wake of growing U.S. restrictions. In 2003, 2,563 Indonesian students received visas to study in China, a 50 percent increase. This was nearly double the number of students who came to study in the United States, which saw the number of Indonesian students fall from 6,520 in 2000 to 1,333 in 2003.[5]

## Students: Canaries in the Talent Mine

Students are the canaries of the global competition for talent, and the countries that succeed in attracting them gain advantages on multiple fronts. In 2001, more than 1.5 million students from some seventy-five countries worldwide were attending universities in countries outside their homelands, according to a detailed study by the Institute for International Education.[6] While the United States accounts for roughly 36 percent, of this total, the next five leading nations for international students (the United Kingdom, Germany, France, Australia, and Japan) already take in about 40 percent of students studying abroad worldwide.

But these absolute numbers mask the tremendous effort being made by a host of countries to attract foreign students. Even though the United States takes in the largest absolute number of them, foreign students make up a much larger percentage of the student pool in eleven other countries. Australia already attracts more than four times as many foreign students as a share of its students—17 percent, versus 4 percent for the United States. Foreign students account for 10 percent of all students in the United Kingdom, 7 percent in Sweden, and 6 percent in New Zealand.

A host of countries around the world are stepping up their efforts to recruit international students. Australia and Canada are more actively courting foreign students, emphasizing lower tuitions and less expensive living costs at world-class universities in world-class cities. Australia registered a 16.5 percent increase in foreign college students, attracting 167,000 international students for the 2003 academic year, compared to a 0.6 percent increase for the United States. With a 20 percent increase in Chinese students, Australia now attracts half as many Chinese students (32,000) as the United States (64,700). England and New Zealand stress that their programs are more flexible, involve less classroom work, and take less time to complete. Korea has instituted programs to ease entry and job regulations for foreign students, to underwrite new dormitories for international students, and to encourage more English-language courses.

German universities now run free international degree programs taught in English to attract students from Britain, America, and around the world. "Our idea is to get the best people to the universities," said Nina Lemmens, the London-based director of the German Academic Exchange service, or DAAD. "We hope that students from today will be our partners tomorrow," she added. "If they go back [to their home countries] and go into business, Germany will be the first port of call for their careers."[7] China and India are pumping money into their educational institutions, encouraging more of their own to stay at home for graduate degrees and to consider local employment when their education is done.

Students I've met at colleges and universities across the U.S. and the world are actively pursuing the free tuition and generous stipends provided by prestigious universities in Canada, Europe, and Australia.

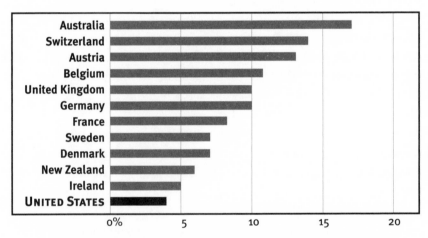

**Foreign Students as a Percentage of Total Student Population**

**Figure 5.6: The Global Competition for Students**

Countries around the world are increasing their efforts to attract foreign students. Australia and Switzerland lead the global competition in the number of foreign students as a percentage of the total student population. The United States ranks twelfth worldwide.

Todd M. Davis, *Atlas of Student Mobility,* Washington, D.C.: Institute of International Education, 2003.

Lisa Craig, director of the office of international education at Carnegie Mellon, the university with the highest percentage of foreign students in the U.S., put it this way: "Students know they can go to Australia. And if there are enough burdens and barriers, guess what—people are doing just that." Thomas Gouttierre, dean of international studies at the University of Nebraska–Omaha, added: "The word is out: It's easier and less demeaning to apply in Canada and the U.K." Or as one of the students at the small Midwestern college told me: "I keep getting recruited by foreign graduate schools—in Spain, in Germany, and other places in Europe. They're saying that if I apply and get accepted, they'll give me a huge scholarship."

The stakes are growing. In 2000, UNESCO estimated 1.7 million students worldwide were educated abroad; by 2025, that figure will rise to more than 8 million. As one report starkly put it: "An increasing number of internationally mobile students at the highest levels—those seeking advanced study and research in the sciences, medicine, technology, and other fields—are looking for academic opportunities outside the United States."[8] A leading higher-education expert summarized the current predicament this way: "There's no question that other countries are making proactive efforts to recruit foreign students. The United States, on the other hand, is doing the opposite. Not only don't we have an active policy of recruiting foreign students, we're putting visa obstacles in the way."[9] Whatever country manages to attract these highly mobile students will have a huge long-run advantage in the burgeoning global competition for talent that is just beginning to be felt.

## The Tolerance Factor

Tolerance, the third T of economic development, is critical to a region's or nation's ability to attract and mobilize creative talent. Openness to people—or what I like to refer to as low barriers to entry for people—enables places to compete more effectively for talent from other countries and also to more effectively mobilize and harness its own talent across race, ethnicity, gender, age, sexual orientation, and class position. Our measure of tolerance, the Global Tolerance Index, is based the comprehensive research by Ronald Inglehart of the University of Michigan.[10] Inglehart's landmark World Values Survey covers the period 1995–1998 and is based on data for sixty-five countries. The survey sample is quite large, with an average of 1,400 respondents per country.

The Values Index measures to what degree a country reflects "traditional" or religious as opposed "modern" or secular values. It is based on a series of questions covering attitudes toward God, religion, nationalism, authority, family, women's rights, divorce, and abortion. The Self-Expression Index captures the degree to which a nation values individual rights and self-expression. It is based on questions covering attitudes toward self-expression, quality of life, democracy, science and technology, leisure, the environment, trust, protest politics, immigrants, and gays. These measures differ considerably from the indexes for U.S. regions used in *The Rise of the Creative Class,* which focus on the actual location of various groups (immigrants, gays, and so on) rather than on the expressed values of the population. Unfortunately, the kinds of comparable data required to develop such measures do not exist. Still, the findings are informative and intriguing.

Tolerance lies at the root of America's growing competitive challenge. While some may find this surprising, the data could not be clearer. The United States ranks twentieth of forty-five nations on the Global Tolerance Index, alongside countries like Italy, Korea, Israel, Spain, and Croatia. While the United States scores very high in terms of commitment to individuals and self-expression, it scores much lower than many other advanced nations on the Values Index. The United States, as Inglehart has said, is the "outlier" among the other economically advanced nations, being much more "traditional" than most.

Americans are exceptionally religious: 92 percent believe in God, 85 percent believe that the Bible is God's word, 74 percent believe in life after death. And the United States is one of the least religiously diverse countries by global world standards. With some 88 percent of Americans declaring themselves as Christian, Daniel Lazare has pointed out, "The United States is more Christian than Israel is Jewish, Egypt is Muslim, or India is Hindu."

A December 2002 study by the Pew Research Center for People and the Press explored religious attitudes across forty-four nations worldwide. Like Inglehart and others, the Pew researchers were struck by the overwhelming role of religion in American life, finding it "much more important to Americans than to people living in other wealthy nations." Nearly six in ten people in the U.S. say religion plays *a very* important role in their lives. That's roughly twice the percentage of self-avowed religious people in Canada, and an even higher proportion compared to Japan and Western Europe. "Ameri-

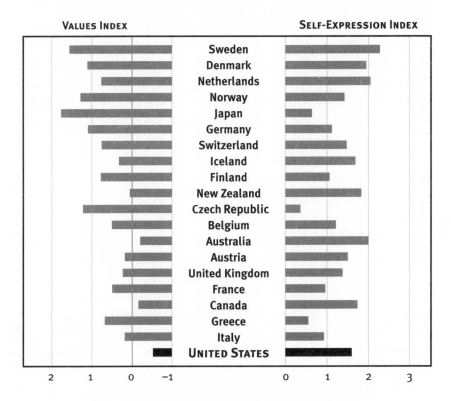

**Figure 5.7: The Global Tolerance Index**

The United States ranks twentieth overall on the Global Tolerance Index. To the left, the Values Index shows the extent to which secularism defines a country's culture. To the right, the Self-Expression Index shows how individualistic a country is.

Ronald Inglehart, *World Values Survey,* 2001.

cans' views," the researchers concluded, "are closer to people in developing nations than to the publics of developed nations."

Religion in America is not fundamentally intolerant. On the contrary, interdenominational, socially conscious, and open-minded organized religion has driven much of the progressive social change of the twentieth century in the United States. It's hard to argue that the world is not better off, more diverse, and more accepting as a result of the efforts of Martin Luther King Jr., for instance. More and more, though, our own people and foreigners alike have come to associate American religion, rightly or wrongly, with its more fundamentalist strains. Groups such as Faithful America have sought to reclaim the tolerant, forward-looking ground in American religion. But the fact remains, for better and for worse: We are an exceptionally traditionally religious people.

While it may be true that the United States has a higher level of immigrants than the European nations, the attitudes of Americans on a wide variety of issues from religion and nationalism to divorce, women's rights, immigrants, and gays are far more conservative or traditional than those of the European nations, especially the Scandinavian and Nordic countries, as well as Canada, for that matter. Inglehart and one of his collaborators have this to say on the subject:

> The United States is not a prototype of cultural modernization for other societies to follow, as some modernization writers of the postwar era naively assumed. In fact, the United States . . . [has] a much more traditional value system than any other advanced industrial society. On the traditional/secular dimension, the United States ranks far below other rich societies, with levels of religious and national pride found in developing societies. . . . The United States does rank among the most advanced societies along the survival/self-expression dimension, but even here, it does not lead the world, as the Swedes and the Danes seem closer to the cutting edge of cultural change than do the Americans.[11]

The "Americanization" of the globe, they add, may be a grossly inaccurate way to paint the situation. Industrializing societies are not, in general, becoming more like the United States. "In fact, the United States seems to be a deviant case," they argue; "its people hold much more traditional values and beliefs than those in any other equally prosperous society."

The tolerance rankings for two other nations, Japan and Germany, also come as some surprise. Here it is important to remember that Inglehart's measures rate countries on how they value "self-expression" and "secular values"—not on their actual openness to immigrants or other groups. Japan, it goes without saying, has historically been a closed country. Germany, too, has a long legacy of intolerance, including continuing battles over the status of foreign "guest workers." According to a 2004 survey, a majority of citizens in both countries continue to see immigrants as a "bad influence" on their societies. The survey, which covered nine countries including the United States, found troubling views of immigrants around the world.[12] The United Kingdom ranked alongside Germany with the most negative views of immigrants and immigration. Sixty percent of British residents and 57 percent of Germans said immigrants had a negative influence on their country. Indeed, the European nations had universally negative views; a majority of respondents in France, Italy, and Spain said immigrants impacted society negatively. Sweden is the unquestioned leader on the Global Tolerance Index, followed by Denmark, the Netherlands, and Norway. A number of other nations have tolerance scores that suggest they have the values and attitudes to effectively compete for talent: Switzerland, Iceland, Finland, New Zealand, Belgium, and Australia.

But the real leader in terms of tolerance and diversity may well be our northern neighbor, Canada. Only the Canadians, of the nine nations surveyed, had a generally positive view of immigrants. The U.S. was more like Europe in its views on immigration: More than half of U.S. respondents saw immigrants as a bad influence. Maybe it's time we stop congratulating ourselves. Immigrants already make up a greater percentage of the population in Canada than in this country. And, of late, Canada has been actively been courting foreign students and scholars, while we have become more restrictive.

## The Global Creativity Index

For a nation or a region to effectively compete, all three Ts have to work together. Being successful on any one T is a necessary but in itself insufficient condition for economic success. Some U.S. regions like Pittsburgh or Cleveland have great universities and do well on technology, but they export people and fail to attract large numbers of immigrants or gay people. Other regions like Miami have lots of immigrants and are open to all sorts of lifestyles but lack the technology base and vibrant job market to attract people. The regions that are the most successful—places like San Francisco, Boston, and Seattle—do all three Ts well: They invest in technology, are talent magnets, and are open to new people and new ideas.

We developed a new composite measure, the Global Creativity Index (GCI), to provide a full assessment of creative competitiveness based on the Ts. The GCI is a composite measure that combines the scores on the Talent, Technology, and Tolerance indices. The GCI compares well to other leading competitiveness indicators, correlating powerfully with Michael Porter's Innovation Index, *Foreign Policy*'s Globalization Index, the United Nations Human Development Index, and other similar measures. But we believe it to be a considerable improvement over them. This is because the conventional measures emphasize technology, and in some cases include some indicators of talent. None includes any measures of tolerance, an important source of competitive advantage. The GCI factors in all three Ts.

The United States ranks fourth on the Global Creativity Index, behind Sweden, Japan, and Finland. The Scandinavian and Northern European countries including Denmark, the Netherlands, Belgium, Norway, and Germany, as well as Canada, Australia, and the United Kingdom, also do well. Several smaller countries—Iceland, Israel, New Zealand, Ireland—also make the global top twenty. Furthermore, none of these nations or regions has to overtake the United States for the damage to be felt. Over the past century, we have dominated the global market for talent. We attracted the best and brightest from everywhere. Imagine what will happen if just several countries, say Canada, Australia, New Zealand, and a number of European Union nations, increase their ability to compete for this critical resource, each taking away say 5 or 10 percent: The numbers add up fast. Rather than a single deathblow, the more likely scenario is to be seriously hobbled by a thousand cuts.

For these reasons, the economic leaders of the future will not, I believe, be emerging giants like India or China, which rank far down the list, in forty-first and thirty-sixth place, even as they are becoming global centers for cost-effective manufacturing and the delivery of basic business processes. Instead they will be a host of smaller countries, such as Finland, Sweden, Denmark, the Netherlands, Ireland, Canada, Australia, and New Zealand, that have built dynamic creative climates, investing in talent, leveraging technology, and increasing their effort and ability to attract creative talent from around the world.

My point with all of this is not that the United States is going to hell in a handbasket, nor that other advanced industrial nations have everything figured out. Between 1992 and 2000, the growth in U.S. GDP (36 percent in real terms) far and away outstripped that of its European competitors (19 percent) and was better than all but a handful of emerging Asian nations. And, according to a report by the Center for European Reform, five years after committing themselves to becoming "the world's most competitive and dynamic knowledge economy by 2010" via the Lisbon Agenda, the vast majority of European nations still lag far behind their own development goals. Denmark and Finland are the only notable exceptions. Despite doing a better job preaching the creative economy sermon, European nations have suffered problems similar to their American counterparts in actually adjusting to new economic realities. Budget deficits, inflexible labor markets, a rapidly aging population, bloated agricultural subsidies, and ongoing EU constitutional strife have all taken their toll on Europe's entrance into the creative age.

Even more damaging is the growing opposition in many quarters to European openness and immigration. While Inglehart rates many Northern European countries high on his value rankings, anti-immigration sentiment has grown ever more steadily as the creative

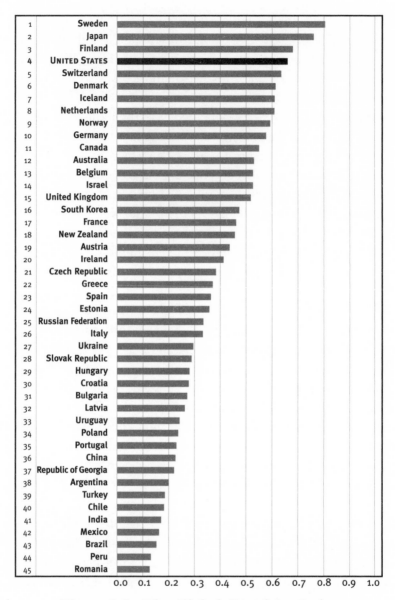

| | | |
|---|---|---|
| 1 | Sweden | |
| 2 | Japan | |
| 3 | Finland | |
| 4 | **UNITED STATES** | |
| 5 | Switzerland | |
| 6 | Denmark | |
| 7 | Iceland | |
| 8 | Netherlands | |
| 9 | Norway | |
| 10 | Germany | |
| 11 | Canada | |
| 12 | Australia | |
| 13 | Belgium | |
| 14 | Israel | |
| 15 | United Kingdom | |
| 16 | South Korea | |
| 17 | France | |
| 18 | New Zealand | |
| 19 | Austria | |
| 20 | Ireland | |
| 21 | Czech Republic | |
| 22 | Greece | |
| 23 | Spain | |
| 24 | Estonia | |
| 25 | Russian Federation | |
| 26 | Italy | |
| 27 | Ukraine | |
| 28 | Slovak Republic | |
| 29 | Hungary | |
| 30 | Croatia | |
| 31 | Bulgaria | |
| 32 | Latvia | |
| 33 | Uruguay | |
| 34 | Poland | |
| 35 | Portugal | |
| 36 | China | |
| 37 | Republic of Georgia | |
| 38 | Argentina | |
| 39 | Turkey | |
| 40 | Chile | |
| 41 | India | |
| 42 | Mexico | |
| 43 | Brazil | |
| 44 | Peru | |
| 45 | Romania | |

0.0  0.1  0.2  0.3  0.4  0.5  0.6  0.7  0.8  0.9  1.0

## Figure 5.8: The Global Creativity Index

The Global Creativity Index is a composite measure of national competitiveness based on the 3 Ts of economic growth: Technology, Talent, and Tolerance. Sweden tops the list, followed by Japan and Finland. The United States ranks fourth overall on the GCI. (See Appendix A for more details.) Compiled by Irene Tinagli based on various sources.

economy advances and puts pressure on existing institutions and class and social structures. While Sweden is rapidly becoming more open, other countries lag badly behind. From France to the Netherlands to Denmark, populist nationalist politics has reasserted itself, and right-wing governments regularly win victories predicated on blatant and vehement xenophobia. Denmark, which does well on many of our measures, has made it harder for couples of native-born Danes married to foreigners to remain in the country. As Tom Bentley of the London-based think tank Demos has written, "many Europeans identify strongly with a quality of life based on both social equality and secular liberalism . . . but economic transition and new global insecurity are forcing a painful reckoning."

For many of Western Europe's traditional powers, Bentley believes, "tolerance and social protection were possible only within the sheltered spaces of the post-war national welfare state and the NATO security umbrella." The economists Alberto Alesina and Edward Glaeser add that more homogeneous populations have for years made Europe's distinctly socialist welfare state more palatable than what its more diverse demographics now seem to allow. As these institutions and geopolitical arrangements have "creaked," Bentley argues, "many have begun to feel exposed."

So it's not as if other countries are immune to the same pressures felt in the U.S. in response to the growth of the creative economy. But neither does the United States continue to have the playing field to itself.

# 6

# Regions on the Rise

*The chief function of the city is to convert power into form, energy into culture, dead matter into the living symbols of art, biological reproduction into social creativity.* —LEWIS MUMFORD

The competition for talent is not just between nations: The real battle is among cities and regions. For the better part of the past century, the United States held an indisputable edge: Its cities were among the most economically vibrant, most open, and most exciting in the world. More importantly, the United States had—and to a great extent still has—the world's most connected, extensive, and productive *system of cities*. With some fifty different 1-million-plus population centers, the U.S. as a system of cities offers varied bundles of economic opportunities and lifestyle offerings—from cosmopolitan global centers of finance, entertainment, and high-technology to quality-of-life communities, industrial centers, and university towns.

Along with our historic openness, this multidimensional system of cities added immensely to our advantage in attracting and retaining talented people. Jane Jacobs once said to me: "What makes the U.S. great as a nation is that it has lots of great cities, and of various sizes. Canada only has three real cities: Toronto, Montreal, and Vancouver." For it to be a true competitor, she added, it would need to create "more real cities." Not only were United States cities each impressive in its own right; their connectivity allowed them to share creativity, innovations, and ideas on truly national scale.

But just as leading American corporations faced the tsunami of global competition during the 1980s and 1990s, our cities are now seeing the landscape of competition shift under the pressure of globalization. As the economy has globalized, the city system—like the industrial system—has shifted from a set of relatively independent national systems to an increasingly integrated and global one. The number of cities with over a million people grew from twelve in 1900, to eighty-three in 1950, to more than four hundred today. Even if we use U.S. regions (which include cities plus their suburbs) as our units of comparison, America accounts for just 12 percent of those megacities.

Today, U.S. cities are increasingly challenged by the two kinds of world population centers I mentioned earlier. The "Global Talent Magnets" (think Toronto, Amsterdam, Sydney, and Stockholm) are competing more aggressively and effectively for talent from all corners of the world. The "Global Austins" (from Dublin to Taipei and Bangalore) are attracting and retaining their homegrown talent, becoming technology players, and fashioning their own specific niches in the global economy.

## Cauldrons of Creativity

Urban centers have always been cauldrons of creativity. Sir Peter Hall's monumental *Cities in Civilization* demonstrates that cities have been the engines of technological innovation and economic growth for the past five millennia, serving as the cradles of human advancement in the arts, medicine, literature, and politics, as well as science, technology, and entrepreneurship.[1] For Hall, cities follow a pattern of dynamic evolution that is similar to that of technology and industry. Like industries, they rise and fall in a "cycle of creativity" that follows the same basic pattern of "creative destruction" long ago noted by Joseph Schumpeter, the great theorist of technology and economic growth. Schumpeter famously argued that innovation and economic growth came in bursts, as entrepreneurs harnessed new technologies to create new industries and remake existing ones.

The actual geographic locus of the world's centers of creativity and innovation varies from one era to the next. Classical Athens, Hall notes, was the "scene of a unique creative explosion." Florence "pulled off the same trick" some two thousand years later and one thousand miles away. Just as Britain forged the Industrial Revolution but then lost its lead to Germany and America, so were Manchester, Birmingham (UK), the Ruhr Valley, and Detroit once the "smart places." But in the 1990s, advantage migrated to Silicon Valley. Now the question becomes, will a series of new global competitors, whoever and wherever they may be, give the birthplace of high-tech a run for its money.[2] But before we get to that, a brief review of the central role played by cities in economic development is in order.

Even when our economy was primarily dominated by industry and trade, cities were the essential driver of innovation and economic growth. As Jane Jacobs noted in *The Economy of Cities,* her classic analysis of how cities grow, places that were able early on to generate surplus exports and create new divisions of labor became the engines that defined urban economic life. While it once made sense to think that the growth of cities, as well as national economies, was the product of their physical advantages (fertile soil, abundant raw materials) and God-given locational advantages along rivers or natural transportation lines, the role of cities in mobilizing human creativity has become increasingly visible as these physical advantages became less important economically.

Writing in 1965, urban economist Wilbur Thompson described how cities function as incubators on innovation: "The metropolis, with its universities, museums, libraries, and research laboratories, becomes one big, spatially integrated 'coffee house,' where bright minds out of diverse cultures clash and strike sparks that ignite the fires of new products and processes." Such creativity is self-perpetuating, as "inventor-innovators tend to bunch in time and space; dynamic persons create an atmosphere that attracts more of the same."[3] Robert Lucas has argued that—rather than raw materials, labor costs, or even technology—it is urbanization, the geographic concentration and clustering of human beings, that is the true source of productivity growth and competitive advantage. This becomes especially true when creativity, knowledge, and ideas are the key factors of production.

Because of their ability to harness creativity and foster innovation, cities have become increasingly important social and economic organizing units over the course of the past century. The share of the world's population living in urban areas increased from just 3 percent in 1800 to 14 percent in 1900. By 1950, it reached 30 percent, before exploding to nearly half of all people across the globe or 2.8 billion people, by 2000. Today, more than three-quarters of the population of the advanced or developed countries live in urban areas.[4]

In contrast to predictions that technology—from the telephone and the automobile to the computer and the Internet—would lead to the death of cities, the creative economy is taking shape less around national boundaries and industrial sectors and more around cities. Economic geographers and business analysts, most notably McKinsey-consultant-turned-management-guru Kenichi Ohmae, have argued that the forces of globalization are eroding the power of the nation-state and increasing the role of regions as the key economic and social organizing units in the world. Place, as I say in *The Rise of the Creative Class,* has replaced the giant corporation of the industrial age as the central economic and social organizing unit of our time. Place is the factor that organically brings together the economic opportunity and talent, the jobs and the people required for creativity, innovation, and growth.

How did all of this come to be? The earliest cities were, of course, centers for trade and commerce. They grew as places where surpluses of agricultural goods could be traded by farmers. This gave rise over time to naturally evolving divisions of labor, greater specialization of work, and ultimately increased productivity. The surplus these processes produced eventually gave rise to additional income, which allowed people to buy more, which in turn enabled the development of more specialized goods. From spices and farm implements to clothing and books, early consumption-related industries took hold of the marketplace. Over time, cities developed as centers of trade not only in agricultural products, but in a wide variety of both locally produced and imported goods.[5]

By the nineteenth century, urban centers evolved from these market-based systems to industrial powerhouses. Places such as Chicago, Manchester, and Germany's Ruhr Valley became the geographic centers of this great transition to factory production. Many had advantages in raw materials and locations along ports or waterways. From humble beginnings with small factories, a number of these cities evolved into full-blown production complexes; they produced nearly everything required to make a product from raw materials to the finished goods.

The best example is Detroit, the world's center for automobile production and home to Ford's River Rouge Plant. Here, everything required to make a car, from steelmaking and raw-material processing through assembly, final trim, paint, and finish, was integrated in one physical location. While many of these cities came to specialize in one industry or another—Detroit in automobiles or Pittsburgh in steel—almost all of them were distinguished by what economists refer to as tight backward and forward linkages. All the industries, processes, and employees needed to take a product all the way from raw material to ready-to-ship could be found in one tightly knit place—a community of companies, if you will. So, for example, the automotive manufacturer was located "right down the road," relatively speaking, from the steel plant providing the raw materials to make its frames and the glass and rubber manufacturers that would provide its windshields and tires.

And so the Industrial Revolution gave rise to large-scale urban centers as we know them. They massed people, drew immigrants, and organized work in gargantuan factory complexes and downtown office centers. Gradually, these cities became stretched out, sites not only of this mass production, but also for its corollary mass consumption. Suburbanization, particularly in the United States, fueled the engine of Fordist industries, increasing home ownership and the demand for cars, appliances, and other industrial products.[6]

By the 1970s and 1980s, in what some scholars call the "second industrial divide," the hierarchy of industrial cities began to fall apart.[7] Many cities fell victim to lagging investment in technology, oversaturation of consumer markets, and rigid or sclerotic social systems. Gradually, the division of labor that had once been organized within regions began to be stretched across them as more and more elements of a once-integrated production process or value chain were lifted out of established regions and shifted to other parts of the world that offered more malleable environments and lower costs.[8] Instead of being concentrated in integrated regional production systems, production itself became decentralized and global.

As more and more manufacturing shifted inexorably from the older industrial centers to newly emerging production centers in Latin America and Asia, it became obvious that not just U.S. industries, but U.S. cities and the American city system itself, faced serious international competition. Specialization by function and by region occurred, as global locations increasingly came to focus on particular pieces of the production process, rather than an entire industry. Singapore concentrated on disk drives, Taiwan on semiconductors, Tijuana and Guadalajara on electronics assembly, Bangalore on business-process software, and so on down the line.[9] The core characteristics of this new global system of cities is that while cities are specialized by industry, task, or function, the production system or value chain is integrated globally across geography.

At roughly the same time, the economy began to evolve from brawn- to brains-based, giving rise to a new set of knowledge-based regions. These regional centers of innovation were no longer based on natural endowments or giant factory complexes, but on powerful networks linking university research and technology to venture capitalists and entrepreneurs. These propulsive social structures for innovation and new business formation were at the cutting edge of economic development.[10] But more and more of the innovative impulse of capitalism came to be separated, at least geographically, from the actual production of goods and services.

This geographic division of innovation and production was not limited to high-tech industries. It also came to distinguish a growing number of traditional industries. Older regions, like the garment-making areas of Italy, for example, developed niches in design and high value-added production. As Michael Piore, Charles Sabel, and others have shown, regions established competitive advantage by staying at the cutting edge of design, implementing new technology, and organizing themselves into dense but flexible networks of innovators, producers, and consumers. In these ways, they could rapidly change their product mix in tune with—and in time for—consumer demand.[11] Regions throughout the world tried to emulate these processes, reducing their dependence on large companies and attempting to transform themselves into regional innovation centers or technopoles by building high-tech parks, forging linkages between universities and industry, setting up publicly supported venture funds, and encouraging technology transfer.[12] Although only a few of these efforts were actually successful, a consensus gradually emerged that it was networks of knowledge and people—the creative connections, so to speak—that were the motor force of regional economic growth.

## Competing for Niches

The collision of rapid globalization and the rise of the creative economy radically altered the landscape of global competition, transforming the global system of cities itself, enhancing the position of some regions, and desperately damaging the status of others. Older industrial regions such as Pittsburgh, Cleveland, St. Louis, and Detroit were especially hard hit by these twin forces, losing low-skilled industries and jobs to new foreign competitors, and homegrown and foreign high-skilled talent to rising knowledge-based regions. Newly industrializing regions from Taipei to Guadalajara have come to specialize in relatively narrow niches of the production chain, leaving them ever more vulnerable to swings in the economy and in their own cost structures. And while emerging "cities of ideas" have greater economic and creative flexibility, they, too, face vicious competition for talent and a growing divide between creative workers and the rest of their inhabitants.

The end result is that all cities find themselves competing for smaller and smaller niches, causing them to seek advantage by mixing their talent and cost structures in ever more complex and sophisticated ways. These cities essentially perform a "talent arbitrage" by exploiting their niche. Regional economist Ann Markusen argues that American cities are witnessing a remarkable distinctiveness in economic activities: "it is thus an era of heightened specialization, and cities would be well advised to play to their strengths."[13] While U.S. cities and regions remain incredibly vibrant—Silicon Valley still dominates world innovation in fields as diverse as high-technology electronics, software, and biotechnology—a growing number of regions outside the United States are also making significant inroads in key niches of technology and talent. To take just a few examples:

- Tokyo and Osaka, Japan, are the unquestioned world leaders in the development of cutting-edge consumer electronics, and especially new generations of mobile wireless devices. Tokyo has emerged as a leading center for video games and dominates the field of anime, increasingly critical in the production of movies, music videos, and video games.

- Wellington, New Zealand (Peter Jackson's base), Sydney and Melbourne, Australia (home to Mel Gibson, Nicole Kidman, and Russell Crowe, among others), and Toronto (a low-cost alternative to Hollywood) together challenge Los Angeles' long-standing dominance in film production and in key areas of digital technology. Mexico and other Latin American countries, and of course India, have also garnered much attention as of late for leveraging their megalopolises as film-production centers rather than importing more of the standard American fare.

- Finland's Helsinki–Tampere–Oul region, home to world telecom leader Nokia, competes with San Diego, Silicon Valley, and the greater Chicago area, where Motorola is headquartered.

- London, Milan, and Paris have long competed against New York City in fashion, design, and luxury brands. Now add Antwerp and other emerging centers to the mix.

- Toulouse, France, and Hamburg, Germany, challenge Seattle as the world's leading centers for airplane design and manufacture, with Airbus displacing America's number one export earner, Boeing, as the world's leading manufacturer of airplanes.

Of course, advantage here can be fleeting. The very input that generates growth—creative people—can move anywhere in the world, and overly specialized cities are particularly vulnerable to economic oscillations. The trick for cities, then, is to figure out how to make this mobile talent want to come—and, ideally, stay. If they can do this, the talent itself will help to smooth over rough economic patches by remaining economically innovative and entrepreneurial. Easier said than done, though. It's difficult to sustain such creative attraction in an environment of growing global competition, when growth often brings with it both increasing costs and decreasing quality of life.

And consider this: If the competition is ferocious at the top, as New York, San Francisco, Seattle, and Boston vie for top talent with London, Toronto, Vancouver, Amsterdam, and Sydney, what will become of the hundreds of cities and regions that are already economically disadvantaged—the Pittsburghs and Clevelands? As people can choose locations worldwide, they're not going to feel the urge simply to leave their hometown of Cleveland to go to Seattle; they'll think, "Maybe I can go to Vancouver . . . or Sydney." The options will only get more tempting.

# A World of Regions

So how best to get a handle on the emerging set of globally competitive cities? This is a difficult question to answer with a great deal of precision, since much of the data needed to make detailed statistical comparisons simply don't exist. Measuring the extent of the creative class and developing comparable indicators of the 3 Ts for cities and regions around the world is a daunting task. Yet, as I write, many teams of analysts are working on it, and it is certainly a career goal of mine to develop such systematic and comparable ratings and rankings. The fact of the matter is that we're only just beginning. There are, though, a number of data sets compiled by research teams around the world from which we can draw. The figures are not comprehensive, but they allow us to begin to paint a portrait of global creative centers and the challenges they pose to U.S. cities and regions.

A group of economic geographers in the United States and Britain have worked for decades to define what they call "world cities." To do so, they have collected and analyzed detailed data on the concentration and flow of all sorts of economic activity, from bank and company headquartering to flows of capital and immigrants.[14] Their work identifies four great global mega-cities—New York, London, Paris, and Tokyo—that stand at the apex of command, coordination, and control in the world economy. "National and global markets, as well as globally integrated operations," writes Saskia Sassen, the leading student of such global cities, "require central places where the work of running global systems gets done."[15] These cities are linked more closely with one another—through flows of capital, information, and people—than they are with cities in their respective countries. Of course, these cities have huge economic advantages: They didn't need the creative age to draw the attention of the entire world. And they will likely serve as economic nodes for a long time, precisely because they are so enormous and so diverse that they can absorb or breed any kind of human being and likely adapt to any kind of economy.

But U.S. cities face even greater competition down the chain.

These researchers have sorted more than one hundred world cities into three or four major categories based on the strategic function they play in the global economy. I will refer to them as first-, second-, and third-tier cities.

### Big Four First-Tier Cities:
New York, London, Tokyo, Paris

### Other First-Tier Cities
Chicago, Los Angeles, Frankfurt, Hong Kong, Milan, Singapore

### Second-Tier Cities
San Francisco, Sydney, Toronto, Zurich, Brussels, Madrid, Mexico City, São Paulo, Moscow, Seoul

### Third-Tier Cities
Boston, Washington, D.C., Dallas, Houston, Atlanta, Miami, Minneapolis, Amsterdam, Caracas, Düsseldorf, Geneva, Jakarta, Johannesburg, Melbourne, Osaka, Prague, Santiago, Taipei, Bangkok, Beijing, Montreal, Rome, Stockholm, Warsaw, Barcelona, Berlin, Budapest, Buenos Aires, Copenhagen, Hamburg, Istanbul, Kuala Lumpur, Manila, Shanghai

The United States has the most dominant of the four leading global cities, New York, and two others on the first tier—Los Angeles and Chicago—that perform a strategic role comparable to that of Frankfurt, Hong Kong, Milan, or Singapore.[16] San Francisco is the only U.S. city among the ten second-tier cities worldwide, a group that includes Toronto, Sydney, Brussels, and others. U.S. cities make up just seven of the thirty-four third-tier cities: Boston, Washington, D.C., Atlanta, Miami, Houston, Dallas, and Minneapolis—all leading cities on my original Creativity Index. These cities compare with the wide group of international cities from Amsterdam, Geneva, Rome,

Stockholm, Montreal, and Melbourne to Osaka, Taipei, Beijing, and Bangkok. The competition facing U.S. cities, according to these measures, is very significant indeed.

## Global Talent Magnets

The real action in the world economy revolves around a group of cities I refer to as global talent magnets. I call them this because of their openness and ability to compete effectively for outside sources of talent. It's intuitively obvious that these cities are extraordinarily impressive places, and in fact many people choose to live in them precisely because they maintain a standard of living as high as, if not higher than, the first-tier global centers, without all the fuss or tourism or cost. These places offer highly mobile creative talent further inducements such as spectacular waterfronts, beautiful countryside, or great outdoor life. They're safe. They're rarely at war. These cities are becoming the global equivalents of Boston or San Francisco, transforming themselves into creative hotbeds that draw talent from all over—including your city and mine.

It is nearly impossible to get a solid statistical handle on the number and extent of these global talent magnets, say, based on their percentage of the creative class or level of human capital. But Lisa Benton-Short, an economic geographer at George Washington University, and her colleagues have developed extremely useful data on the level of immigration for some 166 cities worldwide, scouring the U.S. Census Bureau's international databases, information from the United Nations' Population Division, and digging deeply into government census data and official Web sites for countries around the world.[17] The level of immigration, measured as percentage of the population that is foreign-born, is a useful proxy measure of how open a city is to global talent.[18] It's important to recall, as we saw earlier, that a substantial body of literature finds a close relationship between the percentage of foreign-born in a city or region and its level of technological innovation and economic growth. Part of what makes the immigration proxy so indicative is that it automatically includes both high- and low-skilled workers. All human beings have the potential to work creatively, and even the high-skilled ones don't want to be around only other high-skilled workers, but prefer a wide variety of immigrants of all skill levels and income groups.

Dubai tops the list with a whopping 82 percent. Looking at the overall level of immigration as a percentage of the population is necessary, but not sufficient. Lumping all foreign-born people together

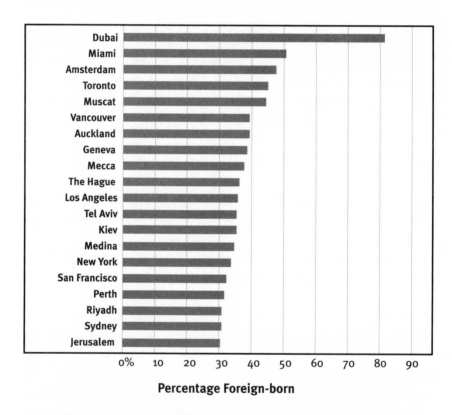

**Percentage Foreign-born**

### Figure 6.1: Immigration Levels in Global Cities

Immigrants account for significant percentages of city populations worldwide, especially in creative centers. Of the top twenty immigrant-populated cities in the world, the United States accounts for just four: New York, Los Angeles, Miami, and San Francisco.

Lisa Benton-Short, Marie Price, and Samantha Friedman, "A Global Perspective on the Connections Between Immigrants and World Cities," The George Washington Center for the Study of Globalization, 2004.

fails to capture the full diversity of immigrants that make up a city. In the case of Dubai, for instance, the figure of 82 percent can be misleading, since a closer examination of the data reveal that 61 percent of the foreign-born came from South Asia (India and Pakistan). Miami is second in terms of percentage of immigrants, with more than half of its population hailing from foreign locations. Again, though, most of this city's immigrants come from one geographical region, in this case Cuba and Latin America. The next most immigrant-heavy cities include Amsterdam (47 percent), Toronto (45 percent), Vancouver (39 percent), Auckland (39 percent), and Geneva (38 percent). What makes these cities such formidable challengers to U.S. regions is that many of them, in particular the Canadian cities, not only boast a high immigrant population, but a diverse one, too. These cities are not dominated by one particular immigrant group, but instead offer a mosaic of ethnic and racial groups from around the world.

While Los Angeles, New York City, and San Francisco follow closely behind (with more than 30 percent of their populations being foreign-born), Australia's Sydney (31 percent), Melbourne (29 percent), Perth (32 percent), and Brisbane (21 percent); European centers like Frankfurt (28 percent), London (27 percent), Brussels (27 percent), Munich (23 percent), and Zurich (23 percent); and Israel's Tel Aviv (36 percent) and Jerusalem (31 percent) boast foreign-born concentrations of 20 percent or better—more than San Diego, Washington, D.C., Seattle, and Boston. Immigrants make up more than 15 percent of the population in several other global hot spots: Singapore, Paris, Stockholm, Vienna, Hamburg, Düsseldorf, and Cologne. All told, the U.S. accounts for ten of the forty-six world cities where immigrants make up more than 15 percent of the population, and just four (Miami, New York, Los Angeles, and San Francisco) of the twenty cities where they make up more than 30 percent of the total population.

To get at the issue of immigrant population diversity within cities, Benton-Short and her colleagues constructed an ingenious measure that I refer to as a "Mosaic Index" because of its ability to capture distinct pieces of the immigrant puzzle in a city. By looking closely at official government documents and Web sites, Benton-Short and her team collected and analyzed data on the actual composition of the foreign-born population, creating a weighted measure based on the total number of foreign-born, the percentage foreign-born, the percentage foreign-born not from a neighboring country, and the mix of foreign-born residents (here they measured cities where no one group made up more than 25 percent of all foreign-born).

New York tops the list on this Mosaic Index, followed by Toronto,

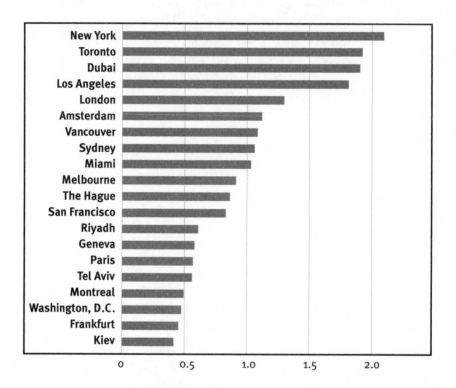

**Figure 6.2: The Mosaic Index**

The diversity of origin of a city's immigrant population is even more important to its economic success than its total percentage of immigrants. Serving as destinations for immigrants from around the world, New York and Toronto top the Mosaic Index list.

Lisa Benton-Short, Marie Price, and Samantha Friedman, "A Global Perspective on the Connections Between Immigrants and World Cities," The George Washington Center for the Study of Globalization, 2004.

Dubai, Los Angeles, and London. Amsterdam, Vancouver, Sydney, Miami, and Melbourne also rank highly on this measure. The second group includes two U.S. cities, San Francisco and Washington, D.C., and a wide range of global competitors—Paris, Montreal, Geneva, Frankfurt, Tel Aviv, Kiev, and Riyadh. The third group includes Boston, Chicago, and Seattle in the U.S., and international cities such as Brussels, Munich, Düsseldorf, Rotterdam, Ottawa, and Perth, among others.

Not all cities are able to compete effectively for global talent. There are a significant number with negative scores on the Mosaic Index, indicating that they are either attracting a very narrow band of immigrants or not attracting many immigrants period. Cities in this group include, not surprisingly, major Asian cities like Seoul, Osaka, Tokyo, Bangkok, Taipei, and even Singapore—but also the European cities of Athens, Naples, Lisbon, and Barcelona, and the Scandinavian centers of Helsinki and Oslo. These places are challenged by their lack of appeal to global talent and will need to improve their diversity and tolerance if they wish to compete at the global cutting edge.

## Competing across the Board

While immigration is a good proxy measure of social and economic openness, what we would really like to have is more detailed data on how global cities stack up on the 3 Ts of economic growth. Such comprehensive data is not available for most global cities, but it is available for the two countries that have the largest concentrations of immigrants in the world: Australia and Canada. And these data suggest once again that regional competition in the creative economy is tougher than many in the U.S. might like to believe. Cities in Canada and Australia garner scores on my 3 Ts that rival or even surpass the most advanced U.S. creative centers.

I first got a hint of the competitive capabilities of Canadian regions while visiting the country in the early 2000s, when I witnessed cities across the country actively investing in their creative assets, from arts and music to film and technology. Toronto had already become a major center for film, while Waterloo, with its remarkable technical university, was a vibrant tech center, home to Research in Motion, the Waterloo University spin-off company that introduced the Black-Berry personal communications devices.

So intrigued was I by the creative vitality of these places that, in 2003, I undertook a study of Canadian regions with Meric Gertler and Tara Vinodrai of the University of Toronto and Gary Gates. Using data from the 1996 Canadian Census, we found that many Canadian city regions, especially Toronto and Vancouver, were poised to compete with the leading U.S. creative centers. In late spring of 2004, Kevin Stolarick updated the Canadian analysis with newly available information from the 2001 Census. Stolarick used Canadian labor-force data to compile estimates of the creative class for Canadian regions and updated the Gay, Bohemian, and other indexes.[19] Here's what he found.

Canada's big-three city regions have concentrations of the creative class rivaling those of leading American regions (Toronto, 36 percent; Montreal, 35 percent; and Vancouver, 35 percent). Of America's ten most populous cities, only Washington, D.C. (40 percent), Boston (37 percent), and San Francisco (36 percent) do better. Smaller Canadian city regions are, if anything, more impressive. Ottawa, the Canadian capital and a burgeoning high-tech center in its own right, employs nearly 45 percent of its workforce in the creative class, while Calgary and Quebec City have creative class percentages in the high thirties.

Canadian regions also do well on tolerance. We have already seen Toronto's and Vancouver's high marks on both overall immigration and immigrant diversity. They perform no less impressively on the Gay Index. While San Francisco boasts the highest Gay Index measure in North America, Vancouver, Montreal, Ottawa, and Quebec are next in line.

By virtue of having quickly repositioned themselves from industrial- to creative economy regions, Canada's population centers score highly on technological competitiveness, too. While there are issues of data comparability, Stolarick's careful comparison indicates that the five largest Canadian regions—Toronto, Montreal, Vancouver, Ottawa, and Calgary—all have concentrations of high tech that rival U.S. cities.

Australian regions are also well poised to compete across the board. As we've already seen, four of its cities—Sydney, Melbourne, Brisbane, and Perth—rank very high in terms of openness to immigration. Indeed, Australia's regions, which boast sun, fun, and some of the world's most successful film and media stars, have become formidable competitors across the board, according to detailed benchmarking data compiled by Australia's National Institute of Economic and Industry Research.[20] Sydney and Melbourne, according to these studies, would rank approximately fourth among U.S. regions on the creative class, fifth on the Bohemian Index, and first on the Gay Index. Overall, they would tie for fourth on the Creativity Index—making them comparable to Boston or Seattle.

The Australian study went one step further than other regional creativity rankings and compiled data for particular inner-city neighborhoods. These results show the incredible creative capacity of Sydney and Melbourne's fashionable, innovative, diverse, and prosperous urban cores. Creative occupations make up a whopping half of the workforce in central Sydney (51 percent) and central Melbourne (50 percent)—well ahead of most U.S. regions. Both cities are also hotbeds of high art, fashion, music, and street-level culture, with Bohemian Index scores that rival those of any U.S. region.

Fundamentally, what these indexes and rankings point to is the reason Australia and Canada are giving the United States a run for its money. Cities like Sydney and Toronto are diverse, tolerant, and already steeped in creative people and occupations. Not to mention they're entertaining, motivating, architecturally magnificent, and in general boast a high quality of life, all without the growing homeland-security concerns that America's large cities must cope with. Quite simply, they're natural havens for global talent to call home, and they're leading their countries headlong into the creative age.

## The Global Austins

The second major group of world cities, the global Austins, follow a development cycle similar to that which moved Austin from a sleepy college town to a major center for technology and talent. Like Austin, these regions emerged as significant players in specific technology niches rather than as across-the-board innovative centers like Silicon Valley. Also like Austin, they initiated their development strategies in part by attracting established technology firms and talent from other regions. They then began to leverage substantial investments in the development of their own homegrown talent, and over time have been able to reverse their historic brain drain, increasing their ability to retain local talent and attract back many who had left for better opportunities elsewhere. Finally, like Austin, these global centers have started to invest in artistic and cultural amenities, and have seen their traditional attitudes toward tolerance and diversity begin to change as they become more vibrant and globally oriented places.

Volumes have been written on the development strategies undertaken by cities around the world to nurture high-technology industries. Indeed, there are many variations on the Global Austin theme, but I will briefly outline just a few of the most interesting.

- Dublin, Ireland, has just about completed its "Austin cycle," moving from an importer and attractor of foreign high-tech companies, to investing in its own human capital, to attracting back its own homegrown talent from abroad. Now it has become a more full-fledged technology center, generating its own technology firms by exploiting niches in global software production. Transforming the city itself into a lifestyle destination has been an equally crucial part of the equation. With its growing base of foreign and homegrown technology companies, superb technical colleges and universities, and thriving artistic and cultural scene, Ireland has emerged as the world's second largest software exporter behind the United States. Dublin is becoming a talent magnet for Europe and the world, developing a considerable innovation and entrepreneurial infrastructure.

- Singapore, through strategic efforts to attract the world's best companies, develop its own talent base, and upgrade its own technological infrastructure, produces the lion's share of the world's disk drives. It's home to a major digital animation studio for *Star Wars* creator George Lucas's Lucasfilm, whose stated goal is to use the facility "as a hub . . . to attract talent from all over the world." Singapore's government has developed a targeted strategy to spur a more broadly creative economy by investing in core creative clusters, pumping funds into higher education, and attracting top foreign universities such as INSEAD to open branches there. Its strategy also includes investing heavily in artistic and cultural activity, including bolstering its Bohemian Index by supporting street-level culture. In the meantime, it has made significant strides toward becoming a more open society by allowing gays to work openly in civil-service jobs and relaxing its restrictive censorship laws.

- Seoul, Korea, has been successful in attracting back many of its best and brightest, too. Korean graduates educated in the United States are now increasingly likely to return home to work. Seoul has become a world center for flat-panel displays, which go in everything from mobile phones and personal computers to television sets and the video panels used in modern offices, conference halls, and convention centers. Seoul is also a major player in mobile wireless technology and in video-game development and production.

- Taipei, Taiwan, hosts the factories of some of the world's best semiconductor manufacturers. With homegrown leaders in contract manufacturing, its production centers produce semiconductors designed, frequently in Taiwanese-owned companies, in Silicon Valley. Taipei focused strategically on the development of its semiconductor industry, exploiting a niche in the production of logic chips. To do so, it invested in technology, developed science parks, and focused on recruiting back top entrepreneurial talent, particularly from the United States, through professional associations and networks that link leading Taiwanese technologists and entrepreneurs in Taipei to those in Silicon Valley. In this way, key people move across borders, linking cutting-edge semiconductor design houses in Silicon Valley to advanced production facilities in Taipei and throughout Taiwan. These cross-border connections enable Taiwanese entrepreneurs to leverage the strategic assistance of venture capitalists in the United States with venture funding available back home.

• Much the same has occurred in Tel Aviv, where entrepreneurs have leveraged the scientific and technical base of Israel's top universities with experienced talent and contacts in the United States. For a time it was said Israeli software firms were taken directly from Tel Aviv to the NASDAQ.

• Bangalore, India, is the destination of choice for the production of routine software code and for the outsourcing of more and more business processes—moving up the value chain from call centers to data processing to full-scale management of computer systems across the board. Indian companies accounted for more than $25 billion in software exports in 2003. With the talent-producing machine of the Indian Institutes of Technology (IIT), Bangalore's initial niche was as a source of imported talent to U.S. software and information technology industries. More than fifty thousand Indian students study in the United States at any given time, and within the U.S., Indians provided a huge share of the temporary H–1B visa workers that filled the high-tech talent gap in the late 1990s. But a budding group of Indian entrepreneurs has transformed Bangalore from a place that exports talent to one that is exploiting a growing niche in the production of software via outsourcing. With a huge medical training infrastructure and close ties between software and medical innovation, India's urban centers are also emerging as a center for medical imaging and biotechnology. According to Ernst & Young, they will generate 1 million jobs in the biotechnology sector between 2004 and 2009. India's budding class of entrepreneurs and high-tech businesses is simultaneously modernizing the culture, bringing Silicon Valley business norms and lifestyles to a once-traditional environment.[21]

- Even Chinese cities (and, remember, there are more than a hundred of them with more than a million people) are increasing their ability to compete in key technology niches, especially mobile technology and consumer electronics. Beijing is home to Microsoft Asia Research, a state-of-the-art software research center with 170 scientists, and Matsushita's Advanced Mobile Communications Laboratory, which is developing cutting-edge technology, including the world's smallest GSM phone. The city's Haidian district is a magnet for creative talent from all over China, with some forty universities and colleges, including the country's two top universities, Beijing and Tsinghua universities (about a hundred meters apart), 138 research institutes, scores of high-tech ventures, and tens of thousands of scientists and engineers. "China was really the No. 1 target from the beginning," Rick Rashid, my former Carnegie Mellon colleague and now vice president for Microsoft Research, told the *New York Times*. "We felt there was a tremendously deep pool of talent there." Beijing is no longer a culturally monolithic town: far from it. The city is at the cultural leading edge, with thriving scenes in music, avant-garde film, video games, and animation. Shanghai is emerging as a technology and creative center in its own right, with world-class capabilities in mobile Internet technology. China is already home to more than 800,000 research scientists and engineers and is

attracting upward of two hundred global research laboratories a year.[22] And the Chinese government is finally pump-
ing up its investments in science, technology, research, and
cultural creativity.

## What's at Stake

Clearly, cities across the world are upping the ante in the competition
for talent. From a global perspective, this is a good thing. Cities and
nations are investing in technology, bolstering their creative climates,
and beginning to become more open and tolerant. Even some of the
most repressive of political and cultural climates are giving way under
the pressure of international flows of talent. Cities can no longer
compete for that talent just by providing economic opportunity and
high-paying jobs; people have come to expect a certain working environment and lifestyle, too. As a result, many of these places are for
the first time becoming more open, not just to immigrants and
techies, but to women, gays, artists, and other traditionally marginalized groups. The world is also becoming more integrated through the
explosion of cross-border networks that link entrepreneurs and technologists and allow them to mobilize resources and harness creativity
on a more global scale. Leading thinkers see the shift pointed out by
Saxenian; older concerns over brain drain are giving way to a new
paradigm of brain circulation, as talent and technology move more
freely around the globe, stimulating economic development in more
and more regions. This can all be considered progress.

But there is a downside as well. The rise of the creative economy is
producing an ever-more-stratified global economy, where the lines of
demarcation now revolve around the nexus of class and region.
Alongside the global talent magnets and global Austins are a large
group of regions around the world that are failing to make the
creative economy cut. Places like St. Louis, Buffalo, and their global
counterparts are bleeding talent and falling further behind. How will
these places compete with—or even survive—this global onslaught?

The answer lies closer to home than we might think. It's the strategy that all cities will have to employ if they are to survive and prosper: to tap into the great reservoir of creative energy represented by the more than two-thirds of the workforce currently being left behind by the creative economy. How these cities address this critical issue will affect more than just their own destinies; it will be a key measure of the broader success or failure of entire countries and the world as a whole in harnessing the energy and productive potential of the creative age.

**Part III**

## Losing Our Way

# 7

# Creative Class War

---

*If we are to achieve a richer culture, rich in contrasting values, we must
recognize the whole gamut of human potentialities, and so weave a less
arbitrary social fabric, one in which each diverse human gift will find a
fitting place.* —MARGARET MEAD


On a delightful spring evening in 2002, I found myself in a Zen-style
garden in one of Northern California's most upscale neighborhoods.
The garden, enclosed by high walls, with flowering plants and small
sculptures artfully placed amid beds of raked sand, adjoined the home
of a Palo Alto venture capitalist. The audience facing me could have
served as a group portrait for the creative class. There were engineers
and entrepreneurs, artists and musicians, businesspeople and venture
capitalists. Many were tastefully clad in black or neo-hippie garb.
Everyone looked permanently young in that California way. They
asked challenging and provocative questions, most of them having lit-

tle to do with their own stations in life; they wanted to know what the creative age might hold for people who were being left further and further behind by the onslaught of technology-based growth and rising housing prices.

I'd had a firsthand look a few hours before. My cabdriver had taken a wrong turn on the way from the airport, and suddenly we found ourselves in East Palo Alto. Here the streets were lined with shabby storefronts with signs announcing check cashing and *cerveza fría*. Instead of people who looked forever young, here were teenagers who looked old too soon. In fact, East Palo Alto has become a poster child for rising inequality. This is thoroughly disheartening. Not only is Silicon Valley the home of great economic wealth; it's also one of the most innovative and creative regions in the world. If ever a rising tide of prosperity were going to lift all boats, you would expect it to happen here. Yet it doesn't. Instead, the opposite occurs.

As a nation, the United States now faces levels of income inequality unseen since the 1920s. This inequality has consistently worsened in recent decades as the incomes of the top 20 percent of families rose by nearly 25 percent while those of the bottom 20 percent fell by more than 5 percent between 1977 and 1999. Thirty years ago, the average real annual compensation of the top one hundred chief executives was $1.3 million, or thirty-nine times the pay of the average worker. In 2001, that figure hit $37.5 million—over one thousand times what an average worker took home. The top 1 percent of households earned 20 percent of all income and held 33 percent of all net worth. The U.S. hasn't witnessed an income gap like this since the Gilded Age, when robber barons sent their children to private boarding schools and the Senate was controlled by the "millionaires' club." Today, the U.S. is the most unequal of all advanced nations, with rates of inequality nearly double those of Sweden and Japan. The Council on Competitiveness, an organization whose members include the CEOs of leading U.S. companies, went so far as to call the trend a significant "long-term vulnerability" for the U.S. economy.[1] The inequality at work here is not simply the CEO robber-baron kind, between the top 1 percent and the rest of us. It's more pervasive, embedded in the very structure of the creative economy. The creative economy produces two kinds of jobs: high-paying creative occupations and lower-paying, less secure service jobs. Another, more cynical way of saying this is that, in order to keep focused on their high-end work, creative types depend on a veritable army of service workers to tend to the things they don't have time for. Nearly 45 percent of the workforce falls into our largest economic sector, the service class.

This class includes people such as janitors and housecleaners, food-service workers, low-end health-care workers, office clerks, and others. Its members earn, on average, less than half of what creative class workers earn—around $22,000 per year compared to over $50,000—and usually reap fewer intrinsic rewards. As global demand for creative workers increases, so does demand for the service-class workers who will fill in the tasks left behind by time-strapped techies and "ecstatic capitalists," to use Kay Hymowitz's phrase. As one astute Silicon Valley observer told the *New York Times*, "behind every software engineer is a nanny or a food-service worker."

Famed chef and author Anthony Bourdain stirred up controversy at a high-society gourmet gathering in New York when he pointedly but rightly seethed: "The restaurant industry would collapse without the Mexicans and Central Americans who came to this country with no skills at all." Yet, he told the stunned audience, "you look out at the audience [at the James Beard Awards, the culinary arts' Oscars night] and you've never seen so many white people in one place since George Wallace ran for president." This massive functional division of human labor produces the bulk of our income and social divides.

Though this hourglass effect exists throughout our society, it is worst in the very places that are at the vanguard of the creative economy. This is no coincidence; rising inequality is an unplanned but direct creative economy by-product, what economists refer to as an "externality." And it's not the only externality—far from it. The creative age is giving rise to a whole host of such externalities, running the gamut from growing housing inaffordability and worsening traffic congestion to mounting stress and anxiety.

No wonder the people in that high-walled garden felt so uneasy with the arrangement. Regardless of where any one of us places the blame for such circumstances, we all know, somehow intuitively, that employing huge numbers of our fellow citizens in such fashion is a waste, only slightly better than the old English domestic-servant system of the 1800s. The issue isn't simply one of social justice or equitable distribution of rewards. It is a matter of functional daily life for all—not to mention a huge creative waste. A large portion of that 70 percent of the noncreative class workforce never has the opportunity to do rewarding creative work. We are in effect wasting that great reservoir of creative capital.

## The New Geography of Class

The economic divide in America is reflected in a new geography of class. The United States is caught in a pattern of uneven regional development not seen since the Civil War. This is not the old North–South split or a coastal–heartland split. Rather, in all parts of the country, some regions are moving toward higher creative growth (think Austin, Boston, Minneapolis–St. Paul, Denver, and Portland), while others become mired in either slow growth (New Orleans, Grand Rapids, Buffalo), low-end service-economy growth (Las Vegas), or no growth at all. Those in the first group are emerging as the overall winners in the new creative economy, capitalizing on their tolerance and technology bases to draw young and old talent into their buzzing ecosystems.

Driving this split is a massive flow of talent and human creative capital. Robert Cushing of the University of Texas has documented the scope and political effects of this regional talent exchange. By comparing home regions on sequential tax returns, Cushing traced migration patterns between metro areas in Texas and the rest of the country. From 1992 to 2000, for instance, he found more than twice as many people moving from Pittsburgh to Austin as vice versa. Moreover, those leaving Pittsburgh for Austin had a much higher average annual income (more than $58,000) than those coming the other way (about $44,000), a sign that Austin is attracting higher-valued workers while shedding those less valued. In the aggregate, creative regions are losing low-income workers but gaining those with higher incomes. Cushing found, for example, that families moving from high-tech Austin to slower-growth Kansas City in the 1990s earned an average of $25,912 a year. Those going in the other direction, from Kansas City to Austin, earned over $65,000. The same pattern occurred in other creative centers from San Francisco and Los Angeles to Boston and Seattle.

The upshot is this: As a nation, we are beginning to divide into two kinds of regions with very different economic prospects. With housing inaffordability, income inequality, and social stratification all on the rise, our once-great middle-class society is cleaving into two groups: those with property and economic security and those without. The political implications could be dire. The old North–South split not only bred a civil war, but continued to drag on our society and economy well into the ensuing century. What might the repercussions of a new split be ten, twenty, or fifty years from now?

This class divide also takes shape within cities and regions. As we've seen, the highest levels of income inequality are found in the great regional meccas of the creative class. Kevin Stolarick has developed a new index of wage inequality (which compares the wages of creative class members to those in the other classes) and uses this to probe the relationship between inequality and measures of regional prosperity for more than three hundred metropolitan regions nationwide. Silicon Valley ranks first in inequality and second on the Creativity Index. Austin ranks fourth in creativity and seventh in inequality. Creative centers such as New York, Washington, D.C., Orange County, and the North Carolina Research Triangle number among the nation's most unequal regions. By and large, the same basic pattern holds true for regions of all sizes.

A 2004 Brookings Institution study reinforces these findings and sheds additional light on the geography of class in America today.[2] The study examined the patterns of class inequality in the one hundred largest American cities (using the city as the unit of analysis, as opposed to the broader metropolitan region). It found that a larger number of cities in the Midwest and Northeast lost high-income households more rapidly than other income groups between 1979 and 1999. The

study also found that only thirteen cities had a "balanced" class struc-
ture. Eight cities, including San Jose, California, and Raleigh, North
Carolina, had class structures strongly tilted to the high-end groups,
while seven additional cities, including Washington, D.C., and San
Francisco, had divided class structures, characterized by an extreme
U-shaped distribution of wealth between the rich and poor.

The study also found that low-income households predominate in
the remaining forty-three cities, which it divides into two groups.

| THE 10 MOST UNEQUAL REGIONS | INEQUALITY RANKING | CREATIVITY RANKING |
|---|---|---|
| San Jose, CA | 1 | 2 |
| New York, NY | 2 | 12 |
| Dallas, TX | 3 | 15 |
| Washington, DC | 4 | 9 |
| Orange County, CA | 5 | 19 |
| Raleigh—Durham, NC | 6 | 6 |
| Austin, TX | 7 | 4 |
| Middlesex, NJ | 8 | 18 |
| San Francisco, CA | 9 | 1 |
| Houston, TX | 10 | 29 |
| **THE 10 LEAST UNEQUAL REGIONS** | **INEQUALITY RANKING** | **CREATIVITY RANKING** |
| Las Vegas, NV | 61 | 47 |
| Fort Worth, TX | 60 | 28 |
| Grand Rapids, MI | 59 | 53 |
| Buffalo, NY | 58 | 61 |
| Indianapolis, IN | 57 | 33 |
| Riverside, CA | 56 | 54 |
| Louisville, KY | 55 | 55 |
| Greensboro, NC | 54 | 60 |
| Oklahoma City, OK | 53 | 50 |
| St. Louis, MO | 52 | 46 |

**Figure 7.1: U.S. Creative Powerhouses Are Among
the Most Unequal Regions**

Regions shown are those with populations of 1 million or more.
Compiled by Kevin Stolarick from U.S. Bureau of Labor statistics—see
Appendix B.

There were fourteen "stressed" cities—places like Detroit, Baltimore, New Orleans, Miami, Cleveland, and Newark—which had become predominantly lower-class cities having at least twice as many families in the bottom income brackets as the top. These cities, the report concludes, suffer from deep structural problems associated with the decline of manufacturing industry, racial segregation, and the flight of high-income households to other cities and regions. The twenty-nine remaining cities, including New York, Chicago, Houston, and Pittsburgh, are classified as having predominantly low-moderate-income class structures. These cities contain a diverse set of households and boast a substantial number of higher-income households, as well as considerable low-moderate-income families. Like divided cities, the study concludes, these cities face significant gaps between white and minority populations.

## Wasted Opportunities

Why should we be concerned about rising inequality? Simple: Inequality equals creative waste. A good deal of research has shown that high levels of inequality actually retard rather than spur economic growth. Someday, a system that employs millions of human beings to do little more than flip burgers, stack boxes, or assemble widgets may be seen to be as economically and ethically retrograde as compelling them to pick cotton. According to Paul Krugman and others, a key to the post–World War II golden age was the leveling of wages and salaries—referred to as the "Great Compression"—that supported the rise of the mighty middle class, who, in turn, helped power the mass-production industrial engine by buying the suburban houses, automobiles, appliances, and consumer durables that rolled off turbocharged assembly lines. We overcame the Depression of the 1930s not simply by stoking the engine of the industrial economy, but by allowing many, many people to participate in and to benefit from it.

I know about this firsthand: I was a child of this era. My blue-collar family benefited immensely from it. My dad's pay rose to a nice living wage—nice enough, in fact, that my parents could afford a modest home and to send my brother and me to Catholic school and then on to college. Although my father had but an eighth-grade education, I was able to be a scholarship student to Rutgers College and go on to earn a Ph.D. from Columbia University.

To take one step further back: After the attack on Pearl Harbor, my dad left his job at the factory and, with many young men in his neighborhood, marched down to the enlistment office in Newark and signed up for the army. After storming the beaches at Normandy, he served as a medical corpsman. It was grim work. In triage battlefield situations, he helped surgeons with wounds, amputations, and appendectomies. He became good enough that the surgeons occasionally trusted him to do it alone. He successfully removed the appendices of numerous soldiers. His supervising officer called him into a tent one day and said, "Lou, I'd like you to consider something. We want to send you to an accelerated college-and-medical-school plan, and train you to be a doctor." My father paused regretfully, then answered: "I don't think I can go to college and medical school. I never went to high school."

For a man who had dropped out in eighth grade to help support his family during the Depression, my father went on to do well anyway. After the war, he started on the shop floor of an eyeglass factory. By the time he retired, he was production supervisor for the entire plant. Without ever seeing the inside of a high school, my father performed in a single lifetime the duties of both an MD and an MBA. What might a whole host of people today be capable of doing if their talents were actually cultivated and channeled—in school, in creative practice on the job, or perhaps even by other means yet unimagined?

But today it is getting harder and harder for Americans to move up the socioeconomic ladder. Americans can tolerate some level of economic inequality so long as society affords them or their children a good chance of moving up economically. But the new reality is that social mobility in the United States is decreasing in tandem with rising income inequality. A well-known 1978 survey on the subject found that 23 percent of adult men who had been born in the bottom fifth of the population eventually made it into the top fifth. That's not bad, really. But a recent update of the study by University of Indiana sociologists found such mobility to be considerably less likely today. The study, which compared 2,749 father-and-son pairs from 1979 to 1998, found few sons who'd been able to achieve the same sorts of upward mobility. In fact, nearly 70 percent of the sons either remained at the same level or were doing worse than their fathers. This time, only 10 percent of the men born in the bottom quarter had made it to the top quarter. The biggest increase in mobility had been at the top of society, with affluent sons moving upward more than their fathers had. In comparative studies, the correlation between the incomes of fathers and sons is higher in the United States than in Germany, Sweden, Finland, or Canada. In other words, the U.S., for decades seen as the world's beacon of social mobility, is now doing worse in this regard than the world's classic social democracies.

Universities have long been considered the primary vehicle for upward mobility. But today America's universities are reinforcing, rather than reducing, the growing class divide. It's no surprise that affluent Americans have great advantages from an early age: They have access to the best schools, private tutors, and lessons, learning to compete and excel in the fields that will get them ahead. Now, though, universities no longer play the crucial role they once did in facilitating upward mobility. A January 2005 *Economist* article cites the troubling statistic that "three-quarters of the students at the country's top 146 colleges come from the richest socioeconomic fourth, compared with just 3 percent who come from the poorest fourth." And that number includes virtually all of the top public universities. From this, *The Economist* is led to conclude that America is no longer the meritocracy it once was, and instead looks dangerously close to the class-based society of the early Industrial Revolution. The divisions between classes are rising, highlighting our failure to tap into our greatest resource: our people.[3]

We can count on neither trickle-down economics nor conventional social-welfare programs to save us here. Rising inequality is driven by the dynamics of the emerging creative system, and does not promise to be self-healing: On the contrary, these dynamics perversely threaten to make the situation worse. While that 30 percent of U.S.

workers who are employed in creative class occupations is an un-precedented number, the remaining 70 percent don't have the chance to perform high-value-adding creative work.

For a superpower wanting to stay at the forefront of the emerging creative age, that's an awful lot of overhead to carry. It's an awful lot of minds to waste. Rising inequality is a deadweight drag on our eco-nomic competitiveness. As Japan taught us in the 1970s, it's simply not an optimal use of human abilities to divide creative labor so that a rel-ative few do the innovating while the majority carries out rote work. Japanese manufacturing firms leaped ahead of ours with their "cre-ative factory" methods, which tap the intelligence of every worker on the factory floor to make continuous small improvements in the pro-duction process. U.S. firms—stuck in the old Fordist system, whereby the engineers and top managers do all the thinking while the masses are paid to execute—nearly had their doors blown off. Many of our firms have now caught on to the new way. But our economy as a whole replicates the outmoded, inefficient Fordist regime. Unless we can tap the creative talents of many more people, we risk having our doors blown off on an inconceivable scale.

The basic formula is simple: Those companies, regions, and coun-tries that reduce waste and effectively harness their productive assets have a huge advantage in the Darwinian competition that powers cre-ative capitalism. Perhaps Michael Frye, head of London's Creativity Commission, explained it best. Frye grew up working in manufactur-ing industries and ultimately took a degree in industrial engineering. After stints working in various fields, he became interested in lighting and in time he accumulated the skill and capital to start his own light-ing business. Fascinated by the growing interest in quality manufac-turing and management, Frye sought to institute the latest strategies emanating from experts like Edward Deming and Joseph Juran, and Japanese companies like Toyota, to tap into the knowledge and intel-ligence of shop-floor workers to improve his company's quality and productivity. While Frye's business certainly realized gains, they were not dramatic. Then it dawned on him. Why not extend this basic ap-proach to include those who design the lighting? So he set up teams of designers to develop new cutting-edge designs for his already high-quality lights. Sales shot up immediately. When I met with Frye in the London offices of the Creativity Commission, he compared his experience in manufacturing with what cities and countries must do now if they are to prosper and benefit their residents. "What if cities and countries were to harness the one unlimited resource at their disposal—their people?" he asked. "What incredible wealth and improved living standards could that bring?" That is precisely the task that lies before us in completing the creative age.

## Externalities of the Creative Age

But there are other problems that must be addressed if we are to get there. The creative age exacerbates a whole host of other problems, or externalities, that we must overcome in order to build a fully creative society. Limits of time and space preclude me from providing a comprehensive accounting, but ponder for a moment just the following few.

### THE HOUSING BIND

The housing market both reflects and reinforces the worsening class divide in American society. While home owners in places like New York, San Francisco, Boston, and Washington, D.C., have seen their equity double or triple in value over the past decade, people in a far greater number of cities across the country have seen much more modest gains, if any, in their underlying value. This growing split in the housing market—both between regions and within the leading creative centers—adds another potent dimension to the new economic geography of class. For these reasons, place has become a primary axis for class conflict in America, pitting existing owners against those who struggle to gain a toehold in the market. San Francisco, for instance, was ripped apart by battles over housing affordability during the late 1990s. I now see those battles in my everyday life in Washington, D.C., as transitional neighborhoods turn over from lower-income communities to fully gentrified districts in just a few months. The *Washington Post* nervously reported in September 2004 that the city was seeing resurgence in class politics as a result of its housing-affordability crisis.

It's much more than a moral obligation to house all of our people; our economic future rests on our continued ability to build, rebuild,

| THE 10 *LEAST* AFFORDABLE REGIONS | INAFFORDABILITY RANKING |
|---|---|
| Miami, FL | 1 |
| Fort Lauderdale, FL | 2 |
| Los Angeles, CA | 3 |
| San Diego, CA | 4 |
| Riverside, CA | 5 |
| Orange County, CA | 6 |
| New York, NY | 7 |
| San Francisco, CA | 8 |
| Oakland, CA | 9 |
| Bergen County, NJ | 10 |
| THE 10 *MOST* AFFORDABLE REGIONS | INAFFORDABILITY RANKING |
| Grand Rapids, MI | 61 |
| St. Louis, MO | 60 |
| Louisville, KY | 59 |
| Kansas City, MO | 58 |
| Detroit, MI | 57 |
| Oklahoma City, OK | 56 |
| Indianapolis, IN | 55 |
| Minneapolis, MN | 54 |
| Pittsburgh, PA | 53 |
| Greensboro, NC | 52 |

**Figure 7.2: The Housing Affordability Crisis, Large Regions**

Creative regions are among the most unaffordable. Large regions are those with populations of 1 million or more.
Compiled by Kevin Stolarick from U.S. Census Bureau statistics—see Appendix B.

and maintain affordable living spaces in our leading creative centers. If current rates of unaffordable housing continue unabated, they may well cause the U.S. creative engine to stall or even stroke out altogether. Places like Silicon Valley; San Diego; Cambridge, Massachusetts; and even New York City used to be places where young creatives, new immigrant families, social and economic outcasts, and intrepid entrepreneurs could go to get a start. But these places now number among the nation's least affordable housing markets.

A detailed analysis of trends in housing affordability for all U.S. regions by Kevin Stolarick illustrates this disturbing pattern. Stolarick's analysis measures affordability by comparing housing costs to incomes, and he also includes the mix of housing (that is, how much is owned versus how much is rented) in his analysis. The least affordable places in the country include a number of leading creative centers like New York, San Francisco, San Diego, and Los Angeles, as well as many leading university towns—both of which are now on par with classic resort destinations and CEO hamlets like Naples, Florida.

This problem is not unique to the United States. Housing, and particularly mortgage debt, accounts for a large and growing share of household expenditure and gross national product in most advanced nations, and has sucked up even more capital in the wake of the technology bubble. Housing prices increased by more than 50 percent between 1997 and 2004 in Australia, Ireland, Spain, and the United Kingdom. In Japan, mortgage loans as a percentage of GDP increased from 5.6 percent in 1970 to 36.5 percent in 2003, according to the International Monetary Fund (IMF). The IMF also notes that that the boom in housing prices is now "synchronized" across the advanced world, predicting that "just as the upswing in house prices has been a mostly global phenomenon, it is likely that any downturn would also be highly synchronized, with corresponding implications for global economic activity." The consequences for the U.S. and world economies would be dire and dwarf those of the technology bubble of the late 1990s and 2000s. The rush of capital away from productive activity and into the holding pen of housing is one of the fundamental tensions of the nascent creative age. Opening up ways to provide more affordable housing and allow precious investment capital to find its way into more effective areas is a key challenge across the advanced industrial world.[4]

The housing sector not only sucks up tons of capital that could be more effectively used to invest in new technology or cure life-threatening diseases; it also establishes a limit on the ability of these regions to attract talent, continue to innovate, and grow. Thirty years ago, the University of California at San Diego, the veritable hub of the San Diego economic growth engine, could recruit leading scientists and faculty by offering them affordable oceanside living. Today, it is hard to imagine how a young professor or scientist could ever afford a house there. Forget about manufacturing, service, or young entrepreneurial workers; *professors* in these communities—midcareer people in their forties with families—cannot buy in. Consequently, they're forced from apartment to apartment on a yearly basis—or less—as their rentals are converted into condos. As a nation, we pride ourselves on the fact that 60 percent of our population own their own homes. That dream has all but disappeared for *all* classes in cities like San Francisco or San Diego, where the rate of home ownership hovers at 25 or 30 percent.

An international real-estate investor in Cambridge, Massachusetts, put the dilemma to me in this way: In the last thirty years, as Cambridge and the Boston area in general have become creative meccas, more and more high-end creative workers have been attracted to the area—whether for real estate, research, or other opportunities. In his particular line of work as in many others, consultants have traditionally been hired straight out of MIT and Harvard. A superb educational atmosphere has fed the economic success of the region, and vice versa, in a virtuous cycle that benefits all. Now, though, with real-estate prices skyrocketing, the investor's firm can no longer get fresh talent to stay in—let alone move to—the area; they simply can't afford to buy homes in Cambridge anymore. The irony of the fact that young real-estate investors and consultants can no longer afford the housing they sell was not lost on the investor; it's also perfectly emblematic of the larger creative economy inaffordability trend. Whether it's Palo Alto, Berkeley, San Diego, or Austin, many of

America's leading university towns and innovation centers are similarly choking themselves off from further creative development.

High-tech businesses, new bands, and family corner stores have this much in common: They start in cheap garages and fixer-uppers, and they improve the economic and cultural vitality of their surroundings greatly. Now these places are filling up with the kind of (all well-intentioned) affluent people who have already completed the wealth-building cycle and who take much of their economic activity to places outside their neighborhoods. The Cambridge real-estate investor noted not just that talent gaps were developing in his firm's lineup, but that the character of the firm itself was changing as older, stodgier interests (he included himself in this category) dominated the internal functionings of the workplace. Even for these more established players, this is a destructive social cycle; as Jane Jacobs once quipped, "when a place gets boring, even the rich people leave." Without an ability to regenerate itself, the U.S. creative economy may begin to stall.

The fact that there are new global competitors further changes this game. For all the affordability problems the creative economy creates, still it's unlikely that these young MIT and Harvard graduates would desert their creative-center homes for Rochester or St. Louis. Most would sooner desert their home-owning dreams, if it meant maintaining a central place in the creative economy. But with the rise of competing global creative centers, they can have their cake and eat it, too. Not that London or Tokyo is cheaper than New York or Los Angeles (the opposite is true), but the other global centers—Sydney, Toronto, Dublin, and the like—are competing quite readily with their American counterparts. American creative workers are increasingly likely to go to a city or region outside the U.S., and foreign creative workers are more likely to stay in their home countries or regions than they are to come here looking for opportunity. That opportunity is growing up all around them—why shouldn't they be? Housing inaffordability is, as a result, *much* more than just a housing problem; it's already eroding our ability to reproduce and recapitalize the creative advantage we hold.

## JUST GETTING AROUND

The congestion of our roadways—and eventually our lungs—is another example of a consideration that most people think of in aesthetic or moral terms, but that cuts to the core of our economic advantage. It's not just inconvenient traffic jams anymore. Automotive congestion is both a cause and a symptom of our larger social ills, reflecting as it does an unsustainable penchant for full-time private property and working against the density required for creative innovation.

A 2004 study by the Texas Transportation Institute at Texas A&M University found that the average urban motorist was stuck in traffic for almost two whole days (forty-six hours) in 2002, a nearly 300 percent increase over the sixteen hours recorded in 1992, and that the annual financial cost of traffic congestion ballooned from $14 billion in 1982 to more than $63 billion today.

Commuters in leading creative centers fared worst of all, in large part because the demand to live in these centers is so great. Los Angeles topped the list, with an average annual delay of ninety-three hours (about four days), followed by San Francisco (seventy-three hours) and Washington, D.C. (sixty-seven hours). Boston commuters logged fifty-four hours in traffic. Commuters in L.A., San Francisco, and Washington, D.C., average daily commutes of more than ninety minutes, and many endure commutes of two or more hours—*each way.* While the more affluent members of these populations undergo these tremendous headaches because they prefer an ex-urban lifestyle, others do so because the outer rings are the only place they can afford to live.

The sprawl that demands and in turn is demanded by traffic congestion also wreaks havoc on our competitiveness. A stretched-out, sprawled metropolis, where professors no longer live near universities, where laboratories and high-tech firms can not co-locate, where entrepreneurs and newcomers are forced to the economic periphery, will lose the advantages that come from proximity, density, spontaneity, and face-to-face interaction. Factor in the hours upon days upon weeks lost to commuting time, missed meetings, and missed break-throughs that don't occur when people can't get together and pool their brainpower, and it's clear that traffic is clogging more than our streets and the decay is more than environmental.

A common feature of leading creative centers around the world is efficient and heavily trafficked subway and light-rail systems. The availability of subway and rail transportation was a key factor cited by creative people in the interviews and focus groups for *The Rise of the Creative Class,* trumping amenities like bike trails, coffee bars, and music venues. In our largest and most creative centers, such public transportation does exist and provides an edge in attracting creative talent. But it is sorely inadequate in far too many others. On this crit-ical dimension, large cities and regions outside the United States have another powerful advantage in the growing global competition for creative talent.

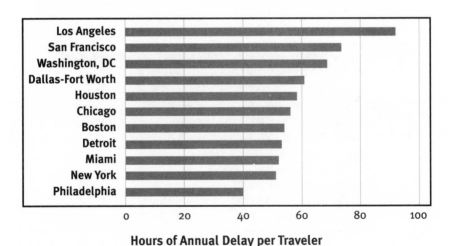

**Hours of Annual Delay per Traveler**

### Figure 7.3: Congested Cities

Commute times for residents of creative centers are among the worst in the nation. This graph shows the number of additional hours beyond the normal free-flowing commute time that a city's residents spend stuck in traffic.
Texas Transportation Institute, *2004 Urban Mobility Report,* Texas A&M University, September 2004.

## The Stressed-out Society

With the elimination of larger institutional and social support structures, the creative economy downloads stress and anxiety directly
onto individuals. A 2004 study of fourteen countries by researchers at
Harvard Medical School and the World Health Organization found
the United States to have the highest rate of mental illness, including
anxiety disorder and depression. The study was based on in-person
interviews with more than sixty thousand adults in Belgium, France,
Germany, Italy, the Netherlands, Spain, and several other nations. It
found that the mental illness rate ranged from 26 percent of people in
the United States to 8 percent in Italy. Even more telling are the findings of a study of rates of stress and anxiety disorder across U.S. regions. The study, which married my regional indicators with mental
illness data compiled by psychiatric researchers Kenneth Thompson
and Roberto Figueroa, found that that the incidence of stress and

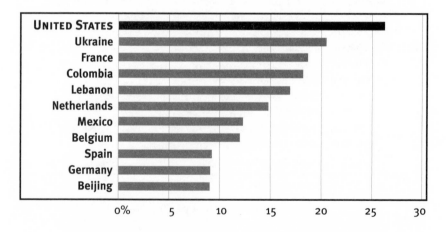

**Figure 7.4: Mental Stress in the Creative Age**

The United States leads the world in the percentage of its citizens who suffer from some form of clinically diagnosed mental disorder.
Ronald Kessler et al., "Prevalence, Severity, and Unmet Need for Treatment
of Mental Disorders in the World Health Organization World Mental
Health Surveys," *Journal of the American Medical Association,* June 2004.

anxiety disorders is markedly higher—across all income and class groups—in regions with high Creativity Index scores.[5]

In Australia, I met a physicist and entrepreneur who owns a major multinational electronics business. His company makes lasers in locations around the world, including several in the U.S. and near major creative centers. When I asked him what motivated his people to do their best, most productive work, he told me they simply needed to be "centered." It's impossible, he added, to be creative when you are stressed and anxious. I know this in my own work; any writer does. So does any software developer. And studies prove it: You need time to get into flow, and once flow is disrupted, it cannot be magically wished back. Stress and anxiety disrupt and damage the creative process. This is what Peter Jackson meant when he said he preferred Wellington because it is free of the "distractions" of daily Los Angeles life. Density and spontaneous interaction are important elements of creative development, but not if they are tethered to too many complications—especially basic safety concerns such as unusable nighttime streets and crime.

Companies across this country and the world are scrambling for ways to reduce stress and anxiety on their workforce. This is why companies like the SAS Institute are developing on-site health centers, day-care facilities, even on-site schools and counseling facilities for kids. They realize that people work more creatively and productively when they're not stressed. Quality of work–life is the wave of the future, not just because it is a good thing to do, but because by relieving stress and anxiety, companies can capitalize on their creative capital and gain a productive advantage. The same is true of cities, regions, and nations: Those that have a higher quality of life for individuals and families, and less stress and anxiety, will enjoy not just a better lifestyle but more productive use of their creative assets.

## Squaring the Circle

Even though the creative economy generates tremendous innovative, wealth-creating, and productive promise, left to its own devices it will

neither realize that promise nor solve the myriad social problems confronting us today. Lasting competitive advantage today will not simply
amass in those countries and regions that can generate the most creative, innovative, or entrepreneurial output but in those that can simultaneously address and ameliorate problems like income inequality,
housing affordability, uneven development, and underutilized human
potential in new and innovative ways. In this sense the formula for
success must shift from simply counting jobs or economic output to
ensuring long-run prosperity that taps and harnesses the full creative
capacities of everyone.

I see little sign that either political party understands this at all. Republicans tend to see inequality as the natural by-product of a Darwinian system in which some people are more competent and
industrious than others. True to a degree, but there's nothing either
natural or desirable about letting it run to extremes. Historical evidence shows that periods of high inequality such as the 1930s are also
periods of low growth, while eras of lower inequality, like the period
following World War II, are accompanied by high growth. Systematic
cross-national research on the growth record of the advanced industrial nations shows without question that high rates of inequality significantly retard growth.

Democrats tend to see inequality as damaging national unity and
weakening consumer demand, and thus something to be remedied by
government assistance or wage supports. Such social-welfare policies
have fallen out of favor as Republicans have blamed them for eroding
the American work ethic and creating a permanently disadvantaged
class. As for the roots of rising inequality, liberal thinkers from
William Julius Wilson to Paul Krugman and others have cited factors
that range from the loss of high-paying manufacturing jobs to an assault by the rich and conservative on unions and other institutions
that help poorer people form politically powerful constituencies.[6]

But the increasing economic disparity between the creative class
and the other classes is not simply the result of tax cuts, welfare reform, or any other conservative agenda. Nor is it a consequence of
loose immigration policies or liberal handouts. It's built into the very
fabric of the unmitigated rise of the creative economy, a direct if

harsh reflection of the kind of work that generates wealth in our global economy. The market alone cannot alleviate the situation. Neither can a welfare state single-handedly solve all our woes. The sheer power of creativity as an economic force means that wealth accumulates very unevenly and that those who are left behind not only become worse off but find it harder to attach themselves to the new socioeconomic system.

Before I go on to describe in the final chapter the principles that must inform our solutions to the economic and social externalities of the creative age, it would be helpful to set the political stage on which these challenges will have to be addressed. I'm referring, of course, to what many see as the worsening polarization of American society. This trend is itself a by-product of the shift from an industrial to a creative economy, and if it continues unabated, it will make it nearly impossible to address the most pressing global economic issues that we as a nation now face.

# 8

## Divided We Fall

*None of us are as smart as all of us.*        —JAPANESE PROVERB

Since the disputed 2000 presidential election, pundits, columnists, and
politicians have told us that the United States is a horribly polarized
country, composed of red and blue states that see eye to eye on almost
nothing and have entirely different views of what's wrong with our
society and how to make it right. This polarization got even uglier in
the hotly contested 2004 election, the argument goes, and has left the
country more divided than ever before. Ron Brownstein of the *Los
Angeles Times* writes that the "boundaries of civilized behavior in the
political world are crumbling." Pundits stoke the flames, blaming
Clinton's profligacy, Cheney's arrogance, Kerry's liberal record, or
Bush's prayer-breakfast conservatism. Whether one agrees with
Brownstein or not, there is a sense everywhere that this country is

deeply divided, that things aren't working, and that the institutions that once provided leadership now offer only conflict.

In this highly charged atmosphere, it's little wonder that the idea that the country is irreconcilably divided has come to pass for the conventional wisdom. Case in point: *The Economist* magazine ticked through an everyman's list for why the nation's politics is a portrait in red and blue. The article contrasts the districts represented by Representatives Nancy Pelosi and Dennis Hastert.[1] "Pelosiville" is "part of vertical America, a land of soaring skyscrapers and high-density living"; it is "the bluest, most liberal city in America," a "mixture of blue bloods and gays, dotcom millionaires and aging hippies," overwhelmingly liberal, pro–gay rights, more secular than religious, more single than family. It is the kind of place where Mark Leno, a state assemblyman, "can find himself labeled a 'conservative' even though he favors 'transgendered rights' and the legalization of cannabis for medical use." Hastertland is part of "horizontal America," a suburb of Chicago, Illinois, stretching "through cornfields to a point just 40 miles south of the Iowa border" and is "deep scarlet," "flat and boring culturally as well as physically," the district is "building new churches and expanding old ones." The "gulf" between these two districts, the article suggests, helps explain "why competition in America's political system is becoming fiercer at the national level. Fifty years ago the differences between the country's two, relatively un–ideological parties seemed small. Now they gape wide."

While it's easy to buy into these political caricatures, a number of America's leading political analysts have come to conclude that the country is not nearly as polarized as the media make it out to be. In his 2004 book, *Culture War?: The Myth of a Polarized America,* the distinguished Stanford University political scientist Morris Fiorina amasses a wealth of data to show that there is little meaningful difference between people in red states and blue states, arguing that "There is little evidence that American ideological or policy positions are more polarized today than three decades ago."[2] But Fiorina agrees with a growing number of political scientists who say that the real divide is between our increasingly partisan leaders in the Congress. "The ex-

planation is that the political figures Americans evaluate are more polarized. A polarized political class makes the citizenry appear polarized,
but it is only that—an appearance." Helping to propagate the polarization myth is the media, always hungry for dramatic stories with considerable shock value. "Thus, the concept of a culture war fits well with
the news sense of journalists who cover American politics."

But viewing American politics through the lens of national elections, the national media, and broad public-opinion polls misses the
underlying conditions causing our divisions. Even analyzing state-by-
state voting trends is misleading. States are enormous places with
many internal differences—economic, political, and cultural. The
ever-feisty James Carville, who cut his teeth on Harris Wofford's Senate campaign, once said that Pennsylvania was really two different
states: "Philadelphia and Pittsburgh, and Alabama in the middle."

The real and enduring change in American political life lies in what
I call the "molecular structure" of our politics—in the economic and
demographic makeup and the political and cultural preferences of
America's regions and cities. The divide I see in this country isn't between Republicans and Democrats, nor does it turn on your view on
gay marriage. The real fault line that threatens our collective future
runs along hidden fissures that shape the economic life chances of people in different parts of this country. Our divisions are between a relatively small group of regions whose openness and tolerance reinforces
their position atop the heap in innovation, creativity, and economic
growth, and a second group that is losing ground domestically and internationally, and whose people are becoming more anxious, less open,
and more resistant to change. The real failure of our time is our collective inability to articulate to this majority of Americans how they,
too, can participate in and benefit from the creative economy.

The economic logic behind this is not only powerful, it poses a serious danger to our national cohesion and may leave our country less
and less able to deal with the broad economic issues required to ensure our long-run competitiveness. As previous chapters have shown,
the U.S. faces stiff competition on the global playing field. As other
nations begin to put their feet to the creative economy pedal, how

will our country's political situation affect its ability to attract talent and prosper globally in the creative age? This question is critical, because the speed of our adjustment to the global creative economy will determine whether our country continues to lead or falls behind. The United States gained a huge advantage during the last economic transformation—the Industrial Revolution—because of our openness and ability to rapidly harness new people and ideas. Our dilemma today is similar: Can we work out our differences and generate consensus quickly enough to regain our ability to attract global talent and effectively leverage the creative economy transformation to our advantage?

## Polarization Pundits

As a look at any daily paper or nightly newscast can attest, polarization is one of the favorite topics on the American political scene. *New York Times* columnist David Brooks has been one of the most outspoken proponents of the demarcations that define our age, devoting much of his *Times* column to the issue of polarization.[3]

> The Year of our Lord 2000 was the year of the map. . . . This election was Hollywood vs. Nashville, "Sex and the City" vs. "Touched by an Angel," National Public Radio vs. talk radio, "Doonesbury" vs. "B.C.", "Hotel California" vs. "Okie from Muskogee." It was the New York Times vs. National Review Online, Dan Rather vs. Rush Limbaugh, Rosie O'Donnell vs. Dr. Laura, Barbra Streisand vs. Dr. James Dobson, the Supreme Court vs.—well, the Supreme Court.

More recently, Brooks has lambasted the polarization of the "educated" (read: creative) class. His new conceptual hinge point lies in the internal split between "knowledge workers" and "managers," the former tending to be more Democratic, the latter more Republican. "As the educated class has grown, it has segmented," he writes, continuing:

The economy has produced a large class of affluent knowledge workers—teachers, lawyers, architects, academics, journalists, therapists, decorators and so on—who live and vote differently than their equally well-educated but more business-oriented peers. . . . This contest between rival elites certainly doesn't explain everything about our politics. But with their overwhelming cultural and financial power, these elite groups do frame the choices the rest of the country must face. If not for the civil war within the educated class, this country would be far less polarized.

Brooks's self-described "comic sociologist" observations make for entertaining reading, but they don't always jibe with my own research and experience, or the analysis of others. Just as the working class was once split into different interest groups—welders, pipe fitters, etc.—so, too, with the creative class. But those differences are declining over time, and will tend to do so even more. In a stinging critique of Brooks, Mickey Kaus writes that the cultural divide between the columnist's two elite classes has been "shrinking, not growing," pointing out that "Even corporate managers want to be hip and edgy—wasn't that the point of Brooks' most famous coinage ('bobos,' or 'bourgeois bohemians')?"[4] It's not, Kaus argues, that the aristocracy of mind is in conflict with the aristocracy of money, but rather that "the aristocracy of mind increasingly *is* the aristocracy of money." The disagreements that do exist can perhaps be attributed to Freud's "narcissism of small differences." The *real* division of the twenty-first century economy, according to Kaus, is "between the unified rich-and-educated bobo elite and the less-educated less rich non-elite."

## Is Polarization a Myth?

It's not just Brooks who's come in for criticism. Many of America's leading political analysts conclude that the polarization thesis is badly overdrawn. Perhaps the most influential critic of the polarization thesis is columnist Robert Samuelson, who writes:

One standard poll item asks respondents to react to this statement: "I don't have much in common with people of other races." In 1987, 23% agreed; by 2002, only 15% did. Of course, strong disagreements (on abortion, for instance) remain. But these disguise large areas of consensus; 80% or more of Americans regularly support environmental regulation. . . . What's actually happened is that politics, and not the country, has become more polarized. By politics, I mean elected officials, party activists, advocates, highly engaged voters and commentators (TV talking heads, pundits). This may be the real polarization: between the true believers on both sides and everyone else.[5]

"Do Americans really despise the beliefs of half of their fellow citizens?" wonders John Tierney of the *New York Times*.[6] The conclusion he extracts in reviewing academic research on the topic: We have Beltway insiders to thank for the dubious distinction between the two Americas, red and blue. "As Norma Desmond might put it," Tierney quips, " 'We're still big. It's the parties that got smaller.' " The state-level red-and-blue map popularized by American media in 2000 and 2004 painted a picture of a starkly divided nation. But a county-level breakdown shows a country whose ideological viewpoints are much more subtly shaded. There are certainly several patches of vibrant red and blue, but the vast majority of America is varying shades of "purple" (see Figure 8.1).

Some of the most important insights on polarization come from the detailed studies of Paul DiMaggio and his collaborators at Princeton University.[7] They find that the American population has, generally speaking, become less divided on most key issues over time, though they agree that polarization has increased slightly in recent years. What coauthors DiMaggio, John Evans, and Bethany Bryson (referred to collectively as "DEB" below) have to say on the subject is worth quoting at length:

Attitudes toward race, gender, and feelings toward liberals and conservatives all are declining in polarization, as found in DEB. However, the additional years of data have suggested a turn-

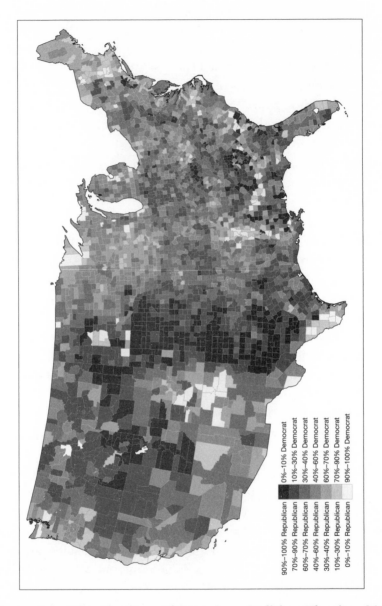

**Figure 8.1: The Shading of American Politics, Election 2004**

The red-state/blue-state divide is misleading. 2004 presidential election returns from America's 3,000+ counties paint a clearer picture.
Robert J. Vanderbei, "Election 2004 Results," http://www.princeton.edu/~rvdb/JAVA/election2004.

around in crime and justice, which now shows evidence of increasing polarization. Similarly, the polarization that DEB found in the general public in attitudes toward abortion continues, and now attitudes toward sexuality are indicating polarization. . . . DEB (the previous report) hypothesized that the well-documented differences in opinion between residents of the South and residents of the rest of the country may reflect polarization processes at work. While the continued growth of a national culture through television and other media would suggest a declining polarization, the growth of the Republican party in the South, which emphasized social issues, suggests at least the possibility of polarization. DEB found no evidence of polarization. Instead, moderate to large differences in attitudes between the South and the Non-South either remained constant over the time series or declined. More recent data confirms that the same variables that were converging then are converging now.

In June 2004, DiMaggio told the *New York Times* that "The two big surprises in our research were the increasing agreement between churchgoing evangelicals and mainline Protestants, even on abortion, and the lack of increasing polarization between African-America and whites. Evangelicals have become less doctrinaire and more liberal on issues like gender roles. African-Americans are showing more diversity in straying from the liberal-line on issues like government programs that assist minorities." DiMaggio's search for division among many subgroups—by age, race, sex, and education—turned up none that exhibited more polarization in 2002 than in 1987, with one exception: the 30 percent of adults who identify as "strong Republicans or Democrats."

In the wake of the 2004 election, though, pundits stampeded en masse toward the "moral values'" explanation as a way of accounting for President Bush's reelection. Democratic strategists lamented that their party had lost its religious way, and was being punished for it by the American people. The failure to understand mainstream America's moral values cost their presidential and congressional candidates election after election, the argument went, and if they were ever to regain a significant amount of those offices, they'd better start relating to the American people on a more spiritual plane. In other words, it wasn't the economy after all, stupid.

But in the rush to find the silver bullet explanation for the elections' decidedly Republican tilt, moral values became more hyped by journalists speaking on behalf of the people than by the people themselves. Sure, one-fifth of all voters cast their ballot for this vaguely defined issue. But that meant four-fifths didn't. Even Karl Rove, when pressed on this question by Tim Russert on *Meet the Press,* said it was one of the three top issues in the campaign, behind national security and the economy. What, then, to make of the supposed revival of the religious vote?

Americans are undoubtedly a religious people—the most religious in the advanced industrial world, as surveys by Inglehart and others demonstrate. But it is also clear that large swaths of America are moving in the kind of postmaterialist direction Inglehart notes. According to American University communications expert Leonard Steinhorn, "Survey after survey of contemporary social attitudes demonstrates social conservatives no more represent the mainstream or the future than Prohibitionists did in the 1920s." If anything, he continues, it is "the baby-boom sensibility spawned in the 1960s that has become mainstream in America today."[8] Broadly speaking, American society is becoming more open-minded on social issue after social issue, from interracial marriage to gender equality.

Even on gay rights, which Ronald Inglehart has called the last frontier of political evolution, Americans are getting there. The percentage of Americans who believe that homosexual relations are "always wrong"" declined from roughly three-quarters (74 percent in 1987) to just slightly more than half (53 percent), while the proportion saying such relations are "not wrong at all" tripled from 12 percent to 32 percent over the same time span, according to the General Social Survey by the National Opinion Research Center at the University of Chicago.

Nowhere is this more evident than in America's youth, who "may be the most inclusive, tolerant, and socially liberal generation in our nation's history," says Steinhorn. In 2004, roughly 40 percent of

Americans between the ages of twenty and thirty said they favored allowing gay marriage, while nearly 90 percent of seventy-year-olds opposed it.[9] "Gay rights could prove to be the issue that ends the culture war," says Alan Wolfe. Without it, "there are no major wedge issues left." And as I argued in *The Rise of the Creative Class,* this younger generation is indeed in the majority because, put simply, their parents agree with them. Though it's common to talk about generational divides and assume that one generation will often be the opposite of the preceding generation, what's striking about the generational divide in America is that it's not between Boomers and their offspring; it's between pre-Boomers on the one hand and the two generations that followed them on the other.

According to a 2002 poll by the Center for Information and Research on Civic Learning and Engagement, the pre-Boomer "greatest generation" is the only age demographic that believes society shouldn't recognize homosexuality as an acceptable lifestyle. Indeed, ideals of tolerance have slowly but steadily become mainstream enough that more than two hundred cities and counties now have laws protecting gays and lesbians from discrimination, 227 of the Fortune 500 companies offer domestic-partner benefits, and election 2004 exit polls found that three in five voters support marriage or civil unions for gays. "The illusion of a predominant' 'moral values' voting bloc," writes Steinhorn, "has much to do with the fact that the most traditional and socially conservative Americans, pre-baby boomers, are living much longer lives and voting in very large numbers." This skews exit polls and thus our image of the mainstream, he explains. Once younger voters begin to replace the pre-Boomers generation "the socially conservative vote will return to the margins of American life."

Pundits on both sides of the aisle seem to believe that "moral values" is synonymous with "traditional family values"—meaning opposing gay marriage and abortion and favoring only traditional family structures and traditional Judeo-Christian religions. In reality, the fastest-growing religious affiliation in America is among people who claim no particular religious identity at all. Their number, according to the 2001 American Religious Identification Survey, nearly equals the number of people who call themselves Baptists. And they tend to be overwhelmingly socially liberal, preferring individual worship over deference to religious authority and embracing modern values over what they see as outmoded religious rules. According to Steinhorn, today's silent majority is composed of the more tolerant Boomers and their children, for whom "diversity is not just a slogan—it's a moral value." Indeed, they've redefined the idea of morality itself.

> Mainstream morality has changed over the last generation . . . most Americans no longer feel comfortable imposing their personal morality on another's private behavior. But that doesn't mean this new majority is any less moral. . . . For baby boomers and younger people, there's nothing equivocal about their views of right and wrong. These Americans condemn bigotry, intolerance, and discrimination. They reject constraints on personal freedom and don't like it when women are not treated as equals. They find pollution objectionable and see nothing moral in imposing religious beliefs on others. They believe a moral upbringing is teaching kids to think for themselves, not to follow another's rules. What they embrace are pluralism, privacy, freedom of choice, diversity and respect for people with different traditions. Perhaps the only thing missing from this new morality is a politician capable of articulating it.

So how to explain the outcry against gay marriage and the resurgence of family values? For Steinhorn and others, the answer lies in the organized effort of a vocal minority. Like the American prohibitionists of the early twentieth century—or even the Luddites of England, a small band of antitechnologists who did great physical damage to the machines that they saw as threatening their own livelihood—this group has been able not only to get out their message but to co-opt the national agenda in the process. If the Democrats have not found a politician capable of articulating the new silent liberal majority, the Republicans have gone for the short-term answer of consolidating their pre-Boomer moral base. Neither party seems very well positioned to describe, let alone harness, the postmodern value system that comes with the creative age.

Here a little historical perspective is useful. Any large-scale economic transition produces political and cultural cleavages. I think most historians would agree that our own twenty-first-century round of polarization is relatively mild in comparison to, say, the outright class warfare that accompanied the late nineteenth and early twentieth centuries' rise of the industrial economy. In such periods, some people (especially those benefiting from the transformation) will embrace that change, while others (most commonly those losing out) will oppose or resist it. "The primary economic conflict," Jane Jacobs wrote more than three decades ago, "is between people whose interests are with already well-established economic activities, and those whose interests are with the emergence of new economic activities." So it should come as little surprise that there are political and cultural cleavages associated with the rise of the creative economy.

To the chagrin of doomsday prophets on all sides of the political game, the fact of the matter is that our current round of polarization is actually less severe, and potentially less damaging domestically and globally, than other, similar periods of economic change. At bottom, I view the cultural cleavages at work today not as some permanent feature of our social and political landscape, but rather as yet another rocky adjustment to our rapid economic transformation. And it will not be solved until more people—many more people—perceive that they, too, can participate fruitfully in the creative economy. It's impossible politically *and* economically to build a fully creative society when just 30 percent of the workforce reaps the full rewards of that economy's productivity. Still, it's an important adjustment to pay attention to.

## The Big Sort

The long and the short of it is that polarization is an overly simplistic misnomer for a more profound shift in the class structure of American society and its complex ripple effects on our politics. These shifts arise not from some master plan or large-scale ideological realignment, but from millions upon millions of individual choices. Their roots lie in the molecular-level demographic and economic earth-quake the creative economy has set in motion—what my colleague Bill Bishop and I refer to as the "big sort."[10]

Several years ago, Bishop and I began to examine this process of regional sorting with colleagues at Carnegie Mellon University, the Urban Institute, and the University of Chicago, and of course Robert Cushing. We quickly noticed a recurring phenomenon. What it boils down to is this: Economic change is driving political differentiation. And the nature of that differentiation is counterintuitive to the way we usually think of class politics in America. As Cushing's detailed region- and county-level analysis show, the more prosperous regions of the country are much more likely to be liberal and Democratic, while the more economically challenged regions are more likely to vote conservative and Republican.

Among the first people to put their fingers on these molecular trends were the political analysts Ruy Teixeira and John Judis.[11] While their predictions of an "emerging Democratic majority" may prove to be overly optimistic, their analysis of the regional economic factors that affect American politics is on target. Democrats, they noted, "are strongest in areas where the production of ideas and services has either redefined or replaced assembly-line manufacturing, particularly in the North and West, but also including some Southern states like Florida. Republicans are strongest in states like Mississippi, Wyoming, and South Carolina (as well as in former Democratic enclaves like Kentucky) where the transition to postindustrial society has lagged." Teixeira and Judis weren't talking about the states themselves, but about the states where the largest concentration of these smaller economic units manifests itself. The exceptions to the rule—culturally conservative Utah, San Diego County with its traditional military ethos, etc.—only serve to prove that the unit of analysis ought to be the city or region, and not the state.

Dubbing the trendsetting tech- and talent-heavy cities "ideopolises," Teixeira later went on to describe the economic side of what is still seen as a primarily political trend: "Between 1990 and 2000, the average ideopolis county grew by 23.2% compared to 11.1% for the average U.S. county and 10% for the average non-

ideopolis county." Ideopolis counties started from a large population base—an average of 475,000 inhabitants, compared to 90,000
for all counties and just 54,000 for the typical nonideopolis county.
Again, the important role of urbanization economies and the impact
of density on innovation and economic growth is evident (see
Chapter 2).

Cushing spent several years working with Bishop to further examine the nature of this sorting process. His research took the nation's
three-hundred-plus metropolitan areas and divided them according to
their economic structures. Cushing grouped the regions from high-
tech to low-tech, and then compared these groupings using the results
of the last six presidential elections. His findings reinforce those of
Teixeira and shed additional light on the big sort.

In 1980, according to Cushing's analysis, there wasn't a significant
difference between how high-tech and low-tech regions voted for
president; the difference between the parties still depended upon
other factors. The high-tech cities were slightly more Democratic
than the country as a whole. The suburbs of these tech cities were the
most Republican cities in the country. By 2000, however, the twenty-
one regions with the largest concentrations of the creative class and
the highest-tech economies voted Democratic at rates 17 percent
above the national average. Regions with lower levels of creative
people and low-tech economies, along with rural America, went
Republican.

The cities adjacent to the high-tech centers—thirty-four metro
areas ranging from Orange County, to Newark, to Salem, Oregon—
switched from being the most dependably Republican in 1980 to the
second most Democratic group of cities in 2000. Blue-collar, manufacturing towns that leaned Democratic in the 1980s became Republican bunkers by 2000. Rural areas, slightly more Republican in 1980
than the rest of the nation, became staunchly Republican by that
time.

In the responses to the annual polls contained in the University of
Chicago's General Social Survey, Cushing found the same divisions.
People in tech cities and their suburbs described themselves as more
liberal and Democratic than their low-tech and rural sisters and

brothers. Cushing examined the polls and surveys collected by Harvard's Robert Putnam in his groundbreaking examination of the nation's civic culture. There were again significant differences between high- and low-tech regions, but this time in the way people thought about life.

In the high-tech regions, people were more likely to be interested in other cultures and places than cities with traditional economies. They were more likely to "try anything once." They had a higher interest in politics, but they were less likely to volunteer, attend church, join clubs, or engage in community projects. In the traditional cities, the social tides reversed. People were more likely to attend church, join clubs, volunteer, and spend time with family. They were also more sedentary, more supportive of traditional authority, and had a declining interest in political affairs.

When Cushing and Gary Gates examined the polling Putnam had conducted in forty communities in 2000, they found the same basic pattern. High-tech cities lagged traditional regions in every measure of civic cohesion—except for two. These fast-growing cities were home to people who had diverse friends. People associated with those who differed in economic class, race, and religion. And, in these cities, citizens were more likely to engage in protest politics. They joined boycotts, protested, and signed petitions. Meanwhile, the tendency of people in low-tech manufacturing or rural areas to describe themselves as conservative or Republican grew from the 1980s to the 1990s. The converse is also true. "Liberals" and Democrats are congregating in high-tech areas, more so now than twenty years ago, Cushing found. What's occurring is a new kind of geographic segregation, based largely on class but refracted in ideology and values and also in voting and politics.

Cushing and Bishop again found the same phenomenon at work when they looked at national voting patterns at an even finer level of geographic detail, the county level, between 1976 and 2000. Overall, they found, the counties growing more Democratic were more high-tech, better educated, and had higher incomes than those growing more Republican. The average per capita income of counties that went from Republican in 1976 to Democratic in 2000 was $27,750 in 2000, compared to $19,750 for counties that turned from Democrat to Republican. The counties that switched from Republicans to Democratic also had 50 percent more people with college degrees than counties that switched the other way around.[12] Democratic counties also grew much denser, reflecting their urban nature. Where just twenty years ago U.S. counties that voted Democratic and those voting Republican had roughly the same concentration of people, by 2000, Democratic counties were likely to be three times denser than their Republican counterparts. In counties where one party experienced a landslide victory of more than twenty percentage points in the 2000 presidential election, the difference was even starker: Democratic landslide counties were, on average, eight times more populous than Republican counties.

The big sort was only exacerbated in the latest election cycle. According to an analysis of county-level returns by Bishop and Cushing, the percentage of Americans living in a county where one presidential candidate won at least 60 percent of the vote increased from just over 25 percent in 1976 to nearly 50 percent—a post–World War II high—in 2004. And the contours of that divide fell along stark geographic lines, with Democrats concentrating themselves in urban and inner suburban areas and Republicans fanning out into exurban and rural America.

The Democratic areas were also far more likely to have higher rates of economic inequality, according to political scientist Thomas Ferguson's analysis of the 2004 election. There, perhaps not surprisingly, economics mattered more to the vote. Ferguson's statistical models examined the relative roles played by such factors as household financial status, voter turnout, religion, and economic inequality for the forty-eight states where data were available. "States that witnessed lesser changes in inequality such as Kansas," he writes, "were far more likely to vote for Bush in 2004." In these states, "talk about values was potent, as the GOP intended." In sharp contrast, states such as Massachusetts, California, New York, and Connecticut, where income inequality rose sharply, went overwhelmingly Democratic. He concludes that while "Republicans tend to portray the liberal vote of these states as the product of snobby cultural elitism," it's actually good old-fashioned material interests that are at work.[13] President Bush skillfully played up moral values in many places that are struggling economically but where inequality has not risen as drastically—a distinction crucial to understanding the landscape of the big sort. In booming creative centers, economics took the day as the issue of utmost importance.

While Ferguson looked at the differences between red and blue states, the trend is even more evident at the molecular regional level. Consequently, the everyday, concrete reality of this sorting process is a drastic split between local communities with increasingly different economic situations—and political worldviews to match. This ideological concentration in turn results in the two major political parties focusing on mobilizing their bases rather than persuading other voters or forming pragmatic coalitions or policy.

## Divided on Top

There's one point on which nearly all political commentators are beginning to agree: Political polarization in the United States is worse at the very top. The disturbing thing, according to George Mason University's James Pfiffner, one of the leading students of American political institutions, is that this political elite has grown not just more polarized, but also practically dysfunctional.[14] "Voting in Congress has become more partisan," he writes, "the use of delaying tactics such as the filibuster have become more common; and the level of civility has declined." In the last fifteen years, conservative Democrats and liberal Republicans in *both* houses of Congress have all but disappeared. "This disappearance of the middle is a convincing demonstration of ideological polarization in Congress," Pfiffner says.

In the middle of the twentieth century, Pfiffner points out, the two political parties in Congress were ideologically diverse. As he puts it, "each party had a significant number of members who were ideologically sympathetic to the other party." The Democratic Party, for example, had Southern conservatives who often voted with conservative Republicans, and the Republican Party contained moderate, "Rockefeller" Republicans who often voted with the Democrats. Such cross-voting members, according to Pfiffner, composed between one-fifth and one-third of the House and Senate at any time from the 1950s to the mid-1980s.

Since then, this stabilizing center of American politics has all but disappeared. The Senate used to have a centrist group of seventeen senators from both parties who often voted with the opposite party; they are almost gone now. Today, he notes, virtually all Republicans have voting records to the right of the most conservative Democrat, while virtually all Democrats have voting records to the left of the most moderate Republican. And consider this: From the mid-1960s to the mid-1990s, the number of conservative Democrats in the House fell from ninety-one in the mid-1960s to eleven in 1995, while the number of moderate Republicans fell from thirty-five to just one. In the Senate, the number of moderate Republicans fell from fourteen to two, while conservative Democrats fell from thirty-five to just one.

Driven in part by a need to turn out the base, the big sort has helped to produce a divide among those who are supposed to lead our country and has contributed to our national government's increasing dysfunction. The big sort has not only resulted in fewer and fewer economically balanced cities and regions, it has simultaneously created fewer and fewer ideologically balanced congressional districts. The driving force here is economic; the by-product is political. As a result, congressional seats have become much safer. Over the last forty years, for instance, the South became solidly Republican, reinforcing partisan differences. One member of Congress summed up the situation this way: "The Democratic districts become more Democratic and the Republican districts become more Republican. There are fewer and fewer districts in the middle. . . . Because the districts in Congress are more and more one-party dominant, the American Congress is more extreme."

This country's institutions and politics were devised in a world where it was expected that people of different income groups, occupations, and ideological predispositions would have to share the same geographic space. In the romantic version of this world, they would all live in the same town or neighborhood and debate their views and positions in town-hall meetings. But when people concentrate in communities with very different economic and class structures, political and ideological differences are magnified. Geographic concentration reinforces ideological views, while higher partisanship leads to greater political participation. The most partisan neighborhoods vote in greater numbers, making primary elections especially ideological. The easiest voters to turn out are those most ideologically committed, and so candidates become more partisan to energize their most likely voters. Under these conditions, the national agenda suffers. In Congress, writes Pfiffner, "It is more likely that votes will be set up to highlight partisan differences and used for rhetorical and electoral purposes, rather than to arrive at compromise policies."

These shifts have worsened with the changing of the political guard in Washington, but their roots go much deeper, to a tectonic shift in the country's socioeconomic demographics. The migrations that have spurred the creative economy also exacerbate its contrasts. It's a sad irony: America's creative economy sparked a demographic shift and a political polarization that now threaten to choke that economy off. What the United States desperately needs now is political leadership savvy enough to bridge that gap.

## Why Neither Party Gets It

But don't expect to see that kind of leadership soon from either major political party, both of whose platforms veer increasingly out of touch with the global realities of the creative economy. The Democrats think of themselves as champions of working people and social justice, but their constituency is strongest in the centers of high-tech growth that have the highest levels of economic inequality and the least manufacturing. Still, they remain loyal to a blue-collar constituency that has largely abandoned them for the hawkish policies of the right. Many favor protective tariffs, workplace regulation, public schools, and at the local level, infrastructure projects that employ a heavily unionized labor force. Democrats have often been too timid to take on the old industry lobbies and too willing to follow the anti-competitive demands of their own industry backers. As social liberals, they support abortion rights, gay rights, affirmative action, and environmental protection—but they are mum on inequality, and prodded by Hollywood interests, they have promoted innovation-curbing policies such as copyright extension. As a set of positions, this reads as if it were created for a different century than the one we're in—as in fact it was.

Republicans, on the other hand, boast that they cultivate the entrepreneurial, wealth-generating edge of capitalism, but they draw their support from areas with relatively higher levels of economic equality, larger proportions of old-style manufacturing, and less-than-vibrant economies. They juggle faith-based initiatives and a halfhearted commitment to free trade that somehow manages to find room for tariff protections for steel, textiles, and agricultural products. On economic issues they look eerily like the party of Calvin Coolidge, with a tax cut on corporate dividends as their catchall solution to a stalled economy. Their idea of economic policy (at least under the latest Bush administration) has essentially been to provide subsidies and regulatory favors to old-economy industries ranging from steel companies and airlines to the energy and defense sectors. These happen to be industries generally located in areas that support the president and the GOP. At best, these favors for the old economy—steel tariffs, farm subsidies, the airline bailout—squander precious public funds in ways that add no entrepreneurial creative class jobs. At worst, they actually undermine such jobs. On sexual orientation, scientific research, the arts, and even civil rights, the current conservative leadership is more backward-looking than ever, although influential dissenters do exist within the party.

Still, the Republican Party may be cleaving in two over the crucial issue of immigration. On one side are the liberalizers, who want more open immigration laws and a guest worker program that will facilitate the gradual introduction of foreigners into the American economy. These are primarily businesspeople and free-traders who see the benefit that controlled immigration can have on the U.S. On the other side are the restrictionists, who want fewer legal immigrants, a tougher border, and sterner treatment for illegal immigrants. The House Republicans now have an anti-immigration caucus, headed by Representative Tom Tancredo of Colorado, that claims some seventy members—up from just fifteen three years ago—including some of the most powerful chairmen in the House. If this is any indication of the future direction of the party, it doesn't look good for our future as an open society.

This wasn't always the case. For a time during the 1980s, and even during the 1990s, it looked as if we might be able to manage the transition to a creative economy in something approaching a bipartisan way. Sure, liberals were mad as hell at Reagan's misadventures in foreign policy, Iran-Contra and the like, and conservatives were more than upset by the long legacy of entitlements and social programs. But on core matters of international and domestic economic policy we had achieved some level of bipartisan consensus. Across the Reagan, George H. W. Bush, and Clinton administrations, there was steadfast support for free trade. Opposition came from fringe quarters of the political spectrum: Recall when Al Gore debated Ross Perot over NAFTA. As a nation, we remained united in our support for open immigration. We opened our borders to a huge wave of foreign investment, which helped rebuild our automotive and related industries. We promoted a policy of low interest rates and fiscal stability. But, by the mid-1990s, all of this began to change, subtly at first, but hitting a flash point sometime after September 11, 2001, with the change in direction of the George W. Bush administration.

What exactly happened? There's more than enough blame to go around. The Clinton administration, despite its progressive rhetoric, failed to make the creative economy something that could benefit a large swath of the population. In doing so, it further alienated a sizable fraction of its working- and middle-class support. It remained steadfast in its support of free trade, open immigration, and high-tech industry, but failed to adequately explain how these stances would benefit working people or address the growing class divide. Most progress on this front was temporary, and due more to the economic boom and tight labor markets than to public policy.

At the same time, Clinton's administration repeatedly failed to stimulate economic growth in ways that reached out to the expanding creative class or developed new programs to connect service and manufacturing workers to the creative economy. The deeply rooted economic and demographic forces at work in this country were therefore left to fester unaddressed. The growing creative centers increased their economic and social distance from the rest of the country, and conservative forces were able to mobilize regular people around resentment at the narrow group of "sophistos, trendoids, and gays" that, it appeared, had hijacked America's economic concerns and cultural priorities.

The Clinton era also saw the rise of partisan enmity. This was personified in the conflict between Clinton and Newt Gingrich, two men who were in many other ways perhaps the most forward-looking and thoughtful leaders of their generation. Clinton well understood the dynamics of the creative economy. With his constant hyping of new technologies and "bridge to the twenty-first century" rhetoric, Clinton was the embodiment of what the sixties became: the creative class nineties, hip but pro-growth, open-minded and progressive but ambitious. Present at the birth of the nineties boom, he developed projects such as wiring poor and middle-class school classrooms around the country for the Internet and beating back Republican efforts to cut immigration. For better and for worse, he also personally symbolized the creative class archetype—its libertine character, its cleverness, its global-mindedness.

Gingrich understood the emerging age, too. He was among the first to call for giving every child a computer. His entire career was about spurring individual effort, achievement, and entrepreneurship—that is what most of his attacks on big government were about. He studied innovative capitalism and immersed himself in the high-tech economy. He wrote rambling but insightful essays on economic and political transitions and Silicon Valley–style innovation. His life's project was to try to make politics and government relevant for an age of high-tech capitalism.

Not surprisingly, these two influential protagonists stood at the center of one of the most dramatic policy conflicts of the past several decades. The rise of the "Contract with America" in the wake of the resounding Republican congressional victory in the 1994 midterm elections signaled a partisan stalemate that would eventually shut down the federal government. The key dynamic at work here, as James Pfiffner points out, was not so much a personal struggle as the transformation of American politics. "As bitter as the battles between Clinton and Gingrich were," he writes, "the fundamental causes of the partisan battles that dominated the four Congresses of the Clinton era have been driven by the polarization of Congress rather than by the personalities of the two men."

By the mid-to-late 1990s, this partisan cleavage had come to a head. The demise of Gingrich and the retirement of other thoughtful conservatives and moderate Republicans, who believed strongly in free trade, open immigration, fiscal propriety, and the need to support scientific research, meant that power within the conservative movement began to shift to Republican leaders like Tom DeLay and Dick Armey. These men thought less in terms of economic transformation and more in terms of raw political power. These leaders in combination with a growing conservative movement began to stoke the growing cultural and political antagonism felt by large segments of the population being left behind in the ongoing economic transformation. Hinging their rhetoric on family values, they made the case for taking back the country from an out-of-touch "liberal," "hedonistic" elite of New York City, Boston, San Francisco, and Washington, D.C., at odds with the moral fabric of the average American and to whom the future security of the nation could not be trusted.

The politician who spoke most subtly and skillfully to these grievances was George W. Bush. His election in 2000 signaled a shift in the leadership of the conservative movement from intellectuals like Gingrich to ideologues like DeLay and Senator Rick Santorum and political strategists like Karl Rove. Not surprisingly, then, the Bush administration, which presented itself as centrist (remember "compassionate conservatism," anyone?), tacked heavily to the right, exacerbating the political pressure points in the country, and especially in the Congress.

As president, Bush chose a group of senior advisers whose economic backgrounds have a century-old flavor. His vice president was an oilman; his treasury secretary, John Snow, a railroad man. The White House's economic and fiscal policies were similarly designed to provide life support for older industrial sectors: billions in subsidies for farmers; tariffs for steel; subsidies, tax breaks, and regulatory relief for logging, mining, coal, and natural gas. Still, it would be a huge oversimplification to blame the Bush administration for America's problems, as liberals are wont to do—just as it is a mistake on the conservative side of the aisle to demonize Bill Clinton.

At a time when increasing numbers of pundits call attention to the culture wars, and when many on the left decry the growing impact of moral values on our voting patterns, it's essential to recognize an important fact. Economic transformations never complete themselves. A political solution is required to fully realize the potential of a new economic and social order. The responsibility of making a case for this new order rests implicitly with the progressive forces within a society. If these progressive forces fail to spell out exactly how a better and more inclusive future can benefit all people—from the creative to the manufacturing to the service sectors—then the de facto choice of the people will be a conservative or reactionary regime. Change is frightening. It is the role of the right—the conservative forces within a society—to hark back to a better time, a golden age long past. For those on the left who would like to blame Karl Rove and the Christian right, it's important to remember that it's the failure of progressive forces to articulate the case for a better and more prosperous society that plays a substantial part in our current predicament.

## Getting Beyond Our Differences

The clock of history is always ticking. What we really need to worry about is not whether or not we're more polarized or conflicted than before, but how it will affect our nation's ability to mobilize creative energy, attract talent, and ensure our long-run prosperity. And here, I fear, there is real cause for concern.

Ronald Inglehart has shown how the politics of all advanced industrial nations is moving toward more open or postmaterialist value systems in tandem with economic progress. Across the world, people have less interest in traditional institutions, political parties, social class, and organized religion; and politics more and more revolves around individual freedom, individual rights, and the right of self-expression. While the jury may still be out on the causes and consequences of our political and cultural divisions, there is one thing we can say for certain: Our inability to embrace the future and plan for it is starting to put us at a structural disadvantage vis-à-vis other nations in the global competition for talent. The real issue is not whether the United States will get there (we will), but whether we are getting there fast enough relative to other countries. And here, unfortunately and according to Ingelhart's own measures, the United States lags behind.

At the end of the day, it may be irrelevant whether it's the people, the Congress, or the media that lie at the root of our so-called polarization problems; if we can't get past cultural issues and get our national act together to deal with the most basic economic concerns that confront us, we will fall behind. Remember, no one country or one region needs to trump us; the more likely scenario is a death by a thousand cuts as a series of competitors collectively combine to erode our lead. It's time to get serious, get beyond the moralistic distractions, and get on with the real business of getting this country and its people equipped to handle the creative age.

Indeed, one of my main aims in this book is to disentangle these core economic issues from the obfuscation that political posturing over the culture wars brings. The politics of morality not only distracts us and takes time away from the crucial economic issues we face; it also creates a much more contentious political culture in dealing with those issues when we do finally get around to them. It's a huge mistake, economically speaking, to make issues like openness to diversity, immigration policy, or gay rights pass through the filter of moral litmus tests. Doing so will cost all of us dearly. My work with cities and regions across the United States convinces me that sanity and good economic horse sense can prevail here. Before I launch into a discussion of what we need to do, let me tell you a story of where the impetus for getting our collective act together might come from.

It was a warm night in coastal Florida and I had just finished a speech. Our hosts brought us to an upscale but funky seafood restaurant where a dozen or so leaders from the local business, political, science, and civic communities had gathered. After introductions and pleasantries, the wine began to flow a bit more freely, and the dinner-table conversation became progressively more open and honest. At some point, the talk turned to what I was working on. I told the crowd that my next book (the one you're now reading) would deal with the global competition for talent and the ways in which the U.S. was responding—or failing to respond—to it. I mentioned what many pundits had already pinned down as the rising political polarization of the U.S. Washington, D.C., was becoming ever more partisan, the debate there increasingly bitter.

This made it difficult, I ventured, for our country to develop a unified response to the biggest economic challenge of our time. I mentioned that in cities and regions I had been visiting around the country, I found much more consensus on the local level than I'd expected. People are able to work cohesively across party lines when it comes to matters of immediate and practical concern. I personally work closely with people from both parties—often on the same project—and can rarely tell who is a Republican and who is a Democrat.

I proposed a simple experiment. We went around the table, one at a time, with my three hosts telling me a bit about themselves—nothing overtly political, just occupation, interests, family life, schooling, and the usual polite conversation. I then tried to identify each member of the dinner party as either a Democrat or a Republican, based on this knowledge.

My host was the founder of a major computer-science institute and an eminent professor and researcher. He, I was certain, had to be a Democrat. The woman across the table from me was a real-estate broker who had just sold a penthouse condominium to an aging, though still very successful, former-rock-star-turned-standards-singer. She had to be a Republican. A wealthy lawyer on the other side who had graciously offered to fly us back to Pittsburgh with him in his private plane was also surely a Republican.

The professor, it turned out, was a Republican and a Bush nominee to the National Science Board. The real-estate broker was a former Democratic state representative who, in the opinion of the other guests, was among the most progressive and liberal in the state's history. The lawyer was a lifelong Democrat and made his fortune suing the tobacco companies. I had been wrong on all counts.

The diners chuckled a bit at the whole idea. But let the experiment continue, I thought: Let's talk about Pensacola. Democrats and Republicans all wanted to invest in the region's creative workforce, strengthen its ability to attract talent, improve the general quality of life, and increase spending for research and development. Sure enough, as long as we stayed on these topics, everyone was on the same page.

But as the conversation inevitably drifted into national and international affairs, it became far more contentious. My own thoughts drifted inward, and two questions sprang to mind: Why, in the first place, had it been impossible for me to identify the political affiliations of the dinner hosts, even given my intimate knowledge of which general group characteristics tend to correspond to such affiliations? How was it that these people whose opinions diverged so significantly on national matters could share a common, consensus agenda about the future of their hometown? And if these people could focus their attention, intelligence, and energy on the future of their hometown, and avoid getting sidetracked by cultural or political diversions, why can't we do the same as a country?

# 9

# Building a Creative Society

━━━━━━━━━━━━━━━━━━━━━━━━━━━━━━━━━━━━━━━━━━━

*As for the future, your task is not to foresee but to enable it.*
—ANTOINE DE SAINT-EXUPÉRY

America has incredible transformative capabilities, that much is certain. We've done it so many times before: leading the world out of the Great Depression, winning World War II, saving Europe and the world from the grip of fascism, overcoming the Soviet threat, and rebounding in the 1980s from the onslaught of European and Asian competition in manufacturing industries.

My father told me long ago of this incredible American capacity. A teenager who went to work to help his family during the Great Depression, an infantry solider who enlisted in the army the day after Pearl Harbor, landed on Normandy, and fought in all the major battles of World War II, and a man who spent his life in manufacturing, he would always say: "Richard, no one should ever count this country out. When I enlisted in the army, they gave us doughboy hats and old uniforms, our boots often did not fit. There weren't enough guns to go around in training, so we used wooden facsimiles. But, boy, did we gear up. I saw it as soon as I got over there." He would continue, the pride of a D-day veteran in his eyes: "We all had heard about the technological prowess of the Germans. Their Lugers, the machine guns, their fighter planes and tanks—works of technology and of art. But you should have seen how we mobilized. Our guns might not have been so state-of-the-art, but they worked and there were lots of them. Whoever we could get to take over the factories—old people, women, whoever—we kept churning out what was necessary. We turned this country on a dime and built an incredible production machine. That's why we won." He would end, "I think when the Germans—their soldiers and the officers—saw this stuff coming and coming, on and on, without end, they just got demoralized."

I recalled his words often in the late 1980s, when, as a young academic, I would visit Japan to discuss the manufacturing competition then bracing the world economy. At the time, I was the studying the increasing prowess of the Japanese manufacturing system and its apparent ability to be transplanted to the United States and around the world—the gleaming new automotive assembly plants and steel-rolling mills that were revitalizing our American Midwest. My Japanese hosts, ever polite, would always interject at the end of my remarks. "Professor Florida," they would say, "isn't it so sad what has happened to your country? You were once the envy of the manufacturing world, with your great automotive assembly in Detroit and the towering steel mills of Pittsburgh. We made pilgrimages there to study and learn from you. But now your factories are falling apart—the technology is low, their productivity poor, and quality truly suffers. We want to help you now. We are building new plants and restoring old ones in your country, to give back to you, the country that taught us so much."

I would recall my father's pride and, struggling to hold back my own emotion, retort as politely as possible: "I think it would be a mistake to write the United States off. We've had some tough times, yes. Your manufacturing system and great factories are now the envy of the world. But America has an uncanny ability to remake itself for new times." Sure enough, the 1990s witnessed the high-tech boom and the amazing recovery of the U.S. economy; even as this happened, the Japanese economy became mired in recession. The U.S. had pulled it together one more time.

Can we do it again? That's the question before each and every one of us. I say this humbly and with great nervousness: This is the toughest economic and social challenge we've faced in a long, long time. For the first time in my life, I'm honestly not so certain.

## The Greatest Competitive Threat of Our Time

This is no time to mince words. I have studied economic competitiveness for more than twenty years, and in my opinion this is the gravest threat to our economic competitiveness of the past century. If left unaddressed, it will make what the Japanese did to our manufacturing prowess in the 1980s and 1990s look like a walk in the park. This threat is similar in my view to the world-shattering economic battle between ourselves, the United Kingdom, and Germany set in motion by the Industrial Revolution, out of which the United States eventually emerged as the world's economic superpower.

But this one is different—very different. And that's what makes it so perplexing and hard to grapple with. Competition today is not limited to one, two, or even several great powers. Rather, it comes from many places simultaneously, and is harder to home in on precisely because it's so diffuse. The most likely scenario, in my view, is not that one nation will overtake the U.S. as the dominant power on the global stage, but just that the world stage will see the rise of many more significant players.

There is perhaps no more popular guessing game in the halls of international affairs than predicting which nation will threaten the United States as the next great power. In *The Rise and Fall of Great Powers,* Paul Kennedy famously laid out the conditions by which nation-states and empires ascend to global power and eventually decline, almost always as a result of their own actions. The United States,

Kennedy famously argued, had become "overstretched" by seeking to maintain and project its military prowess while neglecting its core economic and technological might.[1] This has happened time and again with such regularity in world history that it's hard to completely ignore what might otherwise sound like doomsday comparisons to the British, Dutch, and Spanish empires.

Of late, economic historians and foreign-policy pundits tell us we are in the midst of another great power shift, this one from the United States to Asia. Writes Fareed Zakaria:

> There have been two great shifts in the international balance of power over the past 500 years. The first was the rise of Western Europe, which by the late 17th century had become the richest, most dynamic and expansionist part of the globe. The second was the rise of the United States of America, which between the Civil War and World War I became the single most important country in the world. Right now a trend of equal magnitude is taking place: the rise of Asia, led by China, which will fundamentally reshape the international landscape in the next few decades. . . . India is growing with impressive resilience and determination. And because of its size, it adds another huge weight to the Asian balance.

Such predictions have been going on for some time and are not entirely off base, of course. Much growth over the past two decades has indeed taken place in Asia—first in Japan, then the East Asian tigers (Taiwan, Hong Kong, South Korea, and Singapore), and now in India and China. And certainly Asia has emerged as a sizable market and well-developed economy, larger and faster growing than either North America's or Europe's. Others, like T. R. Reid and Jeremy Rifkin, believe the main challenger is a revitalized, expanded, and emboldened Europe, with its large markets, excellent universities, and social democratic institutions.[2] But it's hard to imagine how either Europe or Asia alone could completely overtake the United States anytime in the near future.

In fact, no single country in the world is ready to emerge as the singular great power—not China or India, not Japan or Germany, not Canada, Australia, or any of the Scandinavian nations. While each of these has certain strengths and advantages, all suffer from weaknesses as well. Canada and Australia are relatively open societies but lack the strong technology base and market size to dominate the global arena. Both rank low not only on our measures of creative class and GCI, but also on the Index of Economic Freedom, coming in well behind Mexico, Brazil, Poland, and the Philippines at 118th (India) and 122nd (China). The Scandinavian nations are centers of tolerance and self-expression, have solid technology infrastructures, but are simply too small to become true world powers. India and China have the market size and potential technology and human capital base, but are far from having the kind of openness and tolerance required to attract talent on the world stage.

Thinking only in terms of the rise and fall of *great* powers, though, blinds us to a more likely scenario. We shouldn't assume an impending shift in power from the U.S. to a single emerging great power. The logic of globalization goes against this. Corporations are now free to locate where they want, and more importantly, people can move freely to places that offer opportunity, freedom, and the ability to build the lives they choose. The mobility of people is perhaps the single greatest fact of the modern global economy—more important than the rise of new technology or the mobility of capital. In such an environment, it is much more likely that *many* places will gain particular advantages and that the shape of the global economy will grow more complicated and multipolar. It will likely be a mosaic of competitors, each with unique abilities to attract and mobilize talent.

The key for the United States, then, is to design a strategy that enables it to prosper in this emerging multipolar world. To do so, it must bolster its great universities and science and technology assets, cultivate new creative industry sectors, prepare its people for the future, and most of all remain an open society. But much of what the U.S. is now doing only serves to undercut its position. For decades, the U.S. has succeeded at attracting and growing talented people because of its creative ecosystem—a densely interwoven fabric of institutions, individuals, and economic and social rights. Attracting people does not just happen; it depends on the care and feeding of the organizations and people that make up this ecosystem. Perturb it or damage it in small ways and, like any ecosystem, it can die. The problem is: We don't yet fully understand how this ecosystem works. We don't know which fauna feed off which flora, and what kind of balances are in place. The ecosystem was easy enough to understand when we assumed it was premised on the one simple credo: economic self-interest. Now, though, the increased mobility of talent has shattered our conceptions of national and even personal boundaries.

How to adapt to the realities of this shifting ecosystem? America must start by confronting the hard fact that it's no longer as unilaterally dominant as it once was. I concur wholeheartedly with Peter Drucker's assessment that America's leadership in both political parties, on the left as well as the right, must get beyond the myth of the U.S. as an unassailable superpower. There are many more players occupying many more niches and competing vigorously on the world stage. When asked if the U.S. would lose its economic dominance at any point in the foreseeable future, Drucker replied: "The dominance of the U.S. is already over. What is emerging is a world economy of blocs represented by NAFTA, the European Union, ASEAN. There's no one center in this world economy."[3]

Rather than a single deathblow, the U.S. is much more likely to see its dominance eroded by the sting of those thousand cuts. America will continue to be squeezed between the global talent magnets of Canada, Australia, and the Scandinavian countries, who are developing their technological capabilities, becoming even more open and tolerant, and competing effectively for creative people; and the large emerging economies of India and China, who rake in a greater share of low-cost production and are now competing more effectively for their own talent. Whether America suffers a long, slow decline, or rebounds to skillfully navigate this new playing field, depends entirely on how willing it is to restore its creativity and openness to full capacity.

## Who Will Carry the Ball?

Perhaps the most troubling thing is that no one seems aware of the problem and ready and able to carry the ball. The United States today lacks the kind of collective effort that pulled it together during previous times of economic change and transformation. Business and government working together got our economy back on track during the New Deal period, the incredible World War II mobilization, and the effort to set up a vibrant framework for the postwar economy. Business responded vigorously to the competitive threat posed a few short decades ago by Asian and European manufacturers, forming organizations like the Council of Competitiveness as the federal government undertook efforts to support greater research and innovation. Where will that thrust come from today?

Business has the clout, but has not yet begun to focus on this problem. Today's companies are more global than they've ever been. Years ago, Robert Reich posed the controversial question "Who Is Us?" At the time, the Big Three carmakers were opening plants offshore while closing plants at home; Honda and other Japanese manufacturers were, in turn, opening plants on and bringing jobs to our own soil. Today, business has gone truly global, operating R&D centers, offices, and production units worldwide. Given the immense effort it takes to shift the policy debate in this country, and to influence gargantuan agencies like Immigration and Naturalization Services (INS), the State Department, and the Department of Homeland Security— all while risking the appearance of not being properly concerned with national security and terrorism—it's simply easier for many companies to open offshore branches or use their existing foreign facilities to recruit top talent where it exists.

Political leadership is also unwilling to pick up the ball. On the one hand, Washington moves slowly, is bureaucratic, overly political, and a hard place to get things done. While many mayors are concerned about these issues, there are very few national-level politicians in either major political party willing to take on the challenge. The Republicans—and especially the Bush administration—have been obsessed with homeland security. Indeed, they have staked their entire reputation of late on this one overriding concern. The Democrats, on the other hand, are scared to touch any political hot potato that might touch off their constituencies' concern for jobs and unemployment.

Part of what now holds us back is actually our previous successes. The U.S. was the dominant player of the industrial age. As Mancur Olson long ago warned, such hegemonic powers face huge disadvantages by virtue of their dominance.[4] The very nature of their substantial advantage makes it difficult for them to change, while up-and-comers have every incentive to try harder. As our macrolevel social and economic realities crystallize, harden, and become set in stone, so do the realities that govern our everyday interactions. Such politics, Olson argued, tends to favor small, focused interests on the political extremes, leaving it structurally unable to focus its attention on the issues that face the majority. Theoretically, representation of causes at the extremes would be a healthy trait for the overall diversity of our democratic system. There is often greater incentive for those with something to lose to organize and influence politics, and outliers keep the status quo honest.

Unfortunately, in recent years the powerful political forces at either end of the spectrum have tended to widen a right–left chasm that grows less and less navigable and a dichotomy between materialistic and moralistic values that grows more and more false. At the same time that truly important issues don't even get mentioned in the public sphere, the extremes have actually become the status quo. The end result is that people grow disillusioned with the political process and choose not to participate. The leading force for political change, the creative class, has for all intents and purposes opted out of the political process. Instead, its members vote with their feet, looking for the city, region, or country that offers the most opportunity and best reflects their values.

Here we confront a deep and insidious tension of the creative age. Unlike previous dominant classes, such as the working class, members of the creative class have little direct incentive to become involved in conventional politics. When we get involved in broader social issues, we're likely to do it in on a local scale or through some alternative way of our own choosing rather than through either of the major political parties. The whole basis of the creative ethos is individual creative pursuit and the shunning of traditional forms. The paradox is that this ethos is not necessarily conducive to the highly organized political effort needed to bring our new age to the fore. When I posed the dilemma of political action to a successful young African-American creative class member, he captured the essence of the problem succinctly: "Our energy is best applied elsewhere."

The end result is a gaping vacuum, and nothing to fill it. The biggest competitiveness crisis in thirty or forty years and no leading-edge group to take it on. Thus the central dilemma of our time: Even though the creative economy generates vast innovative, wealth-creating, and productive promise, left to its own devices it will neither realize that promise nor solve the myriad social problems confronting us today.

## From Creative Economy to Creative Society

If the creative economy is here to stay, it is also terribly incomplete. Like a turbocharged engine lacking a chassis to harness the horsepower it generates, ours is an economic system in search of the institutional and social arrangements that can unleash its full potential. The real challenge of our time, in America and around the world, is to complete the system we have given rise to—to build the fully creative society that can channel the creative economic energy we have unleashed. The potential is immense. Today, for perhaps the first time in human history, we have the opportunity to align economic and human development. Indeed, our future economic prosperity turns on making the most of each and every human being's talents and energies.

New kinds of social institutions and policies will be needed to complete the system and make it work well. We can't know exactly what these will look like in advance. It will take time—a long time—to figure this out. Adapting to the industrial age took decades of give-and-take and plenty of experiments that failed. But eventually we built a broader industrial society that was able to support the remarkable productive capacity of the great industrial engine that had first emerged decades earlier. As we completed that system, we embarked on a golden age of rising productivity and living standards.

The challenge that faces the United States and the world today is similar to that posed by the rise of a modern industrial economy. The Industrial Revolution created enormous productive potential alongside deep social and economic problems. The transformation ushered in a period of incredible innovation, productivity improvement, and wealth creation. New industries were formed: railroad, steel, automobile, chemical, and others. But the returns on that increased productivity were highly unequal, accruing mainly to robber barons and their ilk. Manufacturing workers made little and toiled long hours in deplorable—and often fatal—conditions. Cities were filthy and filled with smoke, refuse flowed down streets, and ecological and public-health nightmares abounded.

The full potential of the nascent industrial age required the development of a much more broadly based industrial *society* in which great masses of people could participate. This industrial society did not emerge on its own, but was spurred into existence by a series of policy interventions that gradually evolved and were institutionalized over the period stretching from the Great Depression and New Deal years into the immediate post–World War II era. So it took politics some time to catch up, but ultimately FDR figured out a way to patch together not just a winning political coalition but, crucially, a growth coalition, which matched business with working-class people and minorities. He bridged the divide between the two dominant classes—business and labor.

The success of his solution rested on the Keynesian nature of these interventions: the fact that they increased wages, boosted demand, and thus also spurred the growth and development of key industrial sectors. These programs encouraged the development of mass-production industries, from cars to appliances, by expanding the availability of home mortgages, investing in the development of a large-scale interstate highway system, expanding higher education, and increasing investments in research and development, among other things. But these policies and approaches also dealt effectively with the externalities of the unmediated industrial economy during its so-called gilded age.

Most amazingly, they did so in a way that didn't stoke the fires of class warfare. These programs actually brought capital and labor closer together by encouraging the development of mass-production unions, by linking wage increases to productivity gains, by improving health and safety in the workplace, and by creating social security for older people and basic social-welfare services for the truly needy. This system thus squared the circle, driving the expansion of the industrial economy by allowing many more people (read: political and socio-economic constituencies) to benefit from it, while simultaneously addressing a whole range of its negative externalities.

Like the Industrial Revolution in its initial days more than a century ago, the creative economy is taking shape in ways that tap but a fraction of its extraordinary potential. Worse yet, it is doing so by concentrating its benefits and rewards on a very narrow faction of the workforce, a phenomenon that can only fan the flames of a deepening class divide. The creative economy is the Schumpeterian growth engine of our age, and the socioeconomic dynamic it sets in motion is the modern-day equivalent of the divide Roosevelt faced—the growth of two divergent classes: the creative and the service sectors. I'm not arguing for the return to the policies and programs of the New Deal. These programs and policies were designed for the industrial age and would thus be ineffective if applied directly to the creative economy. Instead, we need a strategy that is the modern-day *equivalent* of the New Deal—one that stimulates the creative economic engine while at the same time extending its benefits to a broad base of people.

Lasting competitive advantage today will not simply amass in those countries and regions that can generate the most creative, innovative, or entrepreneurial output.[5] The places that will be most able to absorb new energies will be those that are both open to diversity and also capable of internalizing the externalities that the creative economy gives rise to. It will no longer be sufficient to incubate new creative industries or generate more creative people. The most successful places will require a *socially adaptive* capability that will enable them to pioneer new fields and innovative industries even as they effectively cope with problems like income inequality, housing affordability, uneven development, and underutilized human potential in new and innovative ways. Most of all, these solutions must do that in ways that inspire the entrepreneurial drive of these individuals and extend the benefits of the creative economy to a broader segment of the population.

To be effective, a fuller, more creative society will require that a large number of individuals feel they have a real stake in its emergence and expansion. Right now, many people are being left behind by the creative economy. They're anxious, and feel unprepared. They look around and see their economic circumstances worsening, their towns and communities being left behind as growth and prosperity accrue to a curious mix of immigrants, singles, and nontraditional households in places like San Francisco, Boston, Austin, Seattle, New York, or Los Angeles. Their resentment is often heightened by the fact that these are the very places their own children are fascinated by or even move to. They see an old economic order being transformed and the values they live by seemingly undercut. Afraid as they are of what the future holds for them, it's no surprise they look fondly backward.

The great disappointment of our age—of its business and political leadership and of the creative class in general—is our collective failure to provide a clear vision of how the broad swath of society can prosper and succeed in this economy. This is particularly important because the creative age demands that individuals take on tremendous levels of risk. As the institutions that once helped organize our chaotic realities—the corporation, the community, the nation, and the family—have broken down or decentralized, stress and anxiety have been downloaded directly onto the individual.

Those societies that can adapt *socially* to the creative age, that can balance individual achievement against risk—in effect, socializing some of this risk and enabling individuals to be more productive and creative—will gain a huge advantage. America's often unfettered cowboy capitalism and its accompanying high anxiety levels do pump creativity out of certain people, it's true. But in a survival-of-the-fittest economy, only those people will survive. A new group of regions and countries, such as Canada, the Scandinavian and Nordic nations, even Australia, may well have the advantage in addressing the two horns of the new, modern-day economic dilemma. This advantage comes not from any preordained plan, but from the gradually evolved capability to cope with individual and social risk. America has a long way to go to catch up in this regard.

## An Agenda for the Creative Age

To succeed and to prosper in the creative age, the United States and other nations and regions around the world will need to make the transition from industrial to creative societies by investing in their people, building up their creative capital, and remaining open, tolerant societies. This is not just in their individual interest. The creative age holds out the promise to harness the talents and reward the energies of a far greater number of human beings and for the first time to connect economic and human development.

So where to start? We—our business and political leaders, but also each and every one of us—must recognize that building a thriving economy and prosperous, creative society is a nonpartisan, nonideological issue. The challenges facing our nation and the world are too important for the dialogue surrounding them to be clouded by political bickering and polarization, the cultural wars, or short-term economic agendas. One of the great paradoxes of the creative age is that, even as it relies on the entrepreneurial spark of individuals to ignite its flames, its heat and light will only last if they are tended by the broader society. While it's hard to see a leading force for political change today, people are often apolitical only until someone comes along who, for the first time, articulates the positions they care about. Both parties fail to excite large segments of the population today, but there's a huge political windfall awaiting the first politician who can figure out how to incorporate us all into a larger, more productive, and more fulfilling creative economy.

It's impossible—and undesirable—to outline a ten-, fifty-, or one-hundred-point plan for building the creative society; this cannot be a top-down or centralized endeavor, but needs to emerge organically from the insights, efforts, and energies of varied groups of people and organizations working every day on addressing the concerns of our collective future. There are, however, several key principles that I hope can serve as signposts on the road to navigate this future.

## Tap the Full Creative Capabilities of Everyone

First and foremost, we must strive to tap the full creative capabilities of every single human being. The creative class is doing well, and taking care of itself. Addressing the needs of the 30 percent of the workforce employed in this class is important, but it won't be enough. To both prevent widespread social unrest *and* benefit economically from the creative input of the maximum number of its citizens, the U.S. and other countries will have to find ways to bring the service and manufacturing sectors more fully into the creative age. In this respect, our greatest challenge involves both the growing class divide that the creative age is producing and the huge reservoir of untapped creative capital that is being squandered. Addressing this divide is not only socially and morally just; it is an economic imperative for any society interested in long-term innovation and prosperity.

Ambitious goals require ambitious means, and this one must entail a massive effort to upgrade the pay, working conditions, and social status of the huge number of service and manufacturing jobs our economy is generating. We need to expand the purview of the creative economy—to massively augment the numbers of people who participate in it and benefit from it. During the Great Depression and New Deal, the United States succeeded in turning a huge number of formerly low-skill, low-paying, blue-collar occupations into the kind of jobs that could support working-class families and become the launchpad for upward mobility. We did that for a good reason: Those were the growth jobs of the industrial age. But today—painful as it is for the people who lose them—those jobs are declining, and they have been declining for four or five decades.

We are, however, seeing the dramatic rise of two kinds of jobs:

high-paying, high-skilled jobs in the creative sector and much lower-paying, lower-skill jobs in the service sector. As I have said before, it is not enough to prime the pump of the creative sector. Just as we improved manufacturing jobs seventy years ago, we must act to improve the pay, content, and working conditions of the second great source of jobs in today's economy—service-sector jobs—the port-of-entry jobs to the creative economy. What's more, personal-service industries that require close physical proximity are practically impervious to outsourcing. It's hard to have your hair cut by someone in Bangalore. These jobs are immensely rewarding from a personal-creativity standpoint, too, and provide further opportunities for those who hold them to utilize the human creativity inherent in all of us.

When I say every human being is creative, I don't mean we ought to expect every human being to write great symphonies or design monumental buildings. As a group, we wouldn't be very effective if all we did was the kind of work that people usually consider "creative." What I am arguing for is a broadening of the very definition of creativity, one that will ennoble and encourage the everyday efforts of "ordinary" occupations. For all the benefits that our modern-day meritocracy bestows upon us, it has yet to teach us how to truly appreciate the work of a housekeeper or a fieldworker. Even when we do look upon these occupations with admiration, it is often with a sort of wistful nostalgia for the good old days, or with the respect afforded a good workhorse. It is, in short, a condescending appreciation. The idea that barbers, landscapers, or factory line workers might actually be motivated in part by some sort of aesthetic, intellectual, or emotional pleasure escapes us. My father exemplified this zeal for creative investment on the job; he toiled because it paid the bills, of course, but he and his fellow factory workers made improvements in the way the very structure of their institution was run because they cared deeply about their craft.

Again, FDR was ahead of the curve in recognizing this human trait decades ago. "Happiness," he said, "is not in the mere possession of money; it lies in the joy of achievement, in the thrill of creative effort." Later, Studs Terkel would observe the same common yearning: "Even for the lowliest laborers," writes Adam Cohen of the *New York*

*Times,* "Mr. Terkel found, work was a search, sometimes successful, sometimes not, for daily meaning as well as daily bread." This meaning no doubt differed—and still differs—across profession, age group, and background. But its basis, a strong desire to transcend the economic self in search of a higher cause, remains true in this day and age more than ever before.

If these workers are so happy with their daily quests for meaning, why the need to pay them more, or grant some kind of increased social status? Self-actualization on the job is grand, but if the basic needs of food, safety, and shelter are not taken care of, we can't expect these people to continue to contribute in meaningful ways to the shops, properties, factories, and institutions that we all utilize and benefit from. And these are the people whose energies will be needed to move the creative economy forward.

Beyond creating opportunities *for* people, a truly creative society would value the opportunities and ideas flowing *from* its people. I can't help but think here of a woman I met in Oklahoma City whose nine-year-old son had big plans for the future of his downtown. He envisioned a large-scale complex, a sort of community center, where kids and adults from the neighborhood would come to play with LEGOs. Yes, LEGOs. The small plastic bricks of a young child's fantasyland. But there was something more to his fantasy. He wanted the center to be a place where the local homeless population would feel comfortable, and where they could interact with the city's residents. Children and old folks alike would come to talk about their community, making use of the abundant multicolored plastic bricks on hand to model possible future plans, make giant and minuscule works of public art, and, well, just enjoy one another's company.

What are the chances you'd find a politician to sign on to such a plan, dreamed up by a child (he was only nine, and hadn't quite made it through his architectural training)? Slim to none, of course. But this is innovative thinking, nonetheless. To have gathered in one place the fields of art, engineering, civics, social work, and entertainment—*that* is a combination for the creative age. My point is not that our city councils should be funding the daydreams of nine-year-olds everywhere (I imagine you'd rack up quite a bill), but that, as a community, we need to start paying more serious attention to the creative ideas of our youngest, our oldest, and generally our most marginalized members. If this kid is making plans for such multi-use facilities in elementary school, imagine what he'll be doing in another fifteen years—with the right combination of education, practical experience, and civic encouragement.

## INVEST IN CREATIVE INFRASTRUCTURE

Yet we don't seem terribly concerned about investing in the future of innovative inquiry. Instead, the U.S. government is cutting key areas of R&D spending, while corporate R&D funding was also down by nearly $8 billion in 2002, the largest single-year decline since the 1950s.[6] State governments have slashed funds for higher education and for arts and culture while pumping up funds for stadiums, convention centers, and other bricks-and-mortar projects. Never mind that the local economic benefits of such projects often turn into the red the minute the last construction worker drives off the site. These choices signal a profound lack of understanding of what an atmosphere of innovation requires.

Investing in innovation and in our collective creative infrastructure is important for the United States and for the world. As Paul Romer and other leading students of innovation have shown, investments in innovations and ideas have extraordinary rates of return and promise to pay incredible dividends precisely because they are public goods; the benefits they confer are broad and reverberate throughout the entire economy.

Around the world, in fact, leading countries will have to spend significantly more on research and development and on higher education, opening up universities and colleges to take in more of the world's best and brightest. Like earlier efforts to build canals, railroads, highways, and other physical infrastructure to power industrial growth, the United States and countries around the world must invest in their *creative* infrastructure if they want to succeed and prosper in the future. Again, if it is to do any good, the scale of the effort required will dwarf the public-education system, land-grant colleges, and the GI Bill of a previous generation. Investments in human capital are the single most important investments we make. We need a massive increase in our ability and capacity to educate and train people from primary and secondary education through the most advanced stages of higher education.

To make the most of increased education and training investments, countries must redouble their efforts to generate high-end creative jobs in R&D, innovation, higher education, and arts and culture. They must reduce barriers to entrepreneurship and encourage even more new company formation. In short, the world economy requires a wide-reaching effort not just to pump out creative talent but also to increase the *market* for creative opportunities.

Investment in creative infrastructure means more than just increased R&D spending. It must involve massive increases in spending—from both the private and public sectors—in the arts, culture, and all forms of innovation and creativity. For proof of the potential of arts and culture to make big economic waves, we need look no further than the other side of the Atlantic. In the spring of 2003, I had the good fortune to meet with high-ranking British economic officials in Tony Blair's cabinet. We were on the topic of high-tech clusters, and they voiced concern over their ability to ever overtake the U.S. in this field. We began to brainstorm other possible British niches, and, as a way to spur the conversation, I asked the ministers to rattle off the richest people in the UK. They shot back without hesitation, and in their list I began to notice a pattern: Paul McCartney, Mick Jagger, Elton John, and David Bowie. Someone joked that not only were these performers fabulously wealthy—most of them had been knighted, too. Largely without realizing it, the UK had created a killer industrial cluster.

To be honest, it was the first time the culture-cluster connection had ever occurred to me, but on the spot we decided that perhaps one of the industries that warranted attention was popular and rock music. Imagine what could happen if you actually thought consciously about ways to support and grow this field, I said. Why wouldn't the United States, or at least cities within our country, want to do the same thing to boost some of their biggest stars—and, better, rising talents? Instead of turning our national cultural icons into anti-American straw men and turning around the airplanes and visa grants of their international counterparts, it's time we begin to embrace the diversity and freedom of expression—and corresponding economic opportunity—that American and world music embody.

Only when we begin to see all of these investments—scientific, economic, artistic, cultural, and other—as mutually reinforcing parts of the same creative whole will we begin to take advantage of even a fraction of our latent human potential. Unfortunately, one of the places that has the most to teach us about such fusion of creative energies, the university, is also under assault.

## LEVERAGE UNIVERSITIES AS TALENT AND TOLERANCE MAGNETS

Universities are the intellectual hubs of the creative economy. America's vital university system is the source of much of our best scientific, social, and creative leadership. To this point, though, our modern conception of what universities could or should be has been somewhat limited. The tendency to see universities primarily as the laboratories of new research and technology has grown particularly acute in the last twenty years. They do indeed serve our society as technological and scientific laboratories—and amazingly productive ones. But they are much more than that.

Universities also do a remarkable job of fostering the other two Ts of economic growth: talent and tolerance. On the one hand, they are undeniably powerful talent magnets, attracting (as we've seen in previous chapters) the best and brightest to our shores. They are the Ellis Islands of the creative age. A huge percentage of the high-tech entrepreneurs that power places like Silicon Valley; Austin, Texas; and the Research Triangle came here originally to attend graduate school. Not surprisingly, almost all of our leading creative regions have one or more great universities. Hence their incredible potential to continually incorporate top talent from every corner of the earth. Unfortunately, we now seem to want to send our top foreign talent packing. "When you graduate from Stanford University with an advanced degree in the sciences or engineering, we then make you go home," venture capitalist John Doerr told Silicon Valley's Technet Innovation Summit. "We should be stapling a green card to your diploma."

Higher-education institutions are also the community entities that, perhaps more than any other, have opened up city after city and college town after college town to the world. In this respect, they are bastions and breeders of tolerance. A university, with its tendency toward openness to ideas, people, and practices not always considered mainstream, is a natural source of diversity—whether ethnic, socio-economic, or cultural. Readers of my work who come to see creative centers as somehow aligned with the coasts are always surprised to see how highly places such as Iowa City, Iowa; Champaign, Illinois; and Corvallis, Oregon, rank on our creativity indices. In case after case, this occurs when states and communities were forward-looking enough to support great institutions of higher education early on.

In this sense, universities and colleges don't serve just the economic winners of the creative age. They represent the key building blocks that cities such as Cleveland, St. Louis, and Pittsburgh can use to rebuild. Kevin Stolarick and our research team have also found that the "higher education–knowledge–learning cluster" is always among the top employers of both creative class workers and service-sector workers in major U.S. regions. I was once asked what I thought might be one of the keys to saving Detroit's economy. My answer was simple: Ann Arbor. What I mean by this is not that Detroit's downtown and neighborhoods aren't important (they are, of course, crucial), but that the future of the Detroit region in the creative age lies more with the technology, talent, and tolerance engine that is Ann Arbor than in stadiums and a refurbished Renaissance center in downtown Detroit.

But how many political and business leaders in these kinds of regions are ready to act on this? How many of them are willing to believe that their future lies more in something as apparently abstract as using their universities as teachers and exemplars of tolerance? Where is the devotion to rebuilding our communities, economies, and culture around such institutions in any kind of meaningful or authentic way, when it so much easier to build a stadium, downtown mall, in-dustrial park, or business incubator? The latter category delivers—at first glance—more immediate results. In this way it seems we're again locked into an industrial-age materialist mind-set that has trouble ac-counting for the benefits of the more intangible creative age.

As a result, higher education doesn't make the cut in tough eco-nomic times. State after state consistently cuts its public higher-education budget, and the resulting system of American universities is made less and less accessible to those whom it could benefit the most. The federal government expands research funding at the margins while restricting access and politicizing cutting-edge scientific issues like stem-cell research. China and India, in the meantime, are pump-ing money into their universities and graduate schools.

How much longer can we rest on our laurels? It's hard to say. It's certainly true that we built the world's greatest university system and still maintain a commanding lead in that respect. But now we're let-ting this most crucial component of our creative infrastructure atro-phy even as others are biting at our heels more and more aggressively. At best, we're teaching the world's citizens and then forcing them to go back to their home countries. At worst, we're conditioning those students not to come here in the first place. And we're giving ample reason to our own population to begin seeking educational opportu-nities elsewhere. This is not bad in and of itself, of course. We need more than anything to foster globally minded young people in this day and age. But it would be preferable if they went abroad proud of their country and looking to come back and share their insights—rather than discouraged by our increasing political and economic iso-lationism and frustrated by the rising costs of learning skills and ideas that would be beneficial to all.

## EDUCATE PEOPLE FOR THE CREATIVE AGE

The problems with education do not by any stretch of the imagina-tion start when our children turn eighteen. For decades, many in K-12 circles and elsewhere have called for education reform. What is needed is, in fact, a full-scale overhaul in the way we go about teaching our children. We can no longer succeed—or even tread water—with an education system handed down to us from the industrial age, since what we no longer need is assembly-line workers. We need one that instead reflects and reinforces the values, priorities, and requirements of the creative age. Education reform must, at its core, make schools into places where human creativity is cultivated and can flourish. Americans revel in the legendary stories of young creators like Michael Dell building new businesses in dorm rooms or in the garage in their spare time. The question to ask ourselves is: Why are they doing these things in their *spare* time? Isn't this the real stuff of education in the creative age? Schools need to be vehicles for enhancing and mobilizing the creative capacities of all our children so that the tinkering of today can be translated into the creative advancement of tomorrow.

Expanding education in this country is not only a matter of basic human rights; it is an economic imperative. As we've already seen, human capital is the most important investment a country makes. We did it with the public school system. We did it with the land-grant universities. We did it with the GI Bill. Now we have to expand our system by several orders of magnitude more than these previous successful expansions. From Head Start through advanced education, English as a Second Language classrooms through full arts and culture funding, we can no longer afford to cater only to the monolithic notion of rote memorization that was important for the Industrial Revolution but has now become woefully outdated.

Many venues for alternatives to our industrial-age educational system have already sprung up. The "Met" (Metropolitan Regional and Technical Center), a state-funded public school in Providence, Rhode Island, has created a new model of education around the idea of real practice. Children are taught not just to think but to do, a welcome change from a system in which arts, music, and physical-education classes are always the first to go. In a similar move, companies such as the SAS Institute have instituted on-site schools that offer a more well-rounded and in many ways more practical education for the creative age. The Gates Foundation has stepped up as another leading private proponent of small schools and experientially based education. But it's a shame that we can't as a general public get behind anteing up for our children's—and indeed our collective—future. The closest we get to discussing the issue is creating false zero-sum games between standardized, traditional education, and newer models that explore different creative potentials.

Of course, both the fundamentals and the more creative fields are crucial to our economic success. India has a huge advantage over the U.S. because so many of its young people excel in mathematics. This translates into jobs not only in computer science and software programming but also in market research and the development of new financial instruments. So of course we need to get back to basics. The basics are not enough, though. What we really need in order to prepare our children for the creative economy is a comprehensive education, something that takes them from aesthetics to algebra without pretending that the two are mutually exclusive. In an environment mired in homeland security and missile defense systems, it's predictable that one or the other often falls by the wayside.

As the quip goes, it will be a strange day when our schools get all the billions they need and the army has to hold a bake sale to fund its bombers. Instead, we are forced to divvy up the paltry sums of money and support given to our educational system among competing recipients—mathematics and music, for instance—that shouldn't have to be competing in the first place. Forget about altruism; in the future, we boomers would all do well to make sure we're raising smart, creative kids—not just our own, but everyone's—if we ever hope to stop working before we hit eighty-five. To make this happen, we need to see to it that, from an early age, our entire population is encouraged to develop its people skills with its multiplication tables and its creative and entrepreneurial potential with its reading abilities. Not only will such an educational system develop each of its members more fully; it will also be capable of getting more of the population pulled into the mix in the first place.

As society diversifies and specializes, more and more different kinds of education and teaching styles must be made available. Vocational schools, experiential and study-abroad programs, music laboratories—

all will play a vital part in the creative age. At times, in fields such as public policy and economics, we focus a bit myopically on science and engineering. I myself am guilty of this, coming as I do from a technologically based background. Perhaps this is because these are the most easily "translatable" fields, the ones in which we can show the direct economic benefits most clearly to the general public. But make no mistake, disc-jockey schools and art and entrepreneurship seminars are beginning to spring up all over the place, and they are valuable contributors to our nation's culture and economy. Science and engineering will always be important fields, but as part of a renewed educational effort we ought to make sure that our children feel just as socially validated entering the glass-blowing course or culinary arts master's class of their dreams.

Parents also need to be recognized and rewarded more fully for their role in the educational process. Study after study has shown that, in the end, parents are what makes or breaks a child's ability and desire to become lifelong learners. Unfortunately, as Phillip Longman's research shows, parents face perverse disincentives to educate their children. Longman deems it a "curious truth about American politics today" that "elected officials love to talk about 'family values' and 'investing in our kids,' but shy away from proposing anything big or new that would actually help them." On the contrary, the system is configured in such a way that raising a child—let alone sending him or her to a good school—is an enormous economic burden. It's one thing to see the rearing of a young one as a benefit only to the happy parents and therefore to brush off the complaint (as many have) as self-centered or even discriminatory against those without children. But the economic and demographic realities of our time lead to this obvious conclusion: Our future depends more than anything else on smart, creative kids.

And yet, what Longman calls "the deepening dependency all people have on both the quantity and quality of other people's children" falls by the wayside in political and economic discussions. He asks us to consider the following anecdote about "where doctors come from":

Human capital does not just spring into being, nor is it simply a product of higher education. Doctors, for example, must first be born. Doctors must also, for many years, be swaddled, fed, and comforted—by someone. Prodigious human effort is further required to teach them to read their first sentence and to add their first sums. Indeed, teaching them to read almost always requires far more adult effort and pedagogical savvy than teaching them biochemistry, the latter of which is usually performed in large lecture halls by teaching assistants and junior faculty members. Moreover, because doctors must be trusted with highly technical life-and-death decisions, they had also better acquire a strong sense of morality, a balanced personality, sober habits of living, and discipline—all of which will most likely require vast commitments of time and money by parents and other nurturing adults.[7]

The real irony, he continues, is that even as we leave individual parents to bear the lion's share of the growing costs of raising the children who sustain the system, these individuals retain a dwindling share of the value they create. "As a rule," Longman laments, "the more involved one becomes in the nurturing of the next generation, the less compensation one is likely to receive. Those who devote themselves full time to raising their children receive no wages. Day-care workers take home less pay than hotel maids. Elementary school teachers could easily make more money as casino dealers." It's no wonder that in most of the advanced nations reproduction rates have dropped below the necessary repopulation levels.

At the systemic level, too, there are disincentives for cities and local governments to invest heavily in education. The mobile nature of the creative economy has broken the age-old connection between where people are educated and where they work. This fuels concerns by U.S. regions and countries around the world that they are experiencing a brain drain, as their talented and skilled people move to other locations. Consider this: Just 10 percent of U.S. regions have a positive score on our Brain Gain Index, a measure of the number of people a region educates through college versus the number of people with a college degree in their labor force. That means 90 percent of U.S. regions suffer a net export of people. As we used to say about Pittsburgh: "The region's key export is no longer steel, but its talent."

The highly mobile nature of the creative economy hampers the already tenuous public-education system with added disincentive for investment in primary and secondary schools. Regions with topflight universities such as Stanford and MIT also draw the best and brightest high school grads from everywhere and hold on to a disproportionate share of them after graduation. Other regions like Austin import many of their top workers by winning the regional talent exchange, in effect plucking ripe creative workers after they're fully educated elsewhere.

In both scenarios, mobility has broken the connection between local investment in education and regional economic growth. Many regions can do quite well without anteing up a big investment in homegrown talent. Talent-importing hotbeds like the Bay Area and San Diego have thrived in California, home of tax revolt, where public-funding shortfalls often have held back local public-education upgrades. An obvious long-term danger looms: If too many regions begin to rely too heavily on imported talent rather than growing their own, the whole process will peter out.

It's easy enough to give lip service to better school systems, but throwing more money and slogans at the problem will get us only so far. Until we have an overall system that values human creative capital—from our children to the people who raise and educate them—the U.S. will continue to fall behind in educational measures, be they traditional or creative. The looming talent gap will go unfilled, and our national economic competitiveness will decline.

## CITIES AND COMPETITIVENESS

Cities and regions are a country's crucibles of competitiveness in the creative age. Leading scholars concur that urbanization economies are the decisive drivers of economic growth, more important even than technology and innovation. As I argued in *Rise of the Creative Class,* cities are the key economic and social organizing units of the creative age. They promote economies of scale, incubate new technology, and match human capital to opportunities, ideas to places, and innovations to investment. They capitalize on the often chaotic ecosystem that creates previously unforeseen financial, scientific, social, political, and other linkages to one another. Urban centers are therefore a vital element of the infrastructure of creativity and competitiveness. Yet, in the United States as in most other nations, we have relegated cities and urban policy to a social-policy afterthought. At best, cities have been conceived as the responsibility of mayors and city planners. At worst, they have been denigrated as "reservations" where the poor are allowed to exist.

Urban policy must be resurrected from the backwaters of social policy and become a cornerstone of national competitiveness planning. A strong urban policy is as important to our nation's future as a strong innovation policy. Of course, we can't legislate urban creativity any more easily than we can legislate economic growth. What we can do, though, is provide the physical and social space needed for creative and economic opportunities to take root. A simple example of the kind of consideration I'm talking about here would be an initiative in which a city maintained a certain amount of "garage" space. Garages, warehouses, historic buildings, affordable housing—all of these are the places where dreams and economic innovations take hold. Whether for company formation, new music, new film, family business, non-profit or social-service providers, cheap but authentic structures have always served as an inspiration and an invitation to take a chance on our city neighborhoods. Jane Jacobs once again put it best and most simply: "New ideas require old buildings."

In today's creative centers, affordable housing and commercial space is being wiped out at an alarming rate. Artists, musicians, immigrants, and other traditionally marginalized groups are being pushed out of the very neighborhoods they helped to rejuvenate. This is not to say, of course, that real-estate development is evil or that cities can magically revitalize themselves by subsidizing cheap space. But right now the opposite is happening. In our rush to take advantage of the housing booms in our most creative centers, the cranes go up and the people are pushed out. It is yet another irony of the creative age that as we rediscover the importance of vibrant cities, we threaten to choke off the very street-level energy that creates a vibrant creative climate. We must find a healthy balance that allows real-estate development to occur in ways that support rather than inhibit the innovative engines that are our cities.

One strategy that will be crucial in striking this balance in our creative centers will actually be to invest more in other cities around the country. Even as technology allows us to work from virtually anywhere, a key characteristic of the creative age is its tremendous geographic concentration. The creative economy has emerged and remained largely concentrated in perhaps a dozen leading U.S. regions, and a few dozen more around the world. Now we must decentralize and spread the benefits of this economy—to enable people in a much wider range of regions to participate fully. Bringing a wider number of regions into the creative economy will help to take the pressure off the leading creative centers, which are experiencing levels of growth, sprawl, inequality, and housing inaffordability that threaten to choke off the very innovation and growth that created them.

What's more, these older cities are the perfect places to build further extensions of the creative economy. They're filled with the industrial-use architecture, the factory buildings and warehouses, that provide the garage space so crucial to economic innovation. The infrastructure is already in place. As opposed to new suburbs and exurbs where we start anew by clearing fields and forests every day, existing urban centers prove fertile playgrounds for the human imagination— but only if we look at them as an opportunity and not a blight. Such an expansion of urban investment is a win-win-win situation; it reinvigorates older centers, takes the pressure off the new ones, and results in a stronger overall *system* of cities.

Cities function not only as economic drivers, but as laboratories for social and political change. The U.S. would be well advised to pay attention and nurture its traditional status as the world's laboratory of democracy, the place where a federal political system and diversified economies come together to keep us at the forefront of innovation.

Since its inception, this federal system has encouraged not just experimentation at the state and local levels, but also collaboration across states and locales. We may have more problems than we know what to do with, but we also have plenty of latitude in figuring out how to deal with those problems. Other countries with more nationalized or centralized planning and policy have never brought the social and political creativity to the table that the U.S. is able to infuse into its economy.

Luckily, despite the more recent centralization of power in our national government, the United States continues to function in many important ways as a large-scale version of Jacobs's "federation of communities." Even as the federal government may be taking us in perilous directions on one front, on another front a municipal or state government has taken the opportunity to spring up and take the lead. Such laboratories of democracy, as long as they are allowed to exercise some degree of autonomy from the federal government, will continue to provide many of the best solutions in the creative age. But only when we continue to encourage such local experimentation, not choke it off with ever-expanding federal mandates.

In my travels around the country and the world, people often ask me which regions serve as examples or models of what to do. First off I tell them, we are in the early stages of the creative age and it would be a mistake to think that any region has it right. I go on to tell them to craft strategies that are unique to their region, emphasize their distinctive strengths, and focus on what is authentic, real, and different about their community and place. But I also tell them to look beyond the one-sided stories of regions like Silicon Valley, which is a great center of technology and wealth, but suffers from enormous problems of inequality, housing affordability, congestion, and mounting human stress. Go down the Silicon Valley path of unbridled entrepreneurship and technology and be prepared to pay a steep price in terms of an unequal and increasingly dysfunctional and broken-down society. Often I add that it makes sense to look for models outside the United States in regions like Toronto, Stockholm, and Helsinki, all of which combine string technology and creative sectors with relatively low levels of inequality, good schools, low crime, safe streets, and high levels of social cohesion and stability.

But there is at least one region in the United States that may be worth a closer look: Minneapolis–St. Paul. The greater Minneapolis region combines both a strong creative economy with low rates of poverty, affordable housing, and a balanced income distribution, according the detailed research of two of my Carnegie Mellon students, Sarah Kneece and Jennifer Eckstra. It scores among the top U.S regions on my Creativity Index, is one of only 34 U.S. metropolitan regions (out of a total 331) to boast a positive brain-gain index, and is one of just 13 percent of American cities that the Brookings Institution classified as a "balanced" income region.

With large Somali and Hmong immigrant populations, three openly gay city-council members, and an extremely high level of microlevel neighborhood racial integration, the Twin Cities are increasingly known as a bastion of tolerance. Add to this equation affordable housing prices, high wages, low unemployment, and low poverty, and it's easy to see why college students and foreigners alike are flocking to Minneapolis–St. Paul's universities, jobs, and communities. As a result, the region has seen high growth in its creative class occupations—especially in the knowledge and education clusters. The key to its success, then, lies in the fact that not only is it attracting the best and the brightest; it's also taking care of all its citizens and tapping their creative energies. Unfortunately, Minneapolis–St. Paul is the exception to the rule among American regions.

As with many large-scale problems, it makes little sense for one person to make specific recommendations about what many greatly differing regions need. What we will really require, when it comes time to roll up our sleeves and improve our urban centers, is a Manhattan Project on the future of the American city. We owe it to the places that made our country great.


## A TRULY OPEN AND ECONOMICALLY SECURE SOCIETY

The United States and the world face real security concerns. But none of them can trump the need for these advanced nations to remain open societies. As we've seen, openness to people, tolerance, and diversity are critical components of the full equation of economic growth. The United States is impeding its own progress when it makes scientific discovery pass religious tests or tightens visa restrictions unnecessarily. European nations do the same when they give in to domestic political pressure to ban immigrants on the grounds that they cost too much or take away jobs that would otherwise be filled by native-born residents. The record shows that the benefits of being an open, welcoming, diverse, inclusive, and tolerant society far outweigh the costs.

In this regard, we may have much to learn again from our neighbor to the north. Canada has developed a new organizing principle for tolerance and inclusion—one that goes far beyond the melting-pot principle traditionally used as a vehicle for assimilating immigrants to the United States. Canada has replaced the melting-pot metaphor with the principle of a *mosaic society,* which to my mind may be the future organizing principle of the talent-driven creative economy. Rather than assimilate toward defined cultural norms, the idea of the mosaic is that each ethnic group or nationality is welcome for both its ability to contribute to society and for its difference.

It is a principle with which immigrants and all sorts of groups resonate. And it is one that other leading countries, most notably Sweden, a leader in all 3 Ts, have taken note of and are trying to learn from. This point bears emphasis: Sweden is trying to learn about the ability to attract and assimilate immigrants from Canada, rather than from the United States. And there is a more personal dimension as well. Whenever I speak to an international audience, as I related in the story of my visit to Melbourne at the beginning of Chapter 5, someone from Canada will inevitably approach me to discuss the advantages of the mosaic society. Whether they are white or black or Indian, Asian, or Hispanic or mixed race, they always make it a point to express how different it is to be recognized, but not stereotyped or stigmatized, based on one's background—to fit into a multiracial and culturally diverse mosaic society. A Canadian woman who had taken a job with an arts organization in New Jersey characterized the difference this way:

I grew up in Canada asking myself a different set of questions about identity. In Canada, I tried to understand who I was as an individual. In the United States, I am being forced to identify with arbitrary categories. I do not identify as African-American (to the disgrace of black people across the country), nor do I identify as biracial. I am an Indian, black, Portuguese, French, Native American, Trinidadian Montrealer who lives in the United States. I still haven't found the right category for me here.

Ironically, the melting-pot society, which tries to erase ethnic differences, only reinforces their importance. The mosaic model—which says to its citizens: Carve out whatever piece of the puzzle you wish for yourself—leads to a greater emphasis on the human being as an *individual*—a critical advantage in leveraging the creative capacities of each and every person.

To be certain, security is a real issue in the post-9/11 world—and it is not one that is going to disappear soon. Whatever one thinks of the specific issues of Iraq or Afghanistan, Saddam Hussein, or Al Qaeda, the fact is that global terrorism has long been a serious problem—and it is now one that the United States and other advanced countries must deal with effectively. But it is important for both business and political leadership to recognize the economic costs of being overzealous and to think of the serious trade-offs to economic security and long-run competitiveness that are involved. As *Newsweek*'s Fareed Zakaria put it, "Every visa officer today lives in fear that he will let in the next Mohammed Atta. As a result, he is probably keeping out the next Bill Gates."

The United States in particular must act in concrete ways to reassure the world—both Americans and global citizens—that it values openness. Everyone recognizes that security is a profound concern. And of course the Departments of Defense and Homeland Security, the FBI, the Coast Guard, and intelligence agencies naturally think in terms of security first: That's their job. People around the world applaud the country's efforts to improve security. What the world does not like is the arbitrary and sometimes brash methods the U.S. has adopted. As I said at the very beginning of this book, over time, terrorism is less of a threat to U.S. society than the possibility that creative and talented people will stop wanting to live within its borders. To that end, the nation must focus on improving the immigration process immediately and preserve its status and reputation as an open, diverse, and tolerant country.

Concerns with the global movement of people are not just security-based. Americans are concerned as never before about the economic mobility of jobs. I'm referring, of course, to outsourcing. In the last few years, it has finally hit home to the average American how truly global this economy is. Politicians and the populace have in general reacted viscerally, blaming foreign countries for taking away jobs. It would be a huge mistake to impede the movement of talented people to economic opportunity, whether here or abroad. This can only hurt our competitive advantage in the long run.

Neither can we allow the debate on immigration to be framed by a tendency to celebrate high-skilled immigrants. Many in the high-tech community breathed a sign of relief when, in November 2004's lame duck session, Congress exempted 20,000 foreign graduate students from the cap on H-1B visas, which enable skilled foreigners to work in this country. Too often nowadays, we hear calls for the easing of visa restrictions for high-skilled laborers and high-skilled laborers alone. Nobel Prize–winning columnist Gary Becker has called for a prioritization system in which highly skilled and highly educated immigrants would be given preferential access to U.S. residence. His intentions are good: The basic argument is that we need to consider how much these high-end people mean to our economic success. I would expand the call, though, to realizing how much *all* immigrants mean to our economic life.

This is yet another example of the need to change the terms of the usual zero-sum argument. It shouldn't be: "high-skilled vs. low-skilled immigrants, and we can only take in so many total because we only have so many resources to accommodate their entry into the U.S." It should be that we find ways to devote more resources to in-sourcing everyone from computer programmers to maintenance men and women. To those in the United States and Europe who would argue that low-skill immigrants constitute a drain on national or local resources by becoming dependent on social welfare, I have a simple answer: Don't blame immigrants for what's wrong with social welfare policy. We know that immigrants add value and that low-skilled immigrants have helped to propel the American economy. It's time to start acknowledging that fact. Our future economic security depends on our willingness and ability to do so.

## A Truly Global Effort

Building this kind of economy and society in the era of globalization will necessitate a truly international effort. Like it or not, we live in a multilateral world, where economic power is significantly more dispersed compared to even fifty years ago. We're likely to have to live in this increasingly multipolar arrangement for the foreseeable future, and our business and political leaders and all Americans must recognize that we cannot do this on our own. The challenges of our nation and the world are too massive to be addressed by any one country.

To start with, it would be useful if we could all be using the same language, statistically speaking. The challenges of the creative age are hard enough to conceptualize and pinpoint as it is; the lack of a unified, standardized system of economic and social measurements makes that task all the more difficult. It's time to get serious about collecting comparable global statistics—a census for the world, if you will. It took months to gather the necessary national data used in this book, and comparable regional data are simply unavailable. During the Great Depression years, this country created its economic census in order to help businessmen and investors more effectively manage their activities. In a global age, a global equivalent—with meaningful, accurate, and useful statistics—makes sense. Such a system will be enormously difficult to institute, no doubt. All the more reason to start trying as soon as possible.

Similarly, to get a better idea of the scope of activity across the world, a true global forum on creativity is in order. We currently have global summits such as Davos to bring together CEOs to talk about tax rates and other business-climate issues. Why not start comparing the best practices of our creative centers, discussing the business of more open societies with competitive people climates? Today, many international organizations, from the International Monetary Fund to the World Bank, are concerned with investment, trade, and competitiveness, while the United Nations and other groups tackle policy, security, or equity. Left out are the crucial dimensions of the new creative age, the other two Ts, talent and especially tolerance, which are important engines for common prosperity. What we need more than anything now is a focal point for the discussion of global talent flows, for someone to make the case for a fair and equitable global framework for managing the flow of people worldwide.

Such a forum would also look more closely at emerging local models, the micro- or city-level approaches that everyday practitioners are using to confront creative-age challenges. In the United States, such a movement is already under way, as groups like Create Detroit and Creative Tampa Bay spring up. Now it's time to expand on the progress that Creative Melbourne, the Club of Amsterdam, Creative Wellington, and others have made by beginning to link these organizations and bring political, artistic, business, scientific, and other leadership to the table. In order to do this, it will be critical to emphasize a brain-circulation approach; such openness is impossible if any of the players sees it as a zero-sum game.

Where will such changes and institutions come from? Thanks to national-level partisan polarization, it's unlikely that our political leadership will catch on anytime soon. In high-level political discourse, the very word *global* has become taboo, as 2004 presidential candidate John Kerry learned when he used the phrase "global test" to recommend American approaches for tackling international terrorism. If the government is unable or unwilling to take the lead in balancing one type of security with another, then the business and academic communities need to begin the push for a renewed American openness. In the 1980s, Hewlett-Packard chief Jack Young spurred his colleagues to form the U.S. Council on Competitiveness, which did much to bring public attention to lagging industrial competitiveness. At that time, though, U.S. companies had a national orientation. Many of the leaders of those companies, from Young to Lee Iacocca, saw their companies' interests as more or less tied to the interests of the United States. They weren't completely intertwined, of course, but there was an undeniably close relationship. That relationship no longer exists across the board. These days, companies are truly global in nature and can go abroad for whatever they may need. Consequently, this can no longer be a one-country, U.S.-only effort. Such a new effort must take shape as truly global initiative.

Perhaps it's time to establish something like a Global Creativity Commission. This commission could be the first step toward formulating the kind of regional, national, and international policies required for success in the creative age. The globalized creative economy, with its rapid and complex movements of goods, money, and people, requires stronger global institutions precisely because nations are increasingly obsolete units, unable to harness the full productive potential of the creative age or to address its mounting economic and social problems. It's time for the advanced nations to consider what Martin Kenney of the University of California at Davis calls a "Global New Deal." Like the postwar social compacts in the U.S. and other nations, such a program would focus on boosting the innovative and productive potential of the creative age while simultaneously expanding its benefits to a broader and more inclusive range of people and addressing its social and economic externalities. But it would develop and implement those strategies and solutions in the only way they can be effective in an increasingly globally interconnected and multipolar world—on a truly global scale. It would have to reach beyond just world political and business leaders to embrace arts, education, and cultural communities—indeed, communities of all incomes, occupations, and ages—committed to developing strategies to invest in people and ensure that global talent can move freely across borders.

With these measures—more opportunity, more entrepreneurship, more investment in people, more investment in our natural as well as human assets—the United States can reclaim its status as a truly open society and lead the world in becoming a more integrated and prosperous place. More importantly, it can reassert itself as a risk-taking society, one that encourages entrepreneurship and experimentation by caring for its people and providing for their basic security—physical, social, political, and economic. Nothing short of this expanded notion of what security means will be sufficient to guarantee the future prosperity of this nation and the world.

Maybe I'm an eternal optimist, but I think the United States can continue to be a beacon of openness for the creative class—and, indeed, for the whole of humanity. It has a long history of resourcefulness and creativity to draw on, and it has transformed itself many times before, rebuilding after the Great Depression and bouncing back after the Asian manufacturing boom of the 1980s.

The role of the United States in generating creativity and talent is a concern not only for U.S. businesses and policy makers, but for all nations. American universities and corporations have long been the educators and innovators for the world. If this engine stalls—or if political decisions about immigration, visas, and scientific research put sugar in its gas tank—the whole world will have to live with the repercussions.

The creative age requires nothing short of a change of worldview. Creativity is not a tangible asset like mineral deposits, something that can be hoarded or fought over, or even bought and sold. We must begin to think of creativity as a common good, like liberty or security. It's something essential that belongs to all of us, and that must always be nourished, renewed, and maintained—or else it will slip away.

# Appendix A: Global Creativity by the Numbers

Measures of the global creative class and global creativity are based upon my 3 Ts theory of economic growth and include detailed indicators for talent, technology, and tolerance. These measures were developed with Irene Tinagli, a doctoral student at Carnegie Mellon University, and are similar in some respects to more conventional international competitiveness measures in that they consider technology and talent, or human capital. They supplement and extend this conventional framework by adding indicators for tolerance, openness, and diversity.

The full data set covers forty-five countries, including most European countries and Organization for Economic Cooperation and Development (OECD) member nations (except Luxembourg), the major Asian nations, and emerging economies like China and India. These measures should by no means be taken as the last word on global creativity, but rather as a beginning conceptual framework for further assessment and comparison. International comparisons are fraught with technical difficulties. They suffer from the thorny issue that analysts and social scientists refer to as data comparability. Different countries collect data according to different standards and criteria. We deal with this as best we can by using the most standardized and acceptable data, and also by comparing our findings to other widely accepted indicators of global competitiveness (discussed below). Keeping this caveat in mind, we have a great deal of faith in the general picture painted by our rankings, and encourage other scholars and analysts to engage in similar studies in the future.

## Creative Class

This measure of creative occupations is based on International Labour Organisation (ILO) statistics. The ILO collects detailed data on occupations, breaking the workforce down into job categories such as scientists and engineers, artists, musicians, architects, engineers, managers, professionals, and so forth. While the ILO categories differ somewhat from the U.S.-based statistics used in *The Rise of the Creative Class,* they are the best available measures of creative occupations worldwide. All ILO data used here have been classified according to the international standard ISCO-88 in order to ensure comparability across European countries. The U.S. data are from the Bureau of Labor Statistics. We estimate the creative class in two ways because of variations in how different nations treat the category *technicians.* Our "broad" definition includes scientists, engineers, artists, cultural creatives, managers, professionals, and technicians; the "narrow" definition excludes technicians.

Our global creative class measure is strongly correlated with other, more conventional measures of human capital. It is also strongly and positively associated with economic output or GDP. It is less strongly associated with GDP growth, the relationship here being driven in large measure by the strong performance of Ireland. It's important to note that our measure of the global creative class is not intended to capture or account for conventional economic growth, but to serve as a measure of a country's base of creative talent, which affects growth only through its interaction with a broad range of other factors.

## Other Talent Measures

Two other measures of talent are used in the analyses of global creativity. The Human Capital Index is based on the percentage of a country's population holding a bachelor's degree. These data are from the Organization for Economic Cooperation and Development, for the year 2001. I am painfully aware that national differences in post–secondary education and in the way statistics are collected affect the comparability of these data across countries. The Scientific Talent Index represents the number of researchers per million people. It is based on UNESCO data and covers the years 1999–2001. The overall Talent Index combines these three talent measures (creative class, Human Capital Index, and Scientific Talent Index). Creative class data are not available for the following countries: China, India, Japan, France, Chile, and Brazil. In these cases, we use the average of the other two talent indicators to estimate these countries' Talent Index scores.

## Technology

We use two measures for technology. The R&D Index measures R&D expenditures as a percentage of the Gross Domestic Product, and is based on data from the World Bank for the years 1999–2002. The Innovation Index measures the number of patents granted per million people. It is based on data from the U.S. Patent and Trademark Office (USPTO) and is for the year 2001. The overall Technology Index combines these two measures.

## Tolerance

The Tolerance Index combines two measures. Both are based on the most recent versions of Ronald Inglehart's World Values Survey, which covers the period 1995–1998 and is based on data for sixty-five countries. The Values Index measures the degree to which a country espouses traditional as opposed to modern or secular values. It is based on a series of questions about attitudes toward God, religion, nationalism, authority, family, women's rights, divorce, and abortion. The Self-Expression Index captures the degree to which a nation values individual rights and self-expression. Its questions cover attitudes toward self-expression, quality of life, democracy, science and technology, leisure, the environment, trust, protest politics, immigrants, and gays. The World Values Survey is based on national samples that average approximately 1,400 respondents per country. These data were made available to us by Ronald Inglehart and are available from the Inter-University Consortium for Policy and Social Research (ICPSR) survey data archive at the University of Michigan.

## The Global Creativity Index (GCI)

The Global Creativity Index is made up of an equally weighted combination of the Talent Index, the Technology Index, and the Tolerance Index. The country values for each indicator were normalized on a scale from 0 to 1.

Tinagli and I compared the GCI to other measures of competitiveness and to conventional measures of economic output and growth. The GCI is strongly and positively associated with other leading indices of competitiveness and economic development such as Michael Porter's Growth Competitiveness Index, the United Nations Human Development Index, and the Globalization Index developed by A. T. Kearney for *Foreign Policy*. The GCI is also strongly and positively associated with economic output or GDP. The GCI is only weakly associated with growth in GDP from 1995 to 2001. But the relationship is considerably stronger when we compare a composite measure of the trend or growth in the GCI to GDP growth; this is due in part to the strong performances of Ireland and China in both of these areas. It's important to note, though, that the GCI is not intended as a predictor of short-term economic growth. The GCI is intended to capture the ability of a country to harness and mobilize creative talent for innovation, entrepreneurship, industry formation, and long-run prosperity.

## The Global Creativity Index

| Global Creativity Index Rank | Country | Global Creativity Index | TALENT | | | | TECHNOLOGY | | | TOLERANCE | | |
|---|---|---|---|---|---|---|---|---|---|---|---|---|
| | | | Talent Index | Creative Class | Human Capital | Scientific Talent | Technology Index | R&D Index | Innovation Index (Patents) | Tolerance Index | Values Index | Self-Expression Index |
| 1 | Sweden | 0.808 | 0.642 | 22.93 | 16.94 | 5,186 | 0.819 | 4.27 | 195.97 | 0.964 | 1.60 | 2.22 |
| 2 | Japan | 0.766 | 0.702 | — | 19.20 | 5,321 | 0.785 | 3.09 | 261.53 | 0.811 | 1.84 | 0.68 |
| 3 | Finland | 0.684 | 0.728 | 24.66 | 14.80 | 7,110 | 0.626 | 3.40 | 141.09 | 0.698 | 0.80 | 1.04 |
| 4 | United States | 0.666 | 0.601 | 23.55 | 28.34 | 4,099 | 0.827 | 2.82 | 307.06 | 0.571 | -0.53 | 1.64 |
| 5 | Switzerland | 0.637 | 0.541 | 22.05 | 15.83 | 3,592 | 0.625 | 2.64 | 196.38 | 0.744 | 0.77 | 1.45 |
| 6 | Denmark | 0.613 | 0.597 | 21.29 | 21.50 | 3,476 | 0.385 | 2.09 | 89.38 | 0.858 | 1.11 | 1.96 |
| 7 | Iceland | 0.612 | 0.658 | 24.12 | 18.85 | — | 0.463 | 3.04 | 67.38 | 0.717 | 0.37 | 1.72 |
| 8 | Netherlands | 0.611 | 0.643 | 29.54 | 20.87 | 2,572 | 0.366 | 2.02 | 83.05 | 0.824 | 0.81 | 2.05 |
| 9 | Norway | 0.595 | 0.686 | 18.77 | 27.60 | 4,377 | 0.279 | 1.62 | 58.94 | 0.819 | 1.26 | 1.46 |
| 10 | Germany | 0.577 | 0.468 | 20.09 | 13.48 | 3,153 | 0.511 | 2.50 | 136.77 | 0.753 | 1.13 | 1.08 |
| 11 | Canada | 0.548 | 0.603 | 24.96 | 20.38 | 2,978 | 0.400 | 1.85 | 116.02 | 0.641 | -0.18 | 1.78 |
| 12 | Australia | 0.528 | 0.672 | 30.14 | 19.24 | 3,439 | 0.246 | 1.53 | 45.13 | 0.665 | -0.20 | 2.00 |
| 13 | Belgium | 0.526 | 0.571 | 30.41 | 12.70 | 2,953 | 0.338 | 1.96 | 69.80 | 0.670 | 0.48 | 1.20 |
| 14 | Israel | 0.525 | 0.371 | 20.48 | — | 1,563 | 0.670 | 3.62 | 152.45 | 0.533 | 0.25 | 0.37 |
| 15 | United Kingdom | 0.517 | 0.567 | 25.70 | 18.00 | 2,666 | 0.327 | 1.90 | 67.43 | 0.657 | 0.26 | 1.37 |
| 16 | South Korea | 0.465 | 0.371 | 8.80 | 17.47 | 2,880 | 0.465 | 2.96 | 74.73 | 0.560 | 1.08 | -0.43 |

## The Global Creativity Index (*continued*)

| Global Creativity Index Rank | Country | Global Creativity Index | TALENT | | | | TECHNOLOGY | | | TOLERANCE | | |
|---|---|---|---|---|---|---|---|---|---|---|---|---|
| | | | Talent Index | Creative Class | Human Capital | Scientific Talent | Technology Index | R&D Index | Innovation Index (Patents) | Tolerance Index | Values Index | Self-Expression Index |
| 17 | France | 0.462 | 0.378 | — | 11.87 | 2,718 | 0.364 | 2.20 | 68.27 | 0.643 | 0.49 | 0.97 |
| 18 | New Zealand | 0.459 | 0.510 | 27.07 | 13.92 | 2,197 | 0.175 | 1.11 | 32.22 | 0.693 | 0.09 | 1.87 |
| 19 | Austria | 0.438 | 0.311 | 17.20 | 6.83 | 2,313 | 0.339 | 1.94 | 72.43 | 0.665 | 0.22 | 1.48 |
| 20 | Ireland | 0.414 | 0.586 | 33.47 | 13.96 | 2,190 | 0.190 | 1.17 | 37.25 | 0.467 | -0.92 | 1.27 |
| 21 | Czech Republic | 0.382 | 0.317 | 16.60 | 11.13 | 1,466 | 0.148 | 1.30 | 1.56 | 0.681 | 1.19 | 0.42 |
| 22 | Greece | 0.371 | 0.403 | 22.81 | 12.39 | 1,400 | 0.074 | 0.67 | 2.45 | 0.636 | 0.73 | 0.62 |
| 23 | Spain | 0.365 | 0.449 | 19.81 | 16.89 | 1,948 | 0.115 | 0.96 | 6.54 | 0.532 | 0.09 | 0.56 |
| 24 | Estonia | 0.360 | 0.500 | 26.23 | — | 1,947 | 0.082 | 0.76 | 0.73 | 0.498 | 1.24 | -1.14 |
| 25 | Russian Federation | 0.339 | 0.521 | 21.10 | — | 3,494 | 0.112 | 1.00 | 1.62 | 0.385 | 1.08 | -1.86 |
| 26 | Italy | 0.335 | 0.252 | 13.59 | 10.05 | 1,128 | 0.162 | 1.04 | 29.49 | 0.591 | 0.18 | 0.93 |
| 27 | Ukraine | 0.296 | 0.404 | 20.09 | — | 2,118 | 0.103 | 0.95 | 0.43 | 0.380 | 0.90 | -1.68 |
| 28 | Slovak Republic | 0.291 | 0.304 | 15.08 | 10.32 | 1,774 | 0.068 | 0.65 | 0.19 | 0.500 | 0.65 | -0.39 |
| 29 | Hungary | 0.282 | 0.374 | 18.50 | 14.05 | 1,440 | 0.113 | 0.95 | 5.89 | 0.358 | 0.38 | -1.22 |
| 30 | Croatia | 0.280 | 0.224 | 13.74 | — | 1,187 | 0.110 | 0.98 | 1.83 | 0.505 | 0.08 | 0.35 |
| 31 | Bulgaria | 0.275 | 0.329 | 19.76 | — | 1,167 | 0.058 | 0.57 | 0.38 | 0.437 | 1.15 | -1.52 |
| 32 | Latvia | 0.262 | 0.344 | 20.94 | — | 1,078 | 0.038 | 0.40 | 0.42 | 0.403 | 0.70 | -1.25 |

# The Global Creativity Index *(continued)*

| Global Creativity Index Rank | Country | Global Creativity Index | TALENT | | | | TECHNOLOGY | | | TOLERANCE | | |
|---|---|---|---|---|---|---|---|---|---|---|---|---|
| | | | Talent Index | Creative Class | Human Capital | Scientific Talent | Technology Index | R&D Index | Innovation Index (Patents) | Tolerance Index | Values Index | Self-Expression Index |
| 33 | Uruguay | 0.240 | 0.220 | 15.45 | 9.00 | 276 | 0.021 | 0.26 | 0.60 | 0.478 | −0.22 | 0.50 |
| 34 | Poland | 0.239 | 0.331 | 17.01 | 11.89 | 1,473 | 0.070 | 0.67 | 0.41 | 0.315 | −0.44 | −0.56 |
| 35 | Portugal | 0.234 | 0.243 | 13.91 | 6.63 | 1,754 | 0.085 | 0.78 | 1.20 | 0.373 | −0.89 | 0.47 |
| 36 | China | 0.230 | 0.031 | — | 1.43 | 584 | 0.109 | 1.00 | 0.15 | 0.550 | 1.16 | −0.61 |
| 37 | Rep. of Georgia | 0.219 | 0.345 | 15.54 | — | 2,421 | 0.030 | 0.33 | 0.38 | 0.282 | −0.04 | −1.32 |
| 38 | Argentina | 0.199 | 0.193 | 11.43 | 9.12 | 684 | 0.045 | 0.45 | 1.36 | 0.357 | −0.94 | 0.40 |
| 39 | Turkey | 0.186 | 0.212 | 14.74 | 8.90 | 306 | 0.065 | 0.63 | 0.16 | 0.282 | −0.83 | −0.35 |
| 40 | Chile | 0.185 | 0.160 | — | 9.02 | 419 | 0.055 | 0.54 | 0.78 | 0.339 | −0.88 | 0.18 |
| 41 | India | 0.177 | 0.085 | — | 6.00 | 157 | 0.137 | 1.23 | 0.17 | 0.309 | −0.53 | −0.50 |
| 42 | Mexico | 0.164 | 0.150 | 5.28 | 13.29 | 225 | 0.043 | 0.43 | 0.81 | 0.299 | −1.47 | 0.58 |
| 43 | Brazil | 0.159 | 0.128 | — | 7.67 | 323 | 0.083 | 0.77 | 0.64 | 0.266 | −1.27 | 0.06 |
| 44 | Peru | 0.132 | 0.138 | 9.67 | 8.09 | 229 | 0.000 | 0.08 | 0.15 | 0.258 | −1.33 | 0.07 |
| 45 | Romania | 0.127 | 0.131 | 9.76 | — | 879 | 0.035 | 0.37 | 0.45 | 0.214 | −0.25 | −1.62 |

Compiled by Irene Tinagli from various sources. See above for a full description of indicators, methodology, and sources.

## The Global Creative Class

| Rank by Percent Creative Class | Country | Narrow Definition (Excluding Technicians) | | Broad Definition (Including Technicians) | | Total Employment (Thousands) | Creative Class Average Annual Growth Rate (percent) | Years Covered for Average Annual Growth Rate | Global Creativity Index Rank |
|---|---|---|---|---|---|---|---|---|---|
| | | Percent of Workforce | Total (Thousands) | Percent of Workforce | Total (Thousands) | | | | |
| 1 | Ireland | 33.47 | 586 | 39.12 | 685 | 1,750 | 7.64 | 95–02 | 20 |
| 2 | Belgium | 30.41 | 1,238 | 41.40 | 1,685 | 4,070 | 0.88 | 95–02 | 13 |
| 3 | Australia | 30.14 | 2,806 | 43.00 | 4,004 | 9,311 | 1.23 | 97–02 | 12 |
| 4 | Netherlands | 29.54 | 2,323 | 46.98 | 3,695 | 7,865 | 1.47 | 95–01 | 8 |
| 5 | New Zealand | 27.07 | 508 | 38.43 | 721 | 1,877 | 1.28 | 95–02 | 18 |
| 6 | Estonia | 26.23 | 154 | 39.01 | 228 | 586 | 1.59 | 95–02 | 24 |
| 7 | Ukraine | 25.70 | 7,303 | 39.27 | 11,158 | 28,415 | -0.25 | 96–02 | 27 |
| 8 | Canada | 24.96 | 3,847 | 38.09 | 5,870 | 15,412 | -0.67 | 95–02 | 11 |
| 9 | Finland | 24.66 | 590 | 40.99 | 981 | 2,393 | 1.58 | 00–02 | 3 |
| 10 | Iceland | 24.12 | 38 | 38.03 | 60 | 157 | 1.84 | 95–02 | 7 |
| 11 | United States | 23.55 | 30,042 | 27.32 | 34,846 | 127,568 | -1.47 | 95–02 | 4 |
| 12 | Sweden | 22.93 | 973 | 42.44 | 1,801 | 4,244 | 2.73 | 97–02 | 1 |
| 13 | Greece | 22.81 | 901 | 29.82 | 1,178 | 3,949 | 0.97 | 95–02 | 22 |
| 14 | Switzerland | 22.05 | 873 | 41.98 | 1,662 | 3,959 | 2.32 | 95–02 | 5 |
| 15 | Denmark | 21.29 | 578 | 41.81 | 1,135 | 2,715 | 1.80 | 95–02 | 6 |
| 16 | Russian Federation | 21.10 | 12,745 | 36.45 | 22,019 | 60,408 | -2.12 | 97–99 | 25 |
| 17 | Latvia | 20.94 | 207 | 34.20 | 338 | 989 | 0.41 | 96–02 | 32 |

## The Global Creative Class (*continued*)

| Rank by Percent Creative Class | Country | Narrow Definition (Excluding Technicians) | | Broad Definition (Including Technicians) | | Total Employment (Thousands) | Creative Class Average Annual Growth Rate (percent) | Years Covered for Average Annual Growth Rate | Global Creativity Index Rank |
|---|---|---|---|---|---|---|---|---|---|
| | | Percent of Workforce | Total (Thousands) | Percent of Workforce | Total (Thousands) | | | | |
| 18 | Israel | 20.48 | 468 | 35.80 | 818 | 2,284 | 3.23 | 95–02 | 14 |
| 19 | Germany | 20.09 | 7,339 | 40.22 | 14,695 | 36,536 | 2.20 | 95–02 | 10 |
| 20 | UK | 20.09 | 4,098 | 33.76 | 6,888 | 20,401 | −0.34 | 95–02 | 15 |
| 21 | Spain | 19.81 | 3,221 | 30.14 | 4,901 | 16,258 | 0.85 | 95–02 | 23 |
| 22 | Bulgaria | 19.76 | 347 | 34.97 | 614 | 1,757 | 2.99 | 98–01 | 31 |
| 23 | Norway | 18.77 | 429 | 41.64 | 952 | 2,286 | 2.44 | 96–02 | 9 |
| 24 | Hungary | 18.50 | 716 | 32.58 | 1,261 | 3,871 | 1.60 | 95–02 | 29 |
| 25 | Austria | 17.20 | 660 | 32.00 | 1,227 | 3,836 | 0.88 | 95–02 | 19 |
| 26 | Poland | 17.01 | 2,345 | 29.66 | 4,088 | 13,782 | 1.30 | 95–02 | 34 |
| 27 | Czech Republic | 16.60 | 791 | 35.74 | 1,703 | 4,765 | 0.90 | 95–02 | 21 |
| 28 | Rep. of Georgia | 15.54 | 286 | 21.92 | 403 | 1,839 | −5.29 | 98–02 | 37 |
| 29 | Uruguay | 15.45 | 166 | 21.81 | 235 | 1,076 | −1.21 | 00–01 | 33 |
| 30 | Slovak Republic | 15.08 | 321 | 33.77 | 718 | 2,127 | 0.48 | 95–02 | 28 |
| 31 | Turkey | 14.74 | 2,990 | 19.70 | 3,997 | 20,287 | 3.16 | 01–02 | 39 |
| 32 | Portugal | 13.91 | 712 | 21.18 | 1,084 | 5,115 | −1.64 | 95–02 | 35 |
| 33 | Croatia | 13.74 | 210 | 28.73 | 439 | 1,527 | 1.31 | 96–02 | 30 |
| 34 | Italy | 13.59 | 2,980 | 30.62 | 6,713 | 21,922 | 1.41 | 95–02 | 26 |

## The Global Creative Class *(continued)*

| Rank by Percent Creative Class | Country | Narrow Definition (Excluding Technicians) | | Broad Definition (Including Technicians) | | Total Employment (Thousands) | Creative Class Average Annual Growth Rate (percent) | Years Covered for Average Annual Growth Rate | Global Creativity Index Rank |
|---|---|---|---|---|---|---|---|---|---|
| | | Percent of Workforce | Total (Thousands) | Percent of Workforce | Total (Thousands) | | | | |
| 35 | Argentina | 11.43 | 916 | 27.48 | 2,203 | 8,016 | −1.92 | 98–02 | 38 |
| 36 | Romania | 9.76 | 901 | 18.96 | 1,751 | 9,234 | 1.99 | 95–02 | 45 |
| 37 | Peru | 9.67 | 737 | 18.72 | 1,426 | 7,620 | −1.27 | 96–01 | 44 |
| 38 | South Korea | 8.80 | 1,854 | 18.43 | 3,882 | 21,061 | 3.75 | 95–00 | 16 |
| 39 | Mexico | 5.28 | 2,060 | 16.49 | 6,432 | 39,004 | 3.23 | 95–01 | 42 |

Note: Creative Class data are not available for: Brazil, Chile, China, France, India, and Japan.

Compiled by Irene Tinagli from various sources. See above for a full description of indicator, methodology, and sources.

# Appendix B: Measuring the Class Divide

The emergence of the creative economy in the United States has spurred innovation and productivity even as it reinforces and exacerbates economic and social inequality. While many possible measures of inequality are indicative, this book focuses on two in particular: an *Inequality Index* and a *Housing Affordability Index*. Both measures were developed by Kevin Stolarick and cover all 331 metropolitan statistical areas in the United States.

## The Inequality Index

This Inequality Index of economic inequality compares the wages and salaries of the creative class to the other classes. It covers all metropolitan areas and is based on data from the Bureau of Labor Statistics. It uses a statistical technique called Theil's T, which captures complex deviations from a norm and crunches them down to a single number that reflects the overall degree of deviation.* A region with a high Inequality Index score has many people earning either relatively high or low wages, and few earning near the average. There is a strong overall correlation (of 0.72 on a 0 to 1 scale) between inequality and creativity. The more creative a region is, the more income inequality is found there.

## The Housing Affordability Index

This index measures housing costs in relation to income. It includes total housing costs, not just the cost of home ownership, averaging the median costs for different housing types (rental, mortgage, cost if owned, and no mortgage) weighted by the number of people in each type. The Housing Affordability Index is negatively and significantly correlated with total population. As such, this index does not capture city-size effects. Larger regions have higher housing costs, but they also have higher average incomes.

## The Creativity Index

The Creativity Index is the same as that presented in the 2004 paperback edition of *The Rise of the Creative Class*. It is calculated with three equally weighted parts: technology, talent, and tolerance. The High-Tech Index is drawn from the Milken Institute's Tech-Pole measures for 2000. The Innovation Index is based on average annual patent growth from 1990 to 1999. The talent measure is the percent-

---

* Normally, Theil's T is a measure of the variation both within and between groups, and is therefore calculated as two components (the first measures the variation within a group, the second the variation between groups). Since only information on the broad economic groups is available to us, we are actually measuring inequality using only the *between*-group component of Theil's T. (Calculating the first measure would require our having individual salary information.) More specifically, our measure is the sum of the share-weighted log of the ratio of each class's average wage to the overall average wage.

age of the workforce in the creative class, based on the Bureau of Labor Statistics "Occupation and Employment Survey," for 2001. The Tolerance Index includes four dimensions of diversity or tolerance as captured by four distinct measures: the Gay Index, the Melting Pot Index (concentration of foreign-born people), the Bohemian Index (relative concentration of artists, musicians, and entertainers), and a Racial Integration Index. This last index measures how closely racial percentages within each Census Tract of a region compare to the racial composition of that region.

## Measuring the Class Divide
## Regions with Populations of 1,000,000 or more

| | INEQUALITY INDEX* | | HOUSING INAFFORDABILITY† | | CREATIVITY INDEX | | |
|---|---|---|---|---|---|---|---|
| Region | Peer Ranking | Overall Ranking | Peer Ranking | Overall Ranking | Peer Ranking | Overall Ranking | Score |
| San Jose, CA | 1 | 2 | 12 | 30 | 2 | 3 | .961 |
| New York, NY | 2 | 8 | 7 | 17 | 12 | 22 | .872 |
| Dallas, TX | 3 | 9 | 41 | 139 | 15 | 31 | .851 |
| Washington, DC | 4 | 10 | 36 | 126 | 9 | 12 | .907 |
| Orange County, CA | 5 | 11 | 6 | 13 | 19 | 43 | .775 |
| Raleigh-Durham, NC | 6 | 13 | 30 | 95 | 6 | 9 | .915 |
| Austin, TX | 7 | 14 | 33 | 113 | 4 | 5 | .953 |
| Middlesex, NJ | 8 | 15 | 29 | 93 | 18 | 41 | .782 |
| San Francisco, CA | 9 | 16 | 8 | 22 | 1 | 2 | .962 |
| Houston, TX | 10 | 19 | 48 | 179 | 29 | 70 | .695 |
| Boston, MA | 11 | 21 | 23 | 73 | 5 | 7 | .945 |
| West Palm Beach, FL | 12 | 22 | 16 | 39 | 32 | 76 | .685 |
| Fort Lauderdale, FL | 13 | 26 | 2 | 3 | 41 | 98 | .630 |
| Los Angeles, CA | 14 | 28 | 3 | 5 | 16 | 37 | .802 |
| Monmouth, NJ | 15 | 29 | 13 | 31 | 34 | 78 | .680 |
| San Diego, CA | 16 | 30 | 4 | 9 | 13 | 27 | .858 |
| Baltimore, MD | 17 | 33 | 45 | 145 | 21 | 46 | .765 |
| San Antonio, TX | 18 | 34 | 51 | 190 | 27 | 61 | .725 |
| Miami, FL | 19 | 35 | 1 | 1 | 42 | 100 | .619 |
| Atlanta, GA | 20 | 36 | 34 | 120 | 14 | 28 | .855 |
| Tampa, FL | 21 | 41 | 22 | 72 | 31 | 73 | .692 |
| Bergen, NJ | 22 | 42 | 10 | 27 | 45 | 111 | .600 |

## Measuring the Class Divide (*continued*)
## Regions with Populations of 1,000,000 or more

| Region | INEQUALITY INDEX* Peer Ranking | INEQUALITY INDEX* Overall Ranking | HOUSING INAFFORDABILITY† Peer Ranking | HOUSING INAFFORDABILITY† Overall Ranking | CREATIVITY INDEX Peer Ranking | CREATIVITY INDEX Overall Ranking | Score |
|---|---|---|---|---|---|---|---|
| Newark, NJ | 23 | 46 | 14 | 34 | 35 | 81 | .675 |
| New Orleans, LA | 24 | 50 | 39 | 132 | 58 | 180 | .454 |
| Minneapolis, MN | 25 | 51 | 54 | 204 | 10 | 17 | .890 |
| Cincinnati, OH | 26 | 52 | 49 | 185 | 39 | 91 | .648 |
| Orlando, FL | 27 | 53 | 20 | 52 | 44 | 108 | .605 |
| Hartford, CT | 28 | 55 | 37 | 128 | 37 | 89 | .656 |
| Jacksonville, FL | 29 | 56 | 47 | 166 | 48 | 135 | .543 |
| Philadelphia, PA | 30 | 59 | 28 | 89 | 25 | 58 | .728 |
| Nassau, NY | 31 | 64 | 18 | 42 | 36 | 83 | .670 |
| Columbus, OH | 32 | 67 | 40 | 138 | 40 | 93 | .646 |
| Pittsburgh, PA | 33 | 69 | 53 | 192 | 52 | 162 | .493 |
| Denver, CO | 34 | 70 | 24 | 79 | 23 | 51 | .741 |
| Norfolk, VA | 35 | 74 | 21 | 63 | 57 | 177 | .456 |
| Chicago, IL | 36 | 86 | 26 | 83 | 26 | 59 | .726 |
| Seattle, WA | 37 | 88 | 17 | 40 | 2 | 3 | .961 |
| Charlotte, NC | 38 | 91 | 43 | 141 | 43 | 107 | .607 |
| Kansas City, KS–MO | 39 | 92 | 58 | 243 | 30 | 71 | .694 |
| Detroit, MI | 40 | 93 | 57 | 240 | 59 | 183 | .450 |
| Oakland, CA | 41 | 102 | 9 | 26 | 6 | 9 | .915 |
| Phoenix, AZ | 42 | 108 | 25 | 80 | 17 | 38 | .799 |
| Sacramento, CA | 43 | 113 | 15 | 37 | 11 | 20 | .880 |
| Rochester, NY | 44 | 114 | 32 | 112 | 22 | 47 | .760 |
| Cleveland, OH | 45 | 121 | 38 | 131 | 56 | 174 | .464 |
| Providence, RI | 46 | 122 | 27 | 87 | 24 | 56 | .731 |
| Milwaukee, WI | 47 | 128 | 46 | 152 | 51 | 146 | .525 |
| Nashville, TN | 48 | 134 | 44 | 144 | 38 | 90 | .654 |
| Portland, OR | 49 | 149 | 19 | 51 | 8 | 11 | .908 |
| Memphis, TN | 50 | 151 | 35 | 124 | 49 | 140 | .534 |
| Salt Lake City, UT | 51 | 152 | 42 | 140 | 19 | 43 | .775 |
| St. Louis, MO | 52 | 153 | 60 | 267 | 46 | 116 | .591 |
| Oklahoma City, OK | 53 | 156 | 56 | 232 | 50 | 143 | .527 |
| Greensboro, NC | 54 | 176 | 52 | 191 | 60 | 193 | .432 |
| Louisville, KY | 55 | 197 | 59 | 250 | 55 | 172 | .468 |
| Riverside, CA | 56 | 201 | 5 | 10 | 54 | 170 | .478 |
| Indianapolis, IN | 57 | 205 | 55 | 217 | 33 | 77 | .682 |

## Measuring the Class Divide (*continued*)
## Regions with Populations of 1,000,000 or more

| Region | INEQUALITY INDEX★ Peer Ranking | INEQUALITY INDEX★ Overall Ranking | HOUSING INAFFORDABILITY† Peer Ranking | HOUSING INAFFORDABILITY† Overall Ranking | CREATIVITY INDEX Peer Ranking | CREATIVITY INDEX Overall Ranking | Score |
|---|---|---|---|---|---|---|---|
| Buffalo, NY | 58 | 210 | 31 | 103 | 61 | 214 | .395 |
| Grand Rapids, MI | 59 | 224 | 61 | 278 | 53 | 167 | .484 |
| Fort Worth, TX | 60 | 236 | 50 | 189 | 28 | 69 | .698 |
| Las Vegas, NV | 61 | 240 | 11 | 28 | 47 | 120 | .577 |

## Regions with Populations 500,000 to 1,000,000

| Region | INEQUALITY INDEX★ Peer Ranking | INEQUALITY INDEX★ Overall Ranking | HOUSING INAFFORDABILITY† Peer Ranking | HOUSING INAFFORDABILITY† Overall Ranking | CREATIVITY INDEX Peer Ranking | CREATIVITY INDEX Overall Ranking | Score |
|---|---|---|---|---|---|---|---|
| Ventura, CA | 1 | 12 | 1 | 16 | 8 | 88 | .660 |
| Albuquerque, NM | 2 | 25 | 10 | 77 | 3 | 32 | .846 |
| Colorado Springs, CO | 3 | 31 | 13 | 97 | 2 | 29 | .853 |
| Jersey City, NJ | 4 | 32 | 7 | 49 | 7 | 87 | .667 |
| Wilmington, DE | 5 | 44 | 27 | 198 | 16 | 130 | .555 |
| Birmingham, AL | 6 | 45 | 29 | 202 | 12 | 111 | .600 |
| Richmond, VA | 7 | 54 | 23 | 172 | 19 | 143 | .527 |
| McAllen, TX | 8 | 71 | 20 | 136 | 24 | 162 | .493 |
| New Haven, CT | 9 | 72 | 9 | 54 | 6 | 75 | .687 |
| Allentown, PA | 10 | 80 | 19 | 133 | 18 | 137 | .540 |
| El Paso, TX | 11 | 82 | 17 | 119 | 36 | 235 | .353 |
| Akron, OH | 12 | 89 | 24 | 181 | 34 | 202 | .418 |
| Dayton, OH | 13 | 90 | 28 | 200 | 29 | 189 | .444 |
| Mobile, AL | 14 | 94 | 31 | 214 | 32 | 198 | .423 |
| Little Rock, AR | 15 | 96 | 35 | 236 | 11 | 109 | .603 |
| Harrisburg, PA | 16 | 99 | 30 | 210 | 28 | 186 | .447 |
| Charleston, SC | 17 | 100 | 15 | 111 | 14 | 127 | .558 |
| Tucson, AZ | 18 | 105 | 11 | 78 | 4 | 34 | .838 |
| Knoxville, TN | 19 | 106 | 33 | 218 | 23 | 157 | .502 |
| Columbia, SC | 20 | 118 | 22 | 167 | 13 | 114 | .592 |
| Albany, NY | 21 | 123 | 16 | 117 | 9 | 99 | .621 |
| Worcester, MA | 22 | 125 | 21 | 156 | 1 | 16 | .897 |
| Omaha, IA–NE | 23 | 127 | 36 | 237 | 17 | 132 | .547 |

## Regions with Populations
## 500,000 to 1,000,000 (*continued*)

| Region | INEQUALITY INDEX* Peer Ranking | INEQUALITY INDEX* Overall Ranking | HOUSING INAFFORDABILITY† Peer Ranking | HOUSING INAFFORDABILITY† Overall Ranking | CREATIVITY INDEX Peer Ranking | CREATIVITY INDEX Overall Ranking | Score |
|---|---|---|---|---|---|---|---|
| Bakersfield, CA | 24 | 135 | 6 | 41 | 22 | 154 | .506 |
| Gary, IN | 25 | 145 | 39 | 252 | 41 | 319 | .148 |
| Honolulu, HI | 26 | 160 | 2 | 19 | 31 | 194 | .428 |
| Ann Arbor, MI | 27 | 165 | 25 | 188 | 5 | 42 | .779 |
| Baton Rouge, LA | 28 | 174 | 38 | 244 | 39 | 252 | .323 |
| Springfield, MA | 29 | 177 | 14 | 105 | 14 | 127 | .558 |
| Syracuse, NY | 30 | 181 | 18 | 123 | 25 | 168 | .483 |
| Tulsa, OK | 31 | 184 | 37 | 239 | 29 | 189 | .444 |
| Greenville, SC | 32 | 186 | 32 | 216 | 37 | 238 | .348 |
| Sarasota, FL | 33 | 194 | 12 | 96 | 26 | 175 | .463 |
| Youngstown, OH | 34 | 204 | 40 | 276 | 42 | 320 | .144 |
| Fresno, CA | 35 | 221 | 4 | 23 | 20 | 146 | .525 |
| Wichita, KS | 36 | 234 | 41 | 285 | 10 | 101 | .617 |
| Toledo, OH | 37 | 241 | 34 | 220 | 38 | 242 | .337 |
| Scranton, PA | 38 | 257 | 26 | 195 | 27 | 185 | .448 |
| Stockton, CA | 39 | 273 | 3 | 20 | 35 | 228 | .378 |
| Vallejo, CA | 40 | 295 | 5 | 24 | 21 | 151 | .512 |
| Fort Wayne, IN | 41 | 296 | 42 | 318 | 40 | 261 | .291 |
| Tacoma, WA | 42 | 315 | 8 | 50 | 32 | 198 | .423 |

## Regions with Populations 250,000 to 500,000

| Region | INEQUALITY INDEX* Peer Ranking | INEQUALITY INDEX* Overall Ranking | HOUSING INAFFORDABILITY† Peer Ranking | HOUSING INAFFORDABILITY† Overall Ranking | CREATIVITY INDEX Peer Ranking | CREATIVITY INDEX Overall Ranking | Score |
|---|---|---|---|---|---|---|---|
| Stamford, CT | 1 | 1 | 3 | 12 | 15 | 53 | .737 |
| Huntsville, AL | 2 | 3 | 73 | 294 | 26 | 104 | .613 |
| Melbourne, FL | 3 | 5 | 36 | 158 | 21 | 80 | .676 |
| Boulder, CO | 4 | 6 | 14 | 57 | 1 | 1 | .972 |
| Galveston, TX | 5 | 20 | 38 | 171 | 35 | 143 | .527 |
| Santa Barbara, CA | 6 | 23 | 2 | 8 | 24 | 96 | .639 |
| Trenton, NJ | 7 | 24 | 21 | 85 | 22 | 82 | .673 |
| Tallahassee, FL | 8 | 27 | 12 | 46 | 7 | 29 | .853 |
| Binghamton, NY | 9 | 40 | 46 | 197 | 16 | 54 | .732 |

# Regions with Populations
## 250,000 to 500,000 *(continued)*

| | HOUSING | | | | | | |
| | INEQUALITY INDEX* | | INAFFORDABILITY† | | CREATIVITY INDEX | | |
| Region | Peer Ranking | Overall Ranking | Peer Ranking | Overall Ranking | Peer Ranking | Overall Ranking | Score |
|---|---|---|---|---|---|---|---|
| Salinas, CA | 10 | 43 | 5 | 18 | 31 | 127 | .558 |
| Lawrence, MA–NH | 11 | 47 | 16 | 71 | 6 | 25 | .860 |
| Flint, MI | 12 | 48 | 71 | 286 | 40 | 164 | .491 |
| Boise, ID | 13 | 49 | 32 | 137 | 10 | 36 | .805 |
| Daytona Beach, FL | 14 | 57 | 25 | 102 | 23 | 95 | .640 |
| Fort Collins, CO | 15 | 58 | 22 | 90 | 4 | 23 | .866 |
| Pensacola, FL | 16 | 60 | 42 | 180 | 39 | 156 | .505 |
| Montgomery, AL | 17 | 66 | 43 | 183 | 68 | 277 | .259 |
| Augusta, FL | 18 | 68 | 40 | 177 | 50 | 219 | .387 |
| Lansing, MI | 19 | 73 | 62 | 253 | 11 | 39 | .790 |
| Santa Cruz, CA | 20 | 75 | 1 | 4 | 5 | 24 | .863 |
| Bridgeport, CT | 21 | 81 | 11 | 44 | 19 | 62 | .724 |
| Lowell, MA | 22 | 83 | 31 | 130 | 3 | 19 | .884 |
| Killeen, TX | 23 | 85 | 41 | 178 | 34 | 141 | .530 |
| Saginaw, MI | 24 | 87 | 76 | 305 | 63 | 260 | .292 |
| Macon, GA | 25 | 104 | 58 | 228 | 43 | 179 | .455 |
| Kalamazoo, MI | 26 | 109 | 67 | 268 | 41 | 165 | .487 |
| Santa Rosa, CA | 27 | 111 | 4 | 15 | 9 | 35 | .819 |
| Naples, FL | 28 | 116 | 24 | 99 | 46 | 191 | .437 |
| Columbus, GA | 29 | 117 | 35 | 154 | 49 | 211 | .398 |
| Fort Pierce, FL | 30 | 120 | 26 | 104 | 69 | 278 | .257 |
| Brownsville, TX | 31 | 124 | 34 | 146 | 29 | 119 | .578 |
| Lafayette, LA | 32 | 136 | 65 | 263 | 42 | 176 | .457 |
| Corpus Christi, TX | 33 | 137 | 33 | 142 | 60 | 253 | .317 |
| Lincoln, NE | 34 | 138 | 50 | 212 | 17 | 57 | .730 |
| Provo, UT | 35 | 139 | 29 | 122 | 13 | 50 | .743 |
| Des Moines, IA | 36 | 142 | 57 | 227 | 8 | 32 | .846 |
| Reading, PA | 37 | 148 | 49 | 208 | 54 | 230 | .375 |
| South Bend, IN | 38 | 150 | 69 | 283 | 25 | 102 | .616 |
| Charleston, WV | 39 | 155 | 77 | 310 | 48 | 209 | .402 |
| Modesto, CA | 40 | 157 | 7 | 29 | 61 | 254 | .309 |
| Beaumont, TX | 41 | 159 | 78 | 316 | 45 | 183 | .450 |
| Anchorage, AK | 42 | 161 | 17 | 74 | 12 | 40 | .788 |
| Madison, WI | 43 | 162 | 28 | 118 | 2 | 15 | .900 |
| Reno, NV | 44 | 166 | 8 | 33 | 28 | 114 | .592 |

# Regions with Populations
## 250,000 to 500,000 *(continued)*

| Region | INEQUALITY INDEX* Peer Ranking | INEQUALITY INDEX* Overall Ranking | HOUSING INAFFORDABILITY† Peer Ranking | HOUSING INAFFORDABILITY† Overall Ranking | CREATIVITY INDEX Peer Ranking | CREATIVITY INDEX Overall Ranking | Score |
|---|---|---|---|---|---|---|---|
| Ocala, FL | 45 | 168 | 47 | 199 | 79 | 313 | .189 |
| Huntington, WV | 46 | 172 | 63 | 254 | 74 | 296 | .224 |
| Canton, OH | 47 | 173 | 66 | 265 | 70 | 281 | .255 |
| Lexington, KY | 48 | 175 | 60 | 234 | 20 | 63 | .721 |
| Visalia, CA | 49 | 178 | 10 | 43 | 74 | 296 | .224 |
| Peoria, IL | 50 | 179 | 79 | 317 | 38 | 153 | .508 |
| Fort Myers, FL | 51 | 180 | 23 | 94 | 65 | 269 | .278 |
| New London, CT | 52 | 182 | 37 | 161 | 44 | 182 | .452 |
| Savannah, GA | 53 | 185 | 30 | 129 | 62 | 257 | .302 |
| Jackson, MS | 54 | 187 | 48 | 203 | 27 | 106 | .608 |
| Newburgh, NY–PA | 55 | 188 | 13 | 55 | 37 | 149 | .518 |
| Quad Cities, IA–IL | 56 | 190 | 74 | 301 | 53 | 226 | .380 |
| Lakeland, FL | 57 | 199 | 45 | 187 | 73 | 292 | .227 |
| Brockton, MA | 58 | 200 | 27 | 108 | 14 | 52 | .740 |
| Dutchess County, NY | 59 | 207 | 20 | 82 | 18 | 59 | .726 |
| Johnson City, TN–VA | 60 | 212 | 68 | 272 | 66 | 271 | .277 |
| Hamilton, OH | 61 | 214 | 44 | 184 | 52 | 223 | .384 |
| York, PA | 62 | 216 | 52 | 219 | 71 | 282 | .253 |
| Chattanooga, TN | 63 | 218 | 64 | 260 | 77 | 311 | .196 |
| Erie, PA | 64 | 223 | 55 | 224 | 64 | 267 | .279 |
| Lancaster, PA | 65 | 228 | 51 | 213 | 59 | 249 | .326 |
| Rockford, IL | 66 | 229 | 59 | 233 | 51 | 221 | .386 |
| Atlantic City, NJ | 67 | 230 | 6 | 25 | 47 | 207 | .407 |
| Salem, OR | 68 | 233 | 18 | 75 | 30 | 125 | .560 |
| Shreveport, LA | 69 | 244 | 56 | 225 | 78 | 312 | .194 |
| Evansville, IN–KY | 70 | 248 | 75 | 304 | 76 | 300 | .218 |
| Spokane, WA | 71 | 258 | 19 | 81 | 36 | 146 | .525 |
| Fayetteville, AR | 72 | 259 | 61 | 247 | 33 | 139 | .536 |
| Springfield, MO | 73 | 261 | 54 | 223 | 55 | 240 | .341 |
| Biloxi, MS | 74 | 265 | 53 | 221 | 72 | 291 | .232 |
| Utica, NY | 75 | 280 | 39 | 173 | 56 | 243 | .336 |
| Eugene, OR | 76 | 287 | 9 | 38 | 32 | 131 | .552 |
| Fayetteville, NC | 77 | 301 | 15 | 69 | 57 | 244 | .334 |
| Appleton, WI | 78 | 305 | 72 | 288 | 67 | 276 | .266 |
| Hickory, NC | 79 | 324 | 70 | 284 | 58 | 245 | .333 |

# Regions with Populations below 250,000

| Region | INEQUALITY INDEX* Peer Ranking | Overall Ranking | HOUSING INAFFORDABILITY† Peer Ranking | Overall Ranking | CREATIVITY INDEX Peer Ranking | Overall Ranking | Score |
|---|---|---|---|---|---|---|---|
| College Station, TX | 1 | 4 | 1 | 2 | 24 | 93 | .646 |
| Gainesville, FL | 2 | 7 | 6 | 21 | 34 | 123 | .569 |
| Charlottesville, VA | 3 | 17 | 49 | 148 | 19 | 79 | .679 |
| Danbury, CT | 4 | 18 | 31 | 92 | 6 | 21 | .879 |
| Portland, ME | 5 | 37 | 37 | 109 | 22 | 86 | .668 |
| Nashua, NH | 6 | 38 | 44 | 127 | 1 | 6 | .951 |
| Lake Charles, CA | 7 | 39 | 136 | 315 | 124 | 301 | .217 |
| Portsmouth, NH | 8 | 61 | 33 | 100 | 2 | 8 | .938 |
| Corvallis, OR | 9 | 62 | 25 | 70 | 12 | 63 | .721 |
| Las Cruces, NM | 10 | 63 | 36 | 107 | 25 | 97 | .634 |
| Santa Fe, NM | 11 | 65 | 29 | 88 | 17 | 72 | .693 |
| Waterbury, CT | 12 | 76 | 32 | 98 | 20 | 84 | .669 |
| State College, PA | 13 | 77 | 21 | 65 | 13 | 65 | .712 |
| Richland, WA | 14 | 78 | 81 | 226 | 32 | 121 | .576 |
| Kokomo, IN | 15 | 79 | 149 | 331 | 82 | 232 | .368 |
| Punta Gorda, FL | 16 | 84 | 45 | 134 | 41 | 142 | .528 |
| Lubbock, TX | 17 | 95 | 47 | 143 | 45 | 158 | .501 |
| Manchester, NH | 18 | 97 | 38 | 110 | 4 | 14 | .904 |
| Alexandria, LA | 19 | 98 | 77 | 209 | 113 | 285 | .250 |
| Burlington, VT | 20 | 101 | 30 | 91 | 3 | 13 | .905 |
| Roanoke, VA | 21 | 103 | 86 | 238 | 58 | 194 | .428 |
| Laredo, TX | 22 | 107 | 12 | 48 | 42 | 149 | .518 |
| Tyler, TX | 23 | 110 | 93 | 251 | 77 | 224 | .381 |
| Florence, SC | 24 | 112 | 85 | 235 | 128 | 305 | .203 |
| Odessa, TX | 25 | 115 | 102 | 266 | 138 | 318 | .158 |
| Cheyenne, WY | 26 | 119 | 88 | 242 | 55 | 186 | .447 |
| Panama City, FL | 27 | 126 | 68 | 182 | 71 | 215 | .393 |
| Asheville, NC | 28 | 129 | 51 | 150 | 33 | 122 | .575 |
| Pocatello, ID | 29 | 130 | 76 | 207 | 73 | 217 | .391 |
| Rochester, MN | 30 | 131 | 129 | 307 | 7 | 25 | .860 |
| Benton Harbor, MI | 31 | 132 | 109 | 277 | 83 | 233 | .363 |
| Fargo, ND | 32 | 133 | 73 | 201 | 30 | 117 | .589 |
| Missoula, MT | 33 | 140 | 9 | 36 | 35 | 124 | .564 |
| Amarillo, TX | 34 | 141 | 96 | 257 | 123 | 299 | .219 |
| Wheeling, WV | 35 | 143 | 147 | 329 | 110 | 280 | .256 |

# Regions with Populations below 250,000 (*continued*)

| | HOUSING | | | | | | |
| | INEQUALITY INDEX* | | INAFFORDABILITY† | | CREATIVITY INDEX | | |
| Region | Peer Ranking | Overall Ranking | Peer Ranking | Overall Ranking | Peer Ranking | Overall Ranking | Score |
|---|---|---|---|---|---|---|---|
| Dothan, AL | 36 | 144 | 128 | 306 | 77 | 224 | .381 |
| Fort Walton, FL | 37 | 146 | 75 | 206 | 63 | 203 | .417 |
| Columbia, MO | 38 | 147 | 55 | 157 | 14 | 66 | .709 |
| Hattiesburg, MS | 39 | 154 | 54 | 155 | 76 | 222 | .385 |
| Lawrence, KS | 40 | 158 | 34 | 101 | 26 | 102 | .616 |
| Springfield, IL | 41 | 163 | 99 | 261 | 9 | 47 | .760 |
| Lewiston, ME | 42 | 164 | 63 | 169 | 47 | 160 | .496 |
| Iowa City, IA | 43 | 167 | 24 | 68 | 27 | 105 | .610 |
| Muncie, IN | 44 | 169 | 95 | 256 | 64 | 204 | .414 |
| Duluth, MN | 45 | 170 | 144 | 326 | 45 | 158 | .501 |
| Waco, TX | 46 | 171 | 80 | 222 | 94 | 255 | .307 |
| Champaign-Urbana, IL | 47 | 183 | 53 | 153 | 11 | 54 | .732 |
| Parkersburg, OH–WV | 48 | 189 | 130 | 308 | 117 | 289 | .245 |
| Pittsfield, MA | 49 | 191 | 61 | 165 | 43 | 152 | .511 |
| Jackson, MI | 50 | 192 | 142 | 324 | 103 | 267 | .279 |
| Longview, TX | 51 | 193 | 118 | 292 | 119 | 292 | .227 |
| Athens, GA | 52 | 195 | 13 | 53 | 57 | 192 | .435 |
| Abilene, TX | 53 | 196 | 105 | 271 | 80 | 229 | .376 |
| Chico, CA | 54 | 198 | 4 | 11 | 44 | 154 | .506 |
| Enid, OK | 55 | 202 | 137 | 319 | 101 | 265 | .280 |
| Auburn, AL | 56 | 203 | 16 | 59 | 96 | 258 | .298 |
| Great Falls, MT | 57 | 206 | 62 | 168 | 92 | 250 | .324 |
| Fitchburg, MA | 58 | 208 | 56 | 159 | 10 | 49 | .746 |
| Steubenville, OH | 59 | 209 | 145 | 327 | 135 | 315 | .170 |
| Olympia, WA | 60 | 211 | 28 | 86 | 5 | 18 | .889 |
| Eau Claire, WI | 61 | 213 | 106 | 273 | 48 | 161 | .495 |
| Rapid City, SD | 62 | 215 | 66 | 175 | 104 | 269 | .278 |
| Pine Bluff, AR | 63 | 217 | 92 | 249 | 92 | 250 | .324 |
| Lawton, OK | 64 | 219 | 87 | 241 | 97 | 259 | .296 |
| Monroe, LA | 65 | 220 | 78 | 211 | 128 | 305 | .203 |
| Gadsden, AL | 66 | 222 | 124 | 299 | 147 | 329 | .086 |
| Dover, DE | 67 | 225 | 52 | 151 | 74 | 218 | .388 |
| Altoona, PA | 68 | 226 | 101 | 264 | 100 | 264 | .282 |
| Brazoria, TX | 69 | 227 | 126 | 302 | 37 | 132 | .547 |

# Regions with Populations
# below 250,000 (*continued*)

| Region | HOUSING INEQUALITY INDEX* Peer Ranking | INEQUALITY INDEX* Overall Ranking | INAFFORDABILITY† Peer Ranking | INAFFORDABILITY† Overall Ranking | CREATIVITY INDEX Peer Ranking | CREATIVITY INDEX Overall Ranking | Score |
|---|---|---|---|---|---|---|---|
| Lynchburg, VA | 70 | 231 | 112 | 281 | 61 | 200 | .420 |
| Sioux Falls, SD | 71 | 232 | 89 | 245 | 51 | 171 | .472 |
| Casper, WY | 72 | 235 | 140 | 322 | 95 | 256 | .306 |
| Decatur, IL | 73 | 237 | 139 | 321 | 90 | 247 | .332 |
| Billings, MT | 74 | 238 | 58 | 162 | 56 | 188 | .446 |
| Sharon, PA | 75 | 239 | 115 | 289 | 132 | 309 | .199 |
| St. Cloud, MN | 76 | 242 | 116 | 290 | 86 | 237 | .350 |
| Grand Junction, CO | 77 | 243 | 39 | 114 | 61 | 200 | .420 |
| Topeka, KS | 78 | 245 | 119 | 293 | 36 | 126 | .559 |
| Lafayette, IN | 79 | 246 | 65 | 174 | 38 | 134 | .545 |
| Jamestown, NY | 80 | 247 | 79 | 215 | 91 | 248 | .331 |
| Bloomington, IL | 81 | 249 | 84 | 231 | 20 | 84 | .669 |
| Greenville, NC | 82 | 250 | 20 | 64 | 53 | 177 | .456 |
| Kankakee, IL | 83 | 251 | 64 | 170 | 148 | 330 | .078 |
| Johnstown, PA | 84 | 252 | 125 | 300 | 58 | 194 | .428 |
| Greeley, CO | 85 | 253 | 23 | 67 | 70 | 213 | .397 |
| Bremerton, WA | 86 | 254 | 15 | 58 | 8 | 45 | .771 |
| Tuscaloosa, AL | 87 | 255 | 43 | 125 | 88 | 241 | .339 |
| Albany, GA | 88 | 256 | 50 | 149 | 60 | 197 | .426 |
| Wichita Falls, TX | 89 | 260 | 97 | 258 | 142 | 324 | .128 |
| Sumter, SC | 90 | 262 | 69 | 186 | 149 | 331 | .066 |
| Florence, AL | 91 | 263 | 94 | 255 | 146 | 328 | .094 |
| Flagstaff, AZ | 92 | 264 | 19 | 62 | 23 | 92 | .647 |
| Jackson, TN | 93 | 266 | 82 | 229 | 99 | 263 | .283 |
| Victoria, TX | 94 | 267 | 123 | 298 | 141 | 323 | .133 |
| San Angelo, TX | 95 | 268 | 103 | 269 | 69 | 211 | .398 |
| Bismarck, ND | 96 | 269 | 100 | 262 | 66 | 206 | .413 |
| Bangor, ME | 97 | 270 | 46 | 135 | 16 | 68 | .703 |
| La Crosse, WI | 98 | 271 | 91 | 248 | 39 | 136 | .542 |
| Goldsboro, NC | 99 | 272 | 57 | 160 | 75 | 219 | .387 |
| Yuma, AZ | 100 | 274 | 22 | 66 | 84 | 234 | .354 |
| Wilmington, NC | 101 | 275 | 14 | 56 | 49 | 166 | .486 |
| Myrtle Beach, SC | 102 | 276 | 42 | 121 | 125 | 302 | .216 |
| Rocky Mount, NC | 103 | 277 | 60 | 164 | 79 | 226 | .380 |

# Regions with Populations
# below 250,000 (*continued*)

| | HOUSING | | | | | | |
| | INEQUALITY INDEX* | | INAFFORDABILITY† | | CREATIVITY INDEX | | |
| | Peer | Overall | Peer | Overall | Peer | Overall | |
| Region | Ranking | Ranking | Ranking | Ranking | Ranking | Ranking | Score |
| --- | --- | --- | --- | --- | --- | --- | --- |
| Merced, CA | 104 | 278 | 8 | 35 | 71 | 215 | .393 |
| Lima, OH | 105 | 279 | 141 | 323 | 114 | 286 | .247 |
| San Luis Obispo, CA | 106 | 281 | 3 | 7 | 28 | 110 | .602 |
| Pueblo, CO | 107 | 282 | 41 | 116 | 105 | 272 | .271 |
| Sherman, TX | 108 | 283 | 114 | 287 | 50 | 168 | .483 |
| Owensboro, KY | 109 | 284 | 143 | 325 | 122 | 298 | .221 |
| Medford, OR | 110 | 285 | 10 | 45 | 40 | 138 | .539 |
| New Bedford, MA | 111 | 286 | 27 | 84 | 15 | 67 | .708 |
| Green Bay, WI | 112 | 288 | 98 | 259 | 68 | 210 | .399 |
| Vineland, NJ | 113 | 289 | 17 | 60 | 98 | 262 | .287 |
| Anniston, AL | 114 | 290 | 110 | 279 | 116 | 288 | .246 |
| Redding, CA | 115 | 291 | 5 | 14 | 89 | 245 | .333 |
| Kenosha, WI | 116 | 292 | 59 | 163 | 85 | 236 | .352 |
| Elmira, NY | 117 | 293 | 67 | 176 | 67 | 208 | .406 |
| Jonesboro, AR | 118 | 294 | 74 | 205 | 111 | 282 | .253 |
| Houma, LA | 119 | 297 | 146 | 328 | 130 | 307 | .201 |
| Terre Haute, IN | 120 | 298 | 131 | 309 | 81 | 231 | .374 |
| St. Joseph, MO | 121 | 299 | 148 | 330 | 108 | 275 | .269 |
| Cedar Rapids, IA | 122 | 300 | 120 | 295 | 29 | 113 | .597 |
| Grand Forks, ND | 123 | 302 | 72 | 196 | 119 | 292 | .227 |
| Janesville, WI | 124 | 303 | 104 | 270 | 137 | 317 | .163 |
| Waterloo, IA | 125 | 304 | 134 | 313 | 101 | 265 | .280 |
| Dubuque, IA | 126 | 306 | 133 | 312 | 121 | 295 | .226 |
| Bloomington, IN | 127 | 307 | 11 | 47 | 54 | 180 | .454 |
| Texarkana, AR–TX | 128 | 308 | 107 | 274 | 87 | 239 | .347 |
| Wausau, WI | 129 | 309 | 138 | 320 | 139 | 321 | .143 |
| Clarksville, TN–KY | 130 | 310 | 70 | 193 | 127 | 304 | .208 |
| Racine, WI | 131 | 311 | 90 | 246 | 118 | 290 | .233 |
| Williamsport, PA | 132 | 312 | 71 | 194 | 145 | 327 | .117 |
| Yolo, CA | 133 | 313 | 2 | 6 | 52 | 173 | .465 |
| Hagerstown, MD | 134 | 314 | 83 | 230 | 131 | 308 | .200 |
| Sioux City, IA | 135 | 316 | 108 | 275 | 109 | 278 | .257 |
| Glens Falls, NY | 136 | 317 | 48 | 147 | 112 | 284 | .251 |
| Barnstable, MA | 137 | 318 | 40 | 115 | 31 | 118 | .586 |

# Regions with Populations below 250,000 (*continued*)

| | Inequality Index* | | Housing Inaffordability† | | Creativity Index | | |
|---|---|---|---|---|---|---|---|
| **Region** | **Peer Ranking** | **Overall Ranking** | **Peer Ranking** | **Overall Ranking** | **Peer Ranking** | **Overall Ranking** | **Score** |
| Yakima, WA | 138 | 319 | 26 | 76 | 136 | 316 | .168 |
| Danville, VA | 139 | 320 | 113 | 282 | 133 | 310 | .198 |
| Jacksonville, NC | 140 | 321 | 35 | 106 | 126 | 303 | .215 |
| Decatur, AL | 141 | 322 | 111 | 280 | 105 | 272 | .271 |
| Joplin, MO | 142 | 323 | 135 | 314 | 143 | 325 | .119 |
| Cumberland, MD | 143 | 325 | 121 | 296 | 107 | 274 | .270 |
| Elkhart, IN | 144 | 326 | 132 | 311 | 114 | 286 | .247 |
| Sheboygan, WI | 145 | 327 | 127 | 303 | 140 | 322 | .140 |
| Yuba City, CA | 146 | 328 | 18 | 61 | 64 | 204 | .414 |
| Bellingham, WA | 147 | 329 | 7 | 32 | 18 | 74 | .688 |
| Fort Smith, AR–OK | 148 | 330 | 117 | 291 | 134 | 314 | .187 |
| Mansfield, OH | 149 | 331 | 122 | 297 | 144 | 326 | .118 |

Peer ranking is based upon all regions in a given size category. Overall ranking covers all 331 metropolitan statistical areas. Some MSA names ae shortened due to space considerations.
* Ranking based on increasing wage inequality.
† Ranking based on increasing inffordability of housing.

Developed by Kevin Stolarick from various sources. See Appendix B for a complete description of indicators, sources, and methodology.

# Notes

## Chapter 1

1. AnnaLee Saxenian, *Silicon Valley's New Immigrant Entrepreneurs*. San Francisco: Public Policy Institute of California, 1999.
2. Sharon Levin and Paula Stephan, "Are the Foreign-Born a Source of Strength for U.S. Science?" *Science's Compass*, 20, August 1998.
3. Statistic from Susan Martin, "Heavy Traffic: International Migration in an Era of Globalization." *Brookings Review*, September 22, 2001.
4. For more on Porter's Innovation Index, see Michael Porter and Scott Stern, *The New Challenge to American Prosperity: Findings from the Innovation Index*. Washington, D.C.: Council on Competitiveness, 1999. Davos, the World Economic Forum, publishes annual rankings based on Porter's indicators as the *Global Competitiveness Report*. On the Globalization Index, see "The Fourth Annual Globalization Index." *Foreign Policy*, March–April 2004.
5. Kenneth Prewitt, "Demography, Diversity and Democracy: The 2000 Census." *Brookings Review*, Winter 2002, 20(1), pp. 6–9.
6. Data on international student mobility are from the Institute of International Education. See especially Todd M. Davis, *Atlas of Student Mobility*. New York: Institute of International Education, 2003.

7. Steven Camarota, "Economy Slowed, But Immigration Didn't: The Foreign-born Population, 2000–2004." Washington, D.C.: Center for Immigration Studies, November 2004.

8. John Paden and Peter Singer, "America Slams the Door (on Its Foot): Washington's Destructive Visa Policies." *Foreign Affairs,* May–June 2003.

9. "Opening the Door." *The Economist,* October 31, 2002.

10. "Scattering the Seeds of Innovation: The Globalisation of Research and Development." *The Economist,* Intelligence Unit, September 2004.

# Chapter 2

1. See Paul Romer, "Economic Growth." *The Fortune Encyclopedia of Economics,* David R. Henderson (ed.). New York: Time Warner Books, 1993; "Ideas and Things." *The Economist,* September 11, 1993, p. 33; "Beyond the Knowledge Worker." *Worldlink,* January–February 1995; "Endogenous Technical Change." *Journal of Political Economy,* 98(5), 1990, pp. 71–102.

2. Martin Kenney and Richard Florida, *Beyond Mass Production: The Japanese System and Its Transfer to the United States.* New York: Oxford University Press, 1993.

3. Peter Drucker, *Post-Capitalist Society.* New York: HarperBusiness, 1993; Fritz Malchup, *The Production and Distribution of Knowledge in the United States.* Princeton: Princeton University Press, 1962; Steven Brint, "Professionals and the Knowledge Economy: Rethinking the Theory of the Post-Industrial Society." *Current Sociology,* 49(1), July 2001, pp. 101–132; Steven Barley, *The New World of Work.* London: British North American Committee, 1996.

4. W. Michael Cox, Richard Alm, and Nigel Holmes, "Where the Jobs Are." *New York Times,* May 13, 2004.

5. Frank Levy and Richard Murnane, *The New Division of Labor.* Princeton: Princeton University Press, 2004, especially Chapter 3.

6. Serge Coulombe, Jean-François Tremblay, and Sylvie Marchand, *Literacy Scores, Human Capital, and Growth Across 14 OECD Countries.* Ottawa: Statistics Canada, 2004. Also see "Counting Heads: A Breakthrough in Measuring the Knowledge Economy." *The Economist,* August 26, 2004.

7. Cultural Initiatives Silicon Valley, *The Creative Community Index.* San Jose: 2004.

8. Robert Lucas, "On the Mechanics of Economic Development." *Journal of Monetary Economics,* 22, 1988, pp. 1–42; Edward Glaeser, "Are Cities Dying?" *Journal of Economic Perspectives,* 12, 1998, pp. 139–169; Glaeser, "The New Economics of Urban and Regional Growth," in Gordon Clark, Meric Gertler, and Maryann Feldman (eds.), *The Oxford Handbook of Economic Geography.* Oxford University Press, 2000, pp. 83–98.

9. Meric Gertler, Richard Florida, Gary Gates, and Tara Vinodrai, *Competing on Creativity.* Report for the Ontario Ministry of Enterprise, Opportunity and Innovation, November 2002.

10. Gianmarco Ottaviano and Giovanni Peri, "The Economic Value of Cultural Diversity: Evidence from U.S. Cities." University of California at Davis, February 2004.

11. Steven Malanga, "The Curse of the Creative Class." *City Journal,* Winter 2004.

12. Joel Kotkin and Fred Siegel, "Too Much Froth." *Blueprint,* January 8, 2004.

13. "Pick a Place to Live, Then Find a Job." *Wall Street Journal,* January 27, 2002. The original study is by Next Generation Consulting, *Talent Capitals: The Emerging Battleground in the War for Talent: A White Paper,* 2002.

14. Sam Youl Lee, Richard Florida, and Zoltan Acs, "Creativity and Entrepreneurship: A Regional Analysis of New Firm Formation." *Regional Studies,* 2005.

15. David Brooks, "Our Sprawling, Supersized Utopia." *New York Times Magazine,* April 4, 2004; and his book, *On Paradise Drive.* New York: Simon & Schuster, 2004.

16. Glaeser as quoted in Christopher Shea, "Road to Riches." *Boston Globe,* March 1, 2004.

17. Jay Greene and Greg Forster, "Sex, Drugs, and Delinquency in Urban and Suburban Public Schools." Manhattan Institute, Education Working Paper 4, January 2004.

18. William Frey, "Melting Pot Suburbs." Brookings Institution, Center for Urban and Metropolitan Policy, 2001.

19. Jane Jacobs, *The Death and Life of Great American Cities.* New York: Random House, 1961.

20. Brian Knudsen, Richard Florida, Gary Gates, and Kevin Stolarick, "Beyond Spillovers: The Effects of Creative-Density on Innovation." Carnegie Mellon University: Heinz School of Public Policy and Management, 2003; Dora Costa and Matthew Hahn, "Power Couples: Changes in the Locational Choice of the College Educated." National Bureau of Economic Research, Working Paper 7109, May 1999.

21. Terry N. Clark, *The City as Entertainment Machine.* New York: JAI Press, 2003.

22. See Glaeser's "Book Review of Richard Florida's *The Rise of the Creative Class,*" available on his Web site and at www.creativeclass.org.

23. It's also worth pointing out that the precise kind of diversity necessary to cultivate economic growth varies with the size of the region. Obviously, building a creative ecosystem that supports diversity in all its many dimensions is the optimal solution. But my research with Gary Gates has brought us to the interesting conclusion that, as crude as it may sound to prioritize diversity, an openness to bohemians and gays matters much more in large re-

gions with populations over 1 million. Openness to immigrants is a more powerful driver of growth in small- and medium-size regions.

24. James Surowiecki, *The Wisdom of Crowds: Why the Many Are Smarter Than the Few and How Collective Wisdom Shapes Business, Economies, Societies and Nations.* New York: Doubleday, 2004.

25. Joel Kotkin, *The New Geography: How the Digital Revolution Is Reshaping the American Landscape.* New York: Random House, 2001. Kotkin and his frequent collaborator Fred Siegel wrote another homage to the "new economy," "Digital Geography: the Remaking of City and Countryside in the New Economy." Hudson Institute, 2000.

26. Chris Farrell, "Diverse, Not Divided." *BusinessWeek,* August 9, 2004.

# Chapter 3

1. Max Weber, *The Protestant Ethic and the Spirit of Capitalism.* London: Routledge Classics, 2003 (original 1904); Edward Banfield, *The Moral Basis of a Backward Society.* New York: Free Press, 1967; Banfield, *The Unheavenly City Revisited.* Long Grove, IL: Waveland Press, 1990; Daniel Bell, *The Cultural Contradictions of Capitalism.* New York: Basic Books, 1976. This broad literature is excellently summarized in Lawrence Harrison and Samuel Huntington, *Culture Matters.* New York: HarperCollins, 2001, especially the chapters by Harrison and by David Landes.

2. Nathan Glazer and Daniel P. Moynihan, *Beyond the Melting Pot.* Cambridge: MIT Press, 1970.

3. Samuel P. Huntington, *Who Are We?: The Challenges to America's National Identity.* New York: Simon & Schuster, 2004; also his *Clash of Civilizations and the Remaking of World Order.* New York: Simon & Schuster, 1998. Also see Daniel Lazare, "Diversity and Its Discontents." *The Nation,* June 14, 2004; and Alan Wolfe, "Native Son: Samuel Huntington Defends the Homeland." *Foreign Affairs,* May–June 2004. There is an interesting debate between Huntington and Wolfe in "Credal Affairs." *Foreign Affairs,* September–October 2004.

4. See Ronald Inglehart, *Modernization and Post-Modernization,* Princeton: Princeton University Press, 1997; *Culture Shift in Advanced Industrial Society.* Princeton: Princeton University Press, 1989; Ronald Inglehart and Wayne Baker, "Modernization, Cultural Change and the Persistence of Traditional Values." *American Sociological Review,* 65, February 2000, pp. 19–51.

5. See Gary J. Gates, "Racial Integration, Diversity, and Social Capital: An Analysis of Their Effects on Regional Population and Job Growth," Washington, D.C.: Urban Institute, 2003.

6. This history of U.S. immigration policy draws from Rachel Friedberg and

Jennifer Hunt, "The Impact of Immigrants on Host Country Wages, Employment and Growth. *Journal of Economic Perspectives,* 9(2), Spring 1995, pp. 23–44; and Margaret Usdansky and Thomas Espenshade, "The H-1B Visa Debate in Historical Perspective: The Evolution of U.S. Policy Toward Foreign-born Workers." University of California at San Diego, Center for Comparative Immigration Studies, Working Paper 11, May 2000. Data on immigrants and immigration are from the Nolan Malone, Kaarl Beluja, Joseph Costanzo, and Cynthia Davis, "The Foreign-born Population, 2000." U.S. Bureau of the Census, Census 2000 Brief C2KBR-34, December 2003; and the Census Bureau's extensive Web site as well from the Web site maintained by the Center for Immigration Studies, www.cis.org.

7. The best analyses of recent immigration are from Andrew Sum and the Center for Labor Market Studies at Northeastern University; see Andrew Sum, Ishwar Khatiwada, Paul Harrington, and Sheila Palma, "New Immigrants in the Labor Force and the Number of Employed New Immigrants in the U.S. from 2000–2003: Continued Growth Amidst Declining Employment Among the Native-born Population." Northeastern University, Center for Labor Market Studies, December 2003.

8. William Carrigan and Enrica Detragiache, "How Extensive Is the Brain Drain?" *Finance and Development,* 36(2), June 1999.

9. "Do Developing Countries Gain or Lose When Their Brightest Talents Go Abroad?" *The Economist,* September 26, 2002.

10. Mihir Desai, Devesh Kapur, and John McHale, "The Fiscal Impact of High-Skilled Emigration: Flows of Indians to the U.S." Harvard Business School, November 2002.

11. On the changing demographic composition of metropolitan America, see David Fasenfest, Jason Booza, and Kurt Metzger, "Living Together: A New Look at Racial and Ethnic Integration in Metropolitan Neighborhoods, 1990–2000." Brookings Institution, Center for Urban and Metropolitan Policy, April 2004.

12. Alain de Botton, "Workers of the World, Relax." *International Herald Tribune* September 7, 2004.

# Chapter 4

1. On outsourcing, see "Extended Mass Layoffs Associated with Domestic and Overseas Relocations, First Quarter 2004." Bureau of Labor Statistics, June 10, 2004; Charles Schultze, "Offshoring, Import Competition and the Jobless Recovery." Washington, D.C.: Brookings Institution, June 2004.

2. Ralph Gomory and William Baumol, *Global Trade and Conflicting National Interests.* Cambridge: MIT Press, 2001; Paul Samuelson, "Where Ricardo and Mill Rebut and Confirm Arguments of Mainstream Economists Sup-

porting Globalization." *Journal of Economic Perspectives,* 18(3), Summer 2004; for the more general debate see Steven Lohr, "A Dissenter on Outsourcing States His Case." *New York Times,* September 7, 2004. Also John Cassidy, "Winners and Losers: The Truth about Free Trade." *The New Yorker,* August 6, 2004, pp. 26–30.

3. Michael Finn, "Stay Rates of Foreign Doctorate Recipients from U.S. Universities, 1999." Oak Ridge Institution for Science and Education, December 2001. Also see "International Mobility of Scientists and Engineers to the United States: Brain Drain or Brain Circulation?" National Science Foundation, Directorate of Social, Behavioral and Economic Sciences, NSF 98-316, June 22, 1998.
4. Sharon Levin and Paula Stephan, "Are the Foreign-born a Source of Strength for U.S. Science?" *Science's Compass,* 20, August 1998.
5. Jagdish Bhagwati, "Borders Beyond Control." *Foreign Affairs,* 82(1), 2003, January–February, pp. 98–100.
6. A concise overview of the intersection of demographic and labor-market trends is provided by Paul Kaihla, "The Coming Job Boom." *Business 2.0,* September 2003.
7. Kenneth Prewitt, "Demography, Diversity and Democracy: The 2000 Census." *Brookings Review,* 20(1), Winter 2002, pp. 6–9.
8. AnnaLee Saxenian, *Silicon Valley's New Immigrant Entrepreneurs.* San Francisco: Public Policy Institute of California, 1999; Saxenian, "Brain Circulation: How High-Skill Immigration Makes Everyone Better Off." *Brookings Review,* 20(1), Winter 2002, pp. 28–31.
9. Victor C. Johnson, associate executive director of NAFSA, Association of International Educators, quoted in Michael Arnone, "Security at Home Creates Insecurity Abroad." *Chronicle of Higher Education,* March 12, 2004. The *New York Times* quote is from William Broad, "U.S. Is Losing Its Dominance in the Sciences," May 3, 2004; Daniel S. Greenberg, "What Scientist Shortage?" *Washington Post,* May 19, 2004.
10. Thomas Friedman, "Losing Our Edge?" *New York Times,* April 22, 2004.
11. Alan Weber, "Reverse Brain Drain Threatens U.S. Economy." *USA Today,* February 23, 2004.
12. Geoff Brumfiel, "As One Door Closes." *Nature,* 427, January 15, 2004, pp. 190–195. Data on visa trends are from the National Science Board, *Science and Engineering Indicators 2004.* Culture exchange visas are discussed in Steven Clemons, "Land of the Free?" *New York Times,* March 31, 2004.
13. The survey was conducted in February 2004 by the American Council on Education, the Association of American Universities, the Council of Graduate Schools, the National Association of State Universities and Land Grant Colleges, and NAFSA, the Association of International Educators. It compared applications for the Fall 2004 academic year with those for Fall 2003. The survey received responses from 530 institutions, 230 regarding graduate

applications, 130 from doctoral-research institutions, and 382 responses regarding undergraduate education. See "Survey of Applications by Prospective International Students to U.S. Higher Education Institutions." Available at the NAFSA Web site: www.nafsa.org/content/PublicPolicy/Forthe Media/appssurveyresults.pdf. A good overview of these trends can be found in Michael Arnone, "Security at Home Creates Insecurity Abroad."

14. "Council of Graduate Schools Survey Finds Widespread Decline in International Graduate Student Applications to U.S. Graduate Schools for Fall 2004." Council of Graduate Schools, March 2, 2004. Available at the Council of Graduate Schools Web site: www.cgsnet.org/pdf/CGS_PR_IntlSurvey.pdf.

15. Mary Beth Marklein, "Fewer Foreigners Enrolling in Grad School." *USA Today,* September 9, 2004.

16. John Paden and Peter Singer, "America Slams the Door (On Its Foot): Washington's Destructive New Visa Policies." *Foreign Affairs,* May–June 2003. Also see Allison Chamberlain, "Science and National Security in the Post 9/11 Environment." American Association for the Advancement of Science, Issue Brief, July 2004.

17. Geoff Brumfiel, "As One Door Closes"; "Border Security: Improvements Needed to Reduce Time Taken to Adjudicate Visas for Science Students and Scholars." U.S. Government Accountability Office Report 04-371, February 24, 2004.

18. Bernard Wysocki Jr., "Foreign Scientists Are Stranded by Post-9/11 Security Concerns." *Wall Street Journal,* January 20, 2003, p. 1.

19. As quoted in Geoff Brumfiel, "As One Door Closes."

20. On the Chinese students, see Doug Payne, "Students Blocked from U.S. Meeting." *The Scientist,* February 2, 2004. On the University of Toronto professor, see Christine Szustaczek, "U.S. Border Laws Keep University of Toronto Professor Home." University of Toronto, *News@UofT,* November 22, 2002.

21. University of California at Berkeley survey of foreign-born scholars and graduate students as reported in Burton Bollag, "Wanted: Foreign Students." *Chronicle of Higher Education,* October 8, 2004, pp. A37–A38.

22. Santangelo Group, *Do Visa Delays Hurt US Business?* Washington, D.C., June 4, 2002.

23. On world musicians, see Tom Moon, "Fear of Music." *Tracks,* 1, 2004. On the Bulgarian opera singer, see "Lost Soprano: Homeland Security Stifles an Opera Singer." *Pittsburgh Post-Gazette,* February 27, 2004.

24. Jon Markman, "For American Brands the World Turns Ugly." *MSN Money,* March 31, 2004.

25. "The Stem Cell Refugee," *Wired,* 11 (12), December 2003; Elizabeth Rosenthal, "Britain Embraces Embryonic Stem Cell Research." *New York Times,* August 24, 2004.

26. Mancur Olson, *The Rise and Decline of Nations.* New Haven: Yale University Press, 1984.


# Chapter 5

1. Richard Florida and Martin Kenney, *The Breakthrough Illusion.* New York: Basic Books, 1990.
2. The data on patents and scientific publications are from the National Science Board, *Science and Engineering Indicators,* 2004. The *New York Times* quote is from William Broad, "U.S. Is Losing Its Dominance in the Sciences," May 3, 2004.
3. "International Mobility of the Highly Skilled." *OECD Observer,* Policy Brief, 2002.
4. See Andres Solimano, "Globalizing Talent and Human Capital: Implications for Developing Countries." Paper Prepared for the Fourth Annual World Bank Conference on Development Economics, Oslo, Norway, June 24–26, 2002; and Mario Cervantes and Dominique Guellec, The Brain Drain: Old Myths, New Realities. *OECD Observer,* May 7, 2002.
5. Jane Perlez, "Chinese Move to Eclipse U.S. Appeal in South Asia." *New York Times,* November 18, 2004.
6. Figures on international students are from Todd M. Davis, *Atlas of Student Mobility.* New York: Institute of International Education, 2003.
7. Burton Bollag, "Australia Sees Strong Gains in the Enrollment of Foreign Students." *Chronicle of Higher Education,* March 9, 2004. On Korea, see Michael Chan, "South Korea Announces Steps to Attract More Foreign Students." *Chronicle of Higher Education,* 2001. Available at www.educationusa.or.kr/english/news/chronicle-foreign-students.html. On German efforts, see Jennifer Carlile, "Germany Woos American Students." *MSNBC online,* March 26, 2004. Available at www.msnbc.msn.com/id/4601000/.
8. "Fewer International Graduate Students Applying to Study in the United States." Report by the American Council of Educators; Association of American Universities; Council of Graduate Schools. NAFSA; and the National Association of State Universities and Land Grant Colleges, 2004.
9. Victor C. Johnson of NAFSA, in the *Chronicle of Higher Education,* March 9, 2004.
10. For a discussion of the World Values Survey, see Ronald Inglehart, *Modernization and Post-Modernization.* Princeton: Princeton University Press, 1997; Inglehart, *Culture Shift in Advanced Industrial Society.* Princeton: Princeton University Press, 1989; Ronald Inglehart and Wayne Baker, "Modernization, Cultural Change and the Persistence of Traditional Values." *American*

*Sociological Review,* 65, February 2000, pp. 19–51. The data were made available by Inglehart and are available from the Inter-University Consortium for Policy and Social Research (ICPSR) survey data archive at the University of Michigan.

11. Quotes are from Inglehart and Baker, "Modernization, Cultural Change and the Persistence of Traditional Values," pp. 31, 49.

12. "Reactions to Immigration in Leading Nations." AP/Ipsos Poll, May 27, 2004.

# Chapter 6

1. Peter Hall, *Cities in Civilization: Culture, Innovation and Urban Order.* London: Weidenfeld & Nicolson. 1998.

2. Peter Hall, "Cycles of Creativity." *Urban: The Urban Age Magazine,* Fall 1999, available at www.worldbank.org/html/fpd/urnan/urb-age/fall99/cycles.htm.

3. Wilbur R. Thompson, *A Preface to Urban Economics,* Prepared for Resources for the Future, Inc. Baltimore: Johns Hopkins Press, 1965, pp. 15 and 45.

4. Figures on world urbanization are from United Nations, *World Urbanization Prospects.* Revision, 1999.

5. On the evolution and development of trading cities, see Jane Jacobs, *The Economy of Cities.* New York: Random House, 1969; Peter Hall, *Cities in Civilization;* and Wilbur R. Thompson, *A Preface to Urban Economics;* also see Fernand Braudel's classic three-volume study, *The Structures of Everyday Life: The Limits of the Possible,* vol. 1; *The Wheels of Commerce,* vol. 2; *The Perspective of the World,* vol. 3; all Berkeley: University of California Press, 1992.

6. On the discussion of industry and the evolution of city and regional economies, see Edward Glaeser, "Are Cities Dying?" *Journal of Economic Perspectives,* 12 (2), 1998, pp. 139–160; Jane Jacobs, *The Economy of Cities;* Paul Krugman, "Increasing Returns and Economic Geography." *Journal of Political Economy,* 99 (3), June 1991, pp. 483–499; Douglass North, "Location Theory and Regional Economic Growth." *Journal of Political Economy,* 63 (3), 1955, pp. 243–258; Arthur O'Sullivan and Charles M. Tiebout, "Exports and Regional Economic Growth." *Journal of Political Economy,* 64 (2), 1956, pp. 160–169; Wilbur R. Thompson, *A Preface to Urban Economics.*

7. Michael J. Piore and Charles F. Sabel, *The Second Industrial Divide: Possibilities for Prosperity.* New York: Basic Books, 1984.

8. Doreen Massey, *Spatial Divisions of Labor.* New York; Metheun, 1984; Bennett Harrison and Barry Bluestone, *The Deindustrialization of America.* New York, Basic Books, 1982; Folker Fröbel, Jürgen Heinrichs, and Otto Kreye, *The New International Division of Labour.* Cambridge: Cambridge University Press, 1980; Mike Savage and Alan Warde, "Cities and Uneven Economic Development," in Richard LeGates and Frederic Stout (eds.), *The City*

*Reader.* New York: Routledge, 1996, pp. 311–32; John Friedmann, The World City Hypothesis," in Paul Knox and Peter J. Taylor (eds.), *World Cities in a World System.* Cambridge: Cambridge University Press, 1995.

9. See the various regions and industries discussed in Martin Kenney, *Locating Global Advantage: Industry Dynamics in the International Economy.* Palo Alto: Stanford University Press, 2003.

10. For more on these types of flexible industrial communities, see Annalee Saxenian, *Regional Advantage: Culture and Competition in Silicon Valley and Route 128.* Cambridge: Harvard University Press, 1994; Manuel Castells and Peter Hall, *Technopoles of the World: The Making of 21st Century Industrial Complexes.* London: Routledge, 1994; Peter Hall and Ann Markusen, *Silicon Landscapes.* London: Allen & Unwin, 1985; Allen Scott, *The Cultural Economy of Cities.* London: Sage Publications, 2000; Allen Scott, *Technopolis.* Berkeley: University of California Press, 1993; Michael Storper, *The Regional World: Territorial Development in a Global Economy.* New York: The Guilford Press, 1997.

11. Michael J. Piore and Charles F. Sabel, *The Second Industrial Divide.*

12. Manuel Castells and Peter Hall, *Technopoles of the World.*

13. Ann Markusen, "The Distinctive City: Evidence from Artists and Occupational Profiles," Project on Regional and Industrial Economies. Humphrey Institute of Public Affairs: University of Minnesota. 2004.

14. J. V. Beaverstock, R. G. Smith, and P. J. Taylor, "A Roster of World Cities." *Cities,* 16 (6), 1999, pp. 445–458.

15. Saskia Sassen, "Cities in a World Economy," in Scott Campbell and Susan Fainstein (eds.), *Readings in Urban Theory.* Cambridge: Blackwell, 2002. Also see Sassen's *The Global City: New York, London and Tokyo.* Princeton: Princeton University Press, 2001.

16. Others argue that these global centers of "command and control" are marked by extreme economic polarization, bastions of wealth and knowledge creation but also of a vast, poor underground community of immigrant labor—a "third world service proletariat," one writer calls it—that toils in low-skilled, low-paying jobs. For more on this, see Mike Davis, "Fortress L.A.," in Richard LeGates and Frederic Scout, (eds.), *The City Reader;* Manuel Castells, *End of Millennium,* 2nd Oxford: Blackwell, 2000; and Castells, *The Rise of the Network Society,* 2nd ed. New York: Blackwell Publishers, 2000; John Kasarda, "The Jobs-Skills Mismatch," in LeGates and Stout (eds.), *The City Reader,* pp. 305–310.

17. Lisa Benton-Short, "Global Perspective on the Connections Between Immigrants and World Cities." George Washington Center for the Study of Globalization, Occasional Paper Series, 2004.

18. See the discussion in Chapter 2, in particular, Gianmarco Ottaviano and Giovanni Peri, "The Economic Value of Cultural Diversity: Evidence from U.S. Cities." University of California at Davis, February 2004.

19. Kevin Stolarick provided the updated analysis of Canadian regions. Also see Meric Gertler, Richard Florida, Gary Gates, and Tara Vinodrai, *Competing on Creativity.* Report for the Ontario Ministry of Enterprise, Opportunity and Innovation, November 2002.
20. Detailed benchmarking data from Australian regions is from National Economics, *State of the Regions Report 2002.* National Economics and the Australian Local Government Association, 2002.
21. On India's move up the value chain in computers and software, see "The Latest in Remote Control." *The Economist,* September 9, 2004.
22. For Rashid quote and more on Chinese research centers, see Chris Buckley, "Let a Thousand Ideas Flower: China Is a New Hotbed of Research." *New York Times,* September 13, 2004.

# Chapter 7

1. Figures on inequality are from the Council on Competitiveness data series, *Benchmarking Competitiveness,* available at: www.compete.org/benchmarking. The U.S. has a Gini Coefficient (the standard measure for income inequality) of roughly 0.4, compared to 0.25 for Sweden and Japan. The coefficient can range from 0 (perfect equality, with all families receiving the same income) to 1 (perfect inequality, with only one family receiving all the income). Also see Jared Bernstein, Lawrence Mishel, and Chauna Brocht, "Any Way You Cut It," Economic Policy Institute briefing paper, based on Congressional Budget Office data, September 2002.
2. Alan Berube and Thacher Tiffany, "The Shape of the Curve: Household Income Distribution in U.S. Cities, 1979–1999." Brookings Institution, Center for Urban and Metropolitan Policy, August 2004.
3. "Ever Higher Society, Ever Harder to Ascend," *The Economist,* January 1, 2005, pp. 22–24.
4. On global housing trends, see *World Economic Outlook.* International Monetary Fund, September 2004; and James Woudhuysen, "Metro-miserablists." www.spiked-online.com, October 7, 2004.
5. Ronald Kessler, et al., "Prevalence, Severity, and Unmet Need for Treatment of Mental Disorders in the World Health Organization World Mental Health Surveys." *Journal of the American Medical Association,* 291 (21), June 2, 2004, pp. 2581–2590. Roberto Figueroa and Richard Florida, "The Rise of the Creative Class and Its Impact on Regional Mental Health." Heinz School of Public Policy and Management, Carnegie Mellon University, April 2003.
6. William Julius Wilson, *The Truly Disadvantaged.* Chicago; University of Chicago Press, 1990; Paul Krugman, "For Richer." *New York Times Maga-*

*zine,* October 20, 2002; Krugman, "The Death of Horatio Alger." *The Nation,* January 5, 2004.

# Chapter 8

1. From "A Portrait in Red and Blue." *The Economist,* December 30, 2003.
2. Morris Fiorina, Samuel Abrams, and Jeremy Pope, *Culture War?: The Myth of a Polarized America.* Longman, 2004.
3. On June 5, 2004, Brooks wrote in his *New York Times* column: "Over the next few months, I hope to write a fair bit about the dominant feature of our political life: polarization." His major statement is "One Nation, Slightly Divisible." *Atlantic Monthly,* December 2001. But also see his book *On Paradise Drive.* New York: Simon & Schuster, 2004, as well as his articles and columns: "People Like Us." *Atlantic Monthly,* September 2003; "Democrats Go off the Cliff." *Weekly Standard,* 8 (41), June 30, 2003; "Circling the Wagons." *New York Times,* June 5, 2004; quote below is from "Bitter at the Top." *New York Times,* June 15, 2004.
4. Mickey Kaus, "Who Cooks Your Brooks?" *Slate.com,* June 16, 2004. Kaus is but one of a growing chorus of Brooks's critics. See Sasha Issenberg, "Paradise Glossed." *Philadelphia,* April 2004; Michael Kinsley, " 'On Paradise Drive': Sociology or Shtick?" *New York Times Book Review,* May 23, 2004; Nicholas Confessore, "Paradise Glossed: The Problem with David Brooks." *Washington Monthly,* June 2004; David Plotz, "David Brooks: Why Liberals Are Turning on their Favorite Conservative." *Slate.com,* June 14, 2004.
5. Robert Samuelson, "How Polarization Sells." *Washington Post,* December 3, 2003.
6. John Tierney, "A Nation Divided, Who Says?" *New York Times,* June 13, 2004.
7. The original study is Paul DiMaggio, John Evans, and Bethany Bryson, "Have Americans' Social Attitudes Become More Polarized?" *American Journal of Sociology,* 102, 1997, pp. 690–755; John Evans later updated the study to cover more recent years; see John Evans, "Have Americans' Attitudes Become More Polarized?: An Update." Princeton University, Center for Arts and Cultural Policy Studies, Working Paper 24, Spring 2002. Quote below is from Evans.
8. Steinhorn, Leonard, "60s Morality Is Winning," Salon.com, November 29, 2004. Steinhorn is also the author of *The Greater Generation: In Defense of the Baby Boom Legacy,* New York: St. Martin's Press, 2005.
9. "Religious Beliefs Underpin Opposition to Homosexuality." Pew Research Center, November 18, 2003.

10. This section draws on research and writing conducted jointly with Bill Bishop.

11. John Judis and Ruy Teixeira, *The Emerging Democratic Majority*. New York: Scribner, 2002; Texeira, "Deciphering the Democrats' Debacle." *Washington Monthly*, May 2003.

12. Robert Cushing's findings as summarized in Bill Bishop, "The Blame Game: Who or What Is Behind the Astonishing Divisions in U.S. Politics?" *Austin American-Statesman*, October 23, 2004.

13. Thomas Ferguson, "Holy Owned Subsidiary: Globalization, Religion and Politics in the 2004 Election," in William Crotty (ed.), *A Defining Election: The Presidential Race of 2004*. Armonk, New York: M. E. Sharpe, 2005.

14. These ideas have benefited from discussions with my George Mason colleague Jim Pfiffner. See Pfiffner, "President and Congress at the Turn of the Century: Structural Sources of Conflict," in James Thurber (ed.), *Rivals for Power*. Lanham, MD: Rowan and Littlefield, 2002, pp. 27–47.

# Chapter 9

1. Paul Kennedy, *The Rise and Fall of the Great Powers: Economic Change and Military Conflict from 1500–2000*. New York: Vintage Books, 1989; Fareed Zakaria, "America's Big Challenge: Asia." *Washington Post*, October 19, 2004.

2. See Jeremy Rifkin, *The European Dream: How Europe's Vision of the Future Is Quietly Eclipsing the American Dream*. New York: Jeremy P. Tarcher, 2004; T. R. Reid, *The United States of Europe: The New Superpower and the End of American Supremacy*. New York: Penguin Books, 2004.

3. Brent Schlender, "Peter Drucker Sets Us Straight." *Fortune*, January 12, 2004.

4. Mancur Olson, *The Rise and Decline of Nations*. New Haven: Yale University Press, 1984.

5. The key factor is not just innovative or creative capacity but also *absorptive capacity*. Wesley Cohen and Daniel Levinthal introduced the concept of absorptive capacity to explain why businesses undertake research and development not just to invent new products and processes but to absorb ideas from outside. See Cohen and Levinthal, "Absorptive Capacity: A New Perspective on Learning and Innovation." *Administrative Science Quarterly*, 35(1), March 1990, pp. 128–152.

6. Trends in industrial research and development are from the National Science Foundation, *InfoBrief* 04-320, May 2004.

7. Phillip Longman, "Raising Hell." *Washington Monthly*, March 2004.

# Acknowledgments

A book like this one is truly a team effort, with a huge number of debts incurred along the way. Jesse Elliott managed the project, assisting with virtually every detail of the book's organization, writing and editing, and supervising the development of graphics. Kevin Stolarick provided a good deal of the book's statistical material, particularly the figures on the economic impact of the creative economy in Chapter 2 and on economic inequality and housing affordability in Chapter 7. Irene Tinagli developed the global creativity measures in Chapter 5. Elizabeth Currid has been with me since *The Rise of the Creative Class;* now in the final stages of her doctoral studies in urban planning at Columbia University, she helped me to research and write Chapter 6. Rodgers Frantz and Sarah Gross Fife, my partners in the Creativity Group, have supported my efforts to communicate my ideas to the general public in recent years. Rod also played a central role in helping to frame and communicate the ideas in this book. Timothy Fife designed the book's graphics, and Brian Knudsen assisted with myriad research tasks. I am truly blessed to work with so many kind, inspiring, joyful, and talented people. Their long hours and tireless efforts made all the difference on this project, and my heartfelt thanks goes out to each and every one of them.

In addition to this core team, Gary Gates, Meric Gertler, Martin Kenney, Sam Youl Lee, Timothy McNulty, and Zoltan Acs collaborated on research and studies that inform my ideas and analysis. Louis Musante, George Borowsky, and Rob Yencik, the core team at Catalytix, and our clients throughout the United States, North America, and the world, have helped keep my ideas grounded in reality.

Robert Cushing provided the analysis of talent flows in Chapter 2 and the analysis of elections in Chapter 8. Bill Bishop and I worked together to flesh out the ideas in Chapter 8 on the big sort. Sarah Kneece also assisted with background research on our country's political and economic divisions for that chapter. Paul Glastris of the *Washington Monthly* has been an ongoing source of ideas; he and Ben Wallace-Wells helped me to more sharply define some of the core ideas in this book in two earlier articles published in the *Monthly.* Tom Stewart and Eileen Roche of the *Harvard Business Review* helped me further refine my ideas about creativity ad competitiveness. Jim Pfiffner, my George Mason University colleague, helped me better understand the dynamics of partisan political polarization in the United States. Baykal Eyyuboglu provided additional assistance in the later stages of this project. I am extremely grateful for all of their ideas and efforts.

Susan Schulman is a fabulous agent: She believed in this project and worked tirelessly to find a publisher and editorial team who saw its full potential. Marion Maneker has been terrific editor, a helpful commentator on many big ideas, and a collaborator in shaping the overall trajectory of this project. Mike Vargo provided editorial assistance with some of the background material that led up to this book. The entire HarperBusiness team has been an absolute delight to work with. And of course I could never have brought this project to fruition without the generous support of the Alfred P. Sloan Foundation, the Software Industry Center and Heinz Professorship at Carnegie Mellon University, and the Hirst Professorship at George Mason University's School of Public Policy.

There are so many friends and colleagues, some new and some old, across this country and the world, who support my own creative efforts in scores of untold ways. I am infinitely grateful to them, and in general to the amazing people I have met and continue to meet in my travels who work so hard to bring change to their workplaces and their communities. Your efforts teach me a great deal about the capacity for human creativity, and your energy inspires me to continue working, playing, living, and learning to the fullest.

Family has always meant the world to me. My brother, Robert, is ever able to help me with my writing and to keep my ideas grounded in our family's history. My sister-in-law, Virginia; nieces, Sophia and Tessa; and nephew, Lucca, are a source of great comfort and happiness.

As a student of creativity, I know that projects like this one reward hard work with many joys of the soul. But this one has been particularly extraordinary in that regard: It led me to meet a very special person, Rana Kozouz, who is a source of unwavering support, ongoing inspiration, and incredible happiness. For this, I am grateful far beyond what mere words can say.

*Richard Florida, Washington, D.C., January 2005*

# Index

Page numbers in *italics* indicate charts.